MW01095066

Disclaimer

The views expressed in the book are neither those of the Kendra nor of the publisher, nor are they in agreement with the text. This work is a translation of the sacred and spiritual book of Guru Charitra, which was originally published in Marathi and Kannada. Some of the views are to be understood in the context of the days when it was written. At that time certain practices like Sati, caste distinction, calling Harijans as sudras, etc., were prevalent which have been condemned as being discriminatory in modern times, as also by the publisher and Kendra. Both the publisher and Kendra specifically disclaim any liability personal or otherwise, which is incurred as a consequence, direct or indirect, of the use and application of any of the views and practices discussed in the book. The aim of the publisher and Kendra is to highlight the spiritual significance of the text.

Guru Charitra

Shree Swami Samarth
Vishwa Kalyan Kendra

Sterling Paperbacks

STERLING PAPERBACKS
An imprint of
Sterling Publishers (P) Ltd.
A-59, Okhla Industrial Area, Phase-II,
New Delhi-110020.
Tel: 26387070, 26386209; Fax: 91-11-26383788
E-mail: sterlingpublishers@airtelmail.in
ghai@nde.vsnl.net.in
www.sterlingpublishers.com

Guru Charitra
© 2007, Shree Swami Samarth Vishwa Kalyan Kendra
ISBN 978- 81-207-3348-0
Reprint 2009

Printed and Published by Sterling Publishers Pvt. Ltd.,
New Delhi-110020.

Blessings

Sri *Guru Charitra* is an ancient sacred scripture. It contains the biographies of Sri Vallabha and Sri Narasimha Saraswati. Its sanctity is so profound that repeated reading of the text will yield the blessings of Lord Dattatreya and enable the devotees to fulfil their wishes.

P.B. Paranjpe
9/11/2006

P. B. Paranjape alias *Nana,* is the founder of Shree Swami Samarth Vishwa Kalyan Kendra at Aapta Phata, near Panvel, Mumbai. He is the moving force behind the translation of *Guru Charitra* in English.

Foreword

Guru Charitra, a profoundly revered scriptural text dating back to the 15th century, is devoutly followed by spiritual aspirants, mostly in Karnataka, Maharashtra and Andhra Pradesh. (Most of the spiritual centres referred therein are located in these states.) It is in conversational form between the master and the disciple clarifying all the doubts of the disciple. Mainly, it deals with biographies of Lord Dattatreya and his subsequent incarnations as Sripada Sri Vallabha and Sri Narasimha Saraswati. In fact, the reading of *Guru Charitra* gives strength, and encouragement to spiritual aspirants to continue with their *sadhana* (spiritual disciplines and practices), despite the various troubles and travails they encounter in the process from time to time.

The idea of *Guru Charitra* in English originated in the study circle conducted by Sri Sathya Sai Seva Samithi in Chembur, a suburb of Bombay. The subject was taken up for discussion, chapter by chapter in the weekly meetings. Sri P.B. Paranjape, founder of Shri Swami Samarth Vishwa Kalyan Kendra, participated in the discussions and explained the subtler spiritual aspects contained in the text. It was ultimately decided to compile the chapters in English in book form and make it available to the English readers who could not read the same in other languages.

Shri L.N. Joshi had attempted it but he could not achieve his ambition. Late Shri K.V.R. Rao, an ardent devotee of Sri Sathya Sai Baba, took the initiative and enlisted the co-operation and support of Sri Sathya Sai devotees, Chembur, in getting the manuscripts typed and corrected. The typescript was perused by late Shri N. Kasturi, biographer of *Sri Sathya Sai Baba*, who also effected the necessary corrections and changes. Shri K.V.R. Rao entrusted the responsibility of getting it published to Shri P.B. Paranjape.

Due to lack of facilities, funds and circumstances beyond our control, the book could not be published earlier. Due to divine grace, today we have been able to place this sacred book in the hands of readers. At the same time, we are fully conscious that we could not do full justice to the subject. Many errors also might have crept in the text for which we crave the indulgences of readers. It may not give full satisfaction to devotees of Lord Dattatreya and they may have valuable suggestions to offer. Even if the readers are spiritually benefited in a small way we consider our efforts as fully rewarded.

We regret our inability to name individually and thank all those persons who made this venture a grand success. However we wish to place on record our sincere appreciation and gratitude to all those who helped us.

May Lord Dattatreya shower his choicest blessings on all and lead them to reach their ultimate goal of self-realisation.

Mumbai   Shri Swami Samarth Vishwa Kalyan Kendra

Preface

Guru Charitra, till a few years back, was only available in Marathi and Kannada. In recent years, Telugu translations of the book have become available. It may perhaps be now available in a few other Indian languages also, but, as far as we are aware, there has been no English rendering of the book so far. The present book in English was started by Shri Joshi some years back, so as to make this spiritual treasure available to wider sections of people. Unfortunately for us, Shri L.N. Joshi is now no more, having left his physical body on 30 October 1981, to merge in and abide at the lotus feet of Guru Nath, which was his yearning all through his life. It is a matter of regret for us that he could not see the book in print. But we feel sure that his spirit will rejoice and be happy that the efforts he had begun, have at last borne fruit and that the book has now seen the light of day.

This is but a free-rendering and an abridged version of the original *Guru Charitra.* The original text was compiled by Sri Saraswati Gangadhar, a devotee of Sri Narasimha Saraswati, a fully enlightened soul very well versed in *Guru tattwa.* The text was in Marathi in OVI form of poetry. The same was transcribed into Sanskrit by the great saint Sri Vasudevananda Saraswati (1854–1914), a contemporary of Sainath, i.e., Sri Sai Baba of Shirdi. A complete rendering of the original text into English is a colossal and formidable task and is far beyond our capacity and competence. In the present book, it has been our attempt to bring out the gist of the original text, but at the same time of course ensuring, as best as we can, that the spirit of the original text is not lost.

We do not know to what extent we have been able to achieve the above objective but if this book, in spite of whatever deficiencies and shortcomings it may be having, still succeeds in satisfying the reader's interest even in a small measure and enthuses and awakens in him the desire and yearning for diving deeper into spiritual lore, for which purpose abundant spiritual literature is available, it would be highly gratifying to us indeed.

It is a bold attempt made by us, and it is our firm faith and belief that it is the grace of and guidance from Guru Nath Sri Narasimha Saraswati alone, that has helped us in our venture. We make our obeisance to Sri Guru Nath and his various manifestations including Sri Manik Prabhu, Sri Swami Samarth Akkalkot Maharaj and Sri Sai Baba.

It may be mentioned here, that the manuscript had received the unique blessings of Sri Sathya Sai Baba (Puttaparthi) and Sri Siddharaj Manik Prabhu Maharaj. Earlier, it was also blessed by Sri Swami Amalananda of Pen (Panvel) during the latter's visit to Chembur.

We cannot conclude this preface without acknowledging our deep debt of gratitude to Sri P.B. Paranjape (dearly called as Nana). It was he who has encouraged us all through and instilled in us confidence and helped us complete this sacred book. Sri Nana is a very saintly person and is an example of extreme humility, great devotion, selfless love and all goodness. He is a highly endowed spiritual soul and many come to him for spiritual succour. It is with his endeavours that Shri Swami Samarth Viswa Kalyana Kendra was founded in the year 1981 with its centre at Apta (Karnala) Panvel Taluka, Raigad District, Maharashtra, for the propagation of the teachings and philosophy of Sri Akkalkot Maharaj. With *pranams* unto the *Guru padukas* of Ganagapur, we dedicate this book to Viswa Kalyana Kendra.

Mumbai   K.V.R. Rao

Note for the Readers

Some of the injunctions given for women, and especially those enjoined on them at the time of the death of the husband and thereafter, from our present day understanding and ideas, seem to be far too unjust and 'even barbarous'. The idea of the 'Sati' rite *(Sahagamana)* will be particularly revolting to us and we cannot bear to think of it. It puzzles us indeed how this custom crept in and came into vogue at all.

The custom of Sati seems to have become prevalent in Hindu society from centuries and particularly more in northern India and especially in the regions of Rajasthan. It seems to be more a practice resorted to by their women to keep their honour blemishless on being deprived of the husband's protections, by the latter's defeat and death in wars, especially in the insecure conditions under the rule of the alien invaders. The alien conquerors, generally, lacked religious tolerance and had no respect and regard for the lives of those belonging to other religions, whom they branded as *kafirs* or heathens. This was due to a total misreading and misunderstanding of their own religions, as no religion ever preaches hatred and violence against people of other faiths. Apart from alien invaders, another plausible reason could have been that their security and honour was at stake even in the hands of their own people, who could often be unscrupulous. Thus, the custom of Sati seems to have come into practice due to the force of circumstances rather than religious injunctions.

But unfortunately, there have been some practices which though have lost their relevance in present times, are yet perpetuated in the name of tradition and customs. That is what seems to have happened in the case of Sati practice in Hindu society in the mid-centuries. It is a great boon and relief indeed that through the efforts of Raja Ram Mohan Roy, who was a deeply religious man himself, that the custom of Sati was legally banned and the evil died for ever.

We should also understand that *Sahagamana* has a really different connotation and significance than merely the practice of Sati. As per Hindu religious tradition and philosophy, marriage is conceived as a lifelong partnership between husband and wife, not only in the worldly life, but also in spiritual life. The husband and wife need to march together under all circumstances and should always endeavour to fulfil the four *Purusharthas,* viz., 'Dharma', 'Artha', 'Kama' and 'Moksha' conjointly. The first three should be oriented towards the fulfilment and attainment of the final goal, i.e., 'Moksha'. For this purpose, the wife and husband should move in closest comradeship. This is what is indeed meant by *Sahagamana,* meaning 'marching together' and the same partnership which existed in one life is believed to be conducive in the next life too.

There were many instances that just at the occurrence of death of the husband or of the wife, the other partner also just dropped down dead, and both the bodies were consigned to the fire together, on the same funeral pyre, making them inseparable even in death. But this, of course, does not justify the practice of Sati, and forced *Sahagamana* is certainly most abominable.

There are actually two types of injunctions in our scriptures, one relating to the eternal values like truthfulness, righteous living, etc., which should guide the conduct of men everywhere and at all times and in any age, and the other one relating to *Naimithika* duties, which are incidental and with a bearing and relation to the conditions and needs of the occasion and the times. While the first type of injunctions have an universal and eternal validity, the second type of injunctions may not hold good for all times. With changing conditions and times, they may need to be revoked, modified or reformed and made relevant to the altered times, and are not to be taken as inviolable.

Let us not miss the spirit behind these injunctions. Let us view them in the context of the time they belonged to. Let us bear in mind that circumstances of the times often dictate customs. Instead, ignoring the above, if we sit in judgement and condemn our preceeding generations for everything, who knows what our future generations will do to us? But also at the same time let us not lose sight of the human and humane aspects of the problems. The customs which are inhuman and have no relevance to the present times have to be discarded or reformed. But we should never forget that the one sole motto of our seers and ancient law-givers, was:

Maa Kaschid Dukha Maapnuyaat ...
Lokah Samastha Sukhinobhavantu ...

Let none suffer from misery ...
May all the people be ever happy!

Let us try to relieve the sufferings of whosoever (he/she) be and to whatever extent we can. Let us contribute to others' happiness in every small measure. This is the core message and purpose of all the injunctions our ancients have laid down.

Contents

Vision of Sri Guru Nath

Saraswati Gangadhara begins with invocation prayers for divine grace to endow on him merit and strength to be able to successfully compile the sacred *Guru Charitra*, the glorious account of the divine incarnations of Lord Sri Dattatreya, viz., Sri Sripada Sri Vallabha and Sri Narasimha Saraswati.

Namdharak, an ardent devotee of Sri Narasimha Saraswati, sets out for Ganagapur for the darshan of the holy *padukas*. Tired and exhausted, he fainted on the way. At this time Guru Nath appeared before him in a dream and blessed him.

Sri Gurubhyo Namaha
Sri Ganesaya Namaha
Sri Saraswathyai Namaha
Sri Gur Datttatreyaya Namaha
Sri Mahalaxmayai Namaha
Gurur Bramha, Gurur Vishnuhu,
Gurudevo Maheshwaraha,
Gurur-Sakshaat Para Bramhaha,
Tasmai Sri Gurave Namaha...

Guru (the Spiritual Preceptor) is himself Lord Bramha, the creator of the cosmos; Guru himself is Lord Vishnu, the sustainer of the cosmos; Guru himself is Lord Maheshwara, who absorbs unto himself this creation at the end of each cycle, and verily the Guru himself is

Absolute and Supreme Godhead. And unto that Guru, I offer my total obeisance...

To transcribe into finite language, in the confines of limited vocabulary, the infinite glory and effulgence of Guru Dattatreya, the unified manifestation of the Supreme Trinity — Bramha, Vishnu and Maheshwara, is an impossible task for any. Even the Vedas failed and beat a retreat. But even so, if at least a small and single ray of the Supreme effulgence of the Godhead can be captured, that is enough to redeem the world. And through divine grace, the impossible becomes possible to some or to a little extent at least.

Namdharak Invokes for Divine Grace

Saraswati Gangadhara* (Namdharak), the blessed devotee of Dattavatara Sri Narasimha Saraswati, before setting out to write the sacred *Guru Charitra* (the life story of the avatar), invokes the grace of Lord Ganesa. Without Lord Ganesa's grace, nothing can be achieved. He is *Mangala Murti*, the embodiment of all the auspicious attributes and the abode of all auspiciousness. He is most easily pleased, responds instantaneously, and bestows his grace ever-readily on whosover calls out to him. He makes the impossible possible. With his grace and help the Sage Vyasa could compose the incomparable and monumental Mahabharata. Saraswati Gangadhara extols Lord Ganesa saying: 'You are the remover of all obstacles. You keep your large fan-like ears always waving. The air waves produced thereby drive away all the obstacles in the path of your devotees. In your stomach rests all the worlds, and that is why you are extolled as *Lambodara*. Even all the gods have to worship you alone first, before undertaking any of their divine tasks. I pray to you to bless this venture of mine and help me through...'

---

*   Saraswati Gangadhara lived in the 15th century

Next, Saraswati Gangadhara invokes the grace of Mother Saraswati, the bestower of all knowledge and wisdom. He prays 'You are the mother of all the Vedas. Without your grace, man cannot pronounce even a syllable. You are the life force behind the "sound". You are the indweller in all the four-fold aspects of sound, viz., *Para, Pasyanti, Madhyama* and *Vaikhariis*, from the subtlest to the grossest expressions of sound. I beseech you to bless me and help me in this venture of mine...'

Saraswati Gangadhara next prays to the Trimurtis and to Sri Dattatreya. He prays, 'Oh Lords! You are the primeval Gurus... You are the ones who incarnated in the *Kali Yuga* as Sri Narasimha Saraswati to redeem people from their ignorance and their ills. With full faith, that you alone are going to steer me through this colossal venture, I am setting out upon this task. It is like the child trying to catch the moon by stretching out its hand, but even so I have complete faith in you, that you will help me through.'

Thus Saraswati Gangadhara starts with the divine narrative—the *Guru Charitra*. As a prelude, he gives a brief account of his lineage and of his immediate forbears. He belongs to the *Kaundinyasa Gotra*. He is of the fourth generation in the line reckoning from Sayamdeo. Sayamdeo's son was Nagnath and Nagnath's son was Deorao. All of them were staunch devotees and worshippers of Guru Nath. Sayamdeo and Nagnath has the blessed privilege of being the close disciples of Guru Nath and of serving the master in his lifetime. It is because of the merit earned by them, that one among their family, Saraswati Gangadhara, could become an instrument of the Lord to write about the divine *leelas* of the great Dattavatara for the benefit of humanity and the world. It should, however, be understood that the life of any great saint or master, and much more so of an avatar like that of Sri Narasimha Saraswati, is like a huge iceberg lying submerged in the frozen waters of the ocean, and showing but a tiny crest or pinnacle afloat on the waters. What will be discernible to human eyes is just the tiny portion afloat above the waters, but not the mountain-sized iceberg submerged under the waters. So also in the following account of Guru Nath's life, it is but a fraction of his glory that will be delineated. It is impossible for anyone to describe the avatar's full glory. He is a mystery beyond all human comprehension.

Namdharak Is Blessed with Guru Darshan

There was once a devotee named Namdharak and who had a great yearning to visit the holy place of Ganagapur for the darshan of the sacred *Guru padukas*, the *Nirguna padukas* of Dattavatar Sri Narasimha Saraswati Deva enshrined there. He heard much, most authentic anecdotes, how Guru Nath continues to shower His grace on all seekers, even after his *Mahaprasthan*, and that a pilgrimage to Ganagapur is sure to soothe the mind, to satiate the yearnings of the heart, to quench the thirst of the soul, and to allay the hunger of the spirit for all the devotees.

With great expectations and hopes, Namdharak sets out from his far off village to Ganagapur. The journey was long and arduous. He was very exhausted and had lost all his stamina. He was seized with despair as to whether he would survive and be able to reach the destination at all.

Resting under a tree, Namdharak cried out in desperation, 'Oh Guru Deva! Don't you have pity and compassion on me? I may be unmerited with so many sin-loads on my head, but what of it? Will a mother ever forsake her son however bad and evil he may be? You know how devotedly my ancestors worshipped and served you. Because of that at least, show me also a little consideration, ignoring and forgiving all my lapses. If you forsake me, who can I look to, Oh my Lord! I will end my life if you are so callous to me.' Wailing thus in anguish and desperation, and fatigued by the journey, he fainted and fell unconscious.

Lo! No mother ever forsakes her child. Even the cow comes seeking its calf. Namdharak had a wondrous dream. Guru Nath Sri Narasimha Saraswati Deva stood there before him, casting his benevolent looks upon him and placing his hand on his (Namdharak's) head as a token of his blessing. Namdharak's joy knew no bounds. He fell at Guru Nath's feet. He sang out long hymns of praise to the Lord. He offered mental worship to him. He collected the dust from under the feet of the Lord and smeared it on his own forehead and all over his body. He was overwhelmed with joy.

THUS ENDS THE FIRST CHAPTER OF SRI
GURU CHARITRA DESCRIBING THE DREAM VISION
VOUCHSAFED TO NAMDHARAK BY SRI GURU NATH.

Glory to the all-merciful, the omnipresent and the ever-responsive Guru Nath!

2

Power and Glory of Guru Bhakti

Namdharak meets Siddha Yogi, the great and close disciple of Guru Nath. Siddha Yogi leads Namdharak to the Bhima-Amaraja Sangam, and seated under the holy Aswatha tree, starts narrating the *Guru Charitra* to him, which the latter listens to with rapt attention.

Siddha Yogi narrates the story of the disciple Deepak and the Guru Vedadharma and about the unexcelled merit that accrue from Guru bhakti and Guru seva. Guru is indeed supreme and all the gods are subsumed in Him. If we can but win the Guru's grace, we will thereby win the grace of all the gods. Guru is indeed supreme.

The names of Vedadharma and Deepak have their own significance. Veda itself is both the dharma and the Guru. And one who is devoted to the scriptures and abides by the dharma which they enunciate is sure to gain enlightenment. This chapter is the key-chapter of the entire text. It charts out the entire path for the spiritual aspirant.

The Kalpataru *can fulfil all your wishes. The* Kamadhenu *can bestow on us all the boons. The* Paras Stone *can transform base metals into gold. But none of them can transform others into the like of themselves. This, Guru alone can do.*

Namdharak, refreshed by the sleep and enlivened by the joy of the dream-vision, now woke up. The dream-vision, of Guru Nath's splendorous form, with ashes smeared all over the body, with tiger skin as his garment and with locks of matted hair, and with looks overflowing with love and compassion, stood indelibly imprinted in his mind. Recapitulating the vision, he was in a state of ecstasy. But it soon flashed on him, that it was after all but a dream. But even so, he realised and felt convinced that it was only because of Guru Nath's grace that he had such a blessed vision, even if it be a dream. But could he ever hope to have even such a dream-vision again? Would Guru Nath ever again shower his mercy upon him? As he was brooding thus, lo! There came near him a yogi (an ascetic) who looked like a near replica of the divine form, which he had seen in his dream. The yogi too had similar face and looks, wore a tiger-skin for his garment and his whole body was smeared with sacred ashes. His face was shining with spiritual splendour and his looks bespeaking of his inner realisation and enlightenment. Namdharak was overwhelmed with joy and wonder and fell at the Yogi's feet and exclaimed, 'Oh! great one! On seeing you, all the agony in my heart has subsided and my whole being is filled with ineffable joy and eternal peace. I am feeling most blessed. I pray to you to let me know who you are and where you are coming from and where you reside. I am certain that it is Sri Narasimha Saraswati Deva who sent you to me, taking pity on me.'

At this, the ascetic replied as follows—'I am known by the name Siddha Yogi (also referred as Siddhamuni), I am the disciple of the great Dattavatar Sri Narasimha Saraswati. The Supreme Bramhan was my Guru. With His grace alone, I have attained the knowledge of the spirit and the possession of all the yogic siddhis. Ever since my Guru's departure from Ganagapur and withdrawing of his avatar a little later, I have been constantly on pilgrimage. I am now on my way back to the holy Ganagapur for the darshan of my Guru Nath's Nirguna padukas enshrined there. I spend all my time revelling in remembrance and recounting the leelas and mahimas of Guru Nath. Oh how great, how divine is my Guru! He is peerless indeed. How blessed is Ganagapur which is hallowed by his grace! How blessed indeed are all those who are devoted to

*him! They are freed for ever from all mundane worries and are for
ever anchored in peace and happiness. Their homes will be ever
prosperous, with everything aplenty and with no want whatsoever.
Cattle, children, wealth—none of these will be ever felt wanting
in the devotees' homes. For that matter, anyone devoted to his own
Guru, let apart to Guru Nath, is most blessed indeed. He will be
all peace and happiness himself. Guru is indeed supreme by himself
and all the gods are no comparison to him at all. Guru is the sole
benefactor and liberator for man, and blessed indeed are those who
are devoted to their Guru.'*

Although Namdharak was so joyous at hearing this, yet some
apprehensions started raising their heads in his mind. He said to
Siddha Yogi, *'I am puzzled at what all you say. I am also devoted to
Guru Nath just as the predecessors in my family were. But I have
no peace at all and am ever haunted by worries. In spite of my
devotion to Guru Nath, I am in a pitiful state. You say that those
devoted to the Guru are freed from all worries and miseries. It
doesn't seem to hold true in my case at least. Further, although I too
believe that great indeed is Guru Nath, how can you say that
Guru whoever he be, is indeed supreme by himself and all the gods
are no comparison to him at all. Guru can hold some place of
honour, like mother and father, but how can you rank him above
all the gods? It puzzles me much and I fail to understand what you
say.'*

Siddha Yogi then said, *'My child! Your faith is wavering and is
not steadfast yet, and you are bedevilled with all sorts of doubts.
Just as a sick person cannot relish food however delicious it is, so also
a doubting heart cannot imbibe the grace of the Guru, however
abundantly it may be overflowing. Just as excessive and wrong diet
is harmful to a sick person, so also doubts are inimical and
detrimental to the progress of men on the path of bhakti. Is it not
said* "Samsayatmaa Vinasyati"—*a wavering and doubting person
perishes and* "Sraddhaavan labhathe gnanam"—*the one with*

faith gains all the wisdom? You should cultivate unalloyed devotion to the Guru. Because of your doubts only, you are not able to derive the benefit of Guru Nath's grace and instead, have enmeshed yourself in misery. Ever remember that the Guru alone can redeem the disciple. Even if he has incurred the wrath of all the gods, if he has his Guru's grace, no harm will ever befall him. Guru's grace will be his invincible armour even if all the gods make an assault upon him. But if one incurs the wrath of the Guru, none can ever rescue him, not even if all the gods together try.

'One should actually never make a distinction between his Guru and God. For the devotee all the forms of god should be subsumed in the form of his own Guru.'

Thereafter, Siddha Yogi started narrating an anecdote from the Bramha Vaivarta Purana *to explain the power of Guru Bhakti.*

In the beginningless times, Bramha Deva created the cosmos, and along with it he also created the four Vedas—the repositories of all wisdom, which enunciate the code of conduct for man for the upkeep of harmony in the universe. He also enunciated the Puranas by way of illustration of the practice of the Vedic dharma in the day-to-day lives of people. He also created the four *Yuga Purushas* assigning to each one of them, the rule of each of the *Yugas* respectively. He does this in each one of the *Kalpas*. Each one of the *Yuga Purushas*, in their respective *Yuga*, has to undertake the responsibility for the upkeep of dharma on earth, for the welfare of all. Each *Yuga* will have its own specific characteristics and special features and Bramha has explained about them in details to each one of the *Yuga Purushas*.

The *Purusha* of *Krita Yuga* is endowed with pure *sattva guna*. The *Purusha* of *Treta Yuga* has *sattva* and *rajas* mixed in him. While the people of the *Krita Yuga* are of contemplative nature, ever-engaged in *Tapas* and contemplating always on the Inner-Self, the people of *Treta Yuga* resort to external and ritualistic disciplines and austerities, especially of performance of sacrifices, etc. The *Purusha* of *Dwapara Yuga* is predominantly *rajasic,* and always carries bow and arrows in his hands. But even so, he is calm and compassionate. The *Kali Purusha* is possessed with *tamasic* traits; the people of *Kali Yuga* are materialistic, who discard all noble values of life, they are atheists and take to unwholesome and evil practices. Moral values will sink to the lowest level in the *Kali Yuga*, and the *Kali Purusha* will tempt and lead people astray, take them away along wrong and evil paths. People will fall slaves to sensual pleasures and throw overboard all noble values of life. Cravings of the tongue and passions of sex are two weapons of the *Kali Purusha* to subdue men.

Lord Bramha, however, had warned the *Kali Purusha* that he should be very cautious when he approaches people devoted to their Guru. He should never try to meddle with and harass people devoted to the Guru. The Guru holds the highest spiritual status, higher than that of even all the Gods. And whosoever is devoted to his Guru, is ever protected against all odds and harm. The Guru's grace will be an impregnable armour around his disciples and devotees. Otherwise, he would be incurring the Guru's wrath and will come to grief and none would be able to help him then, not even the great Trinity. Thereafter, Bramha narrates an anecdote to *Kali* on the power of Guru Bhakti.

On the banks of the holy River Godavari there used to be once the Angeerasa ashram. In the ashram lived many *rishis*, ever engaged in their spiritual pursuits. Many young students used to come for learning to these rishis who were very learned in the Vedas and the scriptures and were realised souls. Vedadharma, son of the great Paila Maharshi, was one of these *rishis*. He was revered for his vast learning as well as for his spiritual stature, and as a worthy son of a great *rishi*.

He used to have a very large group of students. One day, during his daily discourse to his students, he said, 'As a man sows, so shall he reap. No one can escape the bonds of karma. Human birth is a result of his previous karmas only. Just as the law of cause and effect works in the physical world, the law of karma works in the moral sphere. Every thought, word and deed, as it were, is weighed in the scales of eternal justice. The moral law is inexorable and inescapable'. He then slowly added, 'As for me too, in my former lives, in my ignorance, I committed many great sins. I have been able to expiate most of them through the severest of penances in this life, but there is still some *Parabdha Karma* persisting, which I cannot escape and will have to suffer. The time is now coming for me for undergoing this suffering and I will soon be overtaken by a most dreadful disease, which will see me in its grip for a long time, for nearly two years. I need the services of one of you, if any of you are willing. You will have to constantly attend upon me, nurse me and relieve me of my sufferings to whatever extent you possibly can. But, let me tell you, the disease that is going to overtake me is most loathsome and you will not be able to even bear my presence. Those who have to attend to a diseased person will suffer even more than the diseased person himself.' With this he stopped and kept silent.

No sooner than the Guru finished speaking thus, one young disciple, Deepak, rose up, walked to the Guru's feet, prostrated himself there and prayed he be given the chance and privilege to serve him. He said, 'Master! What greater blessing can there be than serving the Master, under all circumstances. Pray, give me the opportunity to serve you.'

Vedadharma said that he was setting out on a pilgrimage to the holy Kasi, as the disease which would be overtaking him could be fatal, and that he would like to breathe his last on the banks of the holy Ganges at the feet of Lord Viswanath.

Vedadharma then entrusted his other disciples to the care of other *rishis*, and he set out to the holy Kasi along with Deepak. There he settled down as Kambleshwar on the northern bank of Manikarnika.

In a few days, the body of Vedadharma was overtaken by leprosy and, day by day, the disease was fast spreading, ravaging the whole body. Files made almost a permanent habitation on the sores of Vedadharma's body. Putrid and foul odour used to emanate from all over the body. Hardly could he sleep; and he was suffering great agony all the time. He grew highly irritable and peevish, and for everything he used to blame Deepak. He used to treat the disciple very harshly. He used to scold him for not cleaning his sores properly, and when he was cleaning the wounds, he used to flare up and howl that he was causing him pain. He used to complain that the food Deepak was getting for him was not good. But Deepak used to bear it all calmly, while at the same time he also felt sorry for the agony and served him. He strove all the time in trying to make the Guru as comfortable as possible. He himself used to hardly sleep, nor used to eat properly, and all the time of the day he was attending upon the Master, catering to his needs. The young boy's dedication and love for his Guru moved the hearts of even the great Trinity.

One day, Lord Siva (Lord Visweswara) appeared before Deepak and said that He was immensely pleased with his Guru bhakti and Guru seva and that he came to him in order to give him whichever boon he might ask for. Deepak said that without his Guru's explicit permission he would not do anything and that he would therefore ask his Guru first as to what he should do and what boon to ask for. Siva said, 'Then you go and get your Guru's permission for asking the boon. I will be waiting here for you. I shall give you whatever you ask for.' Deepak told the Guru about this and said that he would seek boon from Siva for the cure of his (Guru's) dreadful disease. The Guru instantly flared into a rage and said he should not seek any favour from anyone for the redress of his suffering. He said he will have to expiate his karma by his own suffering only. Deepak went back and told Lord Siva that he had nothing to seek from Him. Bramha and Vishnu also later appeared before Deepak and they too offered him boons, pleased with his Guru bhakti. At the behest of the Guru, he turned down the offer of these gods too. Then the gods said, 'When we, the supreme gods, who are higher than any being, are graciously offering you boons, is it not foolish of you to listen to the perverse behests of your Guru and spurn down the blessed opportunity that comes to you?' Deepak replied, 'Pardon me, Sirs! There is none equal to the Guru, Guru is higher than even the highest gods. What I ever yearn for is only my Guru's grace and not the favour of anyone else. If you are still keen on granting me some boon, please bless that my devotion to my Guru will only grow more and more and will never slacken and waver.' The gods blessed him accordingly and disappeared.

Actually Vedadharma wanted only to test Deepak's steadfastness and devotion; for this he put him to the severest of tests. When Deepak thus defied even the gods, Vedadharma was much pleased. The disease was not real, it was just assumed by him for the purpose of testing the faith of his disciple and to give to posterity an example of the supreme power of Guru bhakti.

Vedadharma then gave up the disease and became perfectly well. He embraced Deepak. He lauded him for his steadfast devotion to the Guru even under the severest of trials and tribulation. Vedadharma endowed on Deepak all the knowledge of the scriptures and the highest wisdom and all the *siddhis*. He blessed him thus, 'You will flourish as a *chiranjeevi* for ever in this holy Kasi. Lord Visweswara will ever be at your side. Whoever thinks of you will be rid of all their woes and will enjoy all prosperity and attain enlightenment.' Deepak became as enlightened as his own illustrious Guru himself was, and came to be also known as Sandeepak or Samdeepak.

HERE ENDS THE SECOND CHAPTER OF SRI
GURU CHARITRA GLORIFYING GURU BHAKTI AND
THE SUPREMACY OF THE GURU OVER ALL GODS.

Glory to the all-merciful, the omnipresent and the ever-responsive Guru Nath!

3

Reasons behind Sri Hari's Incarnations

This chapter describes how Lord Sri Hari, in order to save his devotee King Ambareesha from the wrath of Sage Durvasa, draws upon himself the curse which Durvasa intended to pronounce against Ambareesha. As a result of Durvasa's curse, Sri Hari had to take repeated incarnations on earth, which, in a way, was the greatest blessing to the world.

*N*amdharak prayed to Siddha Yogi to accept him as his disciple. He pleaded, 'Pray, enlighten me more and fully on Guru leelas. Also let me know about your way of life, what type of food you take, etc.'

The Siddha Yogi said, 'Unceasing remembrance of Guru Nath's glory, chanting of his (Guru Nath's) name and reading and re-reading (Parayana) of Guru Charitra (which recounts the leelas of Guru Nath) are my sole sustenance and very way of life.' He showed him the bundle of palm-leaves, which was the record of the Guru leelas, which he always carried with him, and which was his priceless treasure. He further said, 'Guru Charitra is the panacea for all the ills of the world, and reading it or listening to its narration, will relieve men of all their mundane worries, and would endow on them enduring peace, happiness and spiritual enlightenment. It is like Kamadhenu (the celestial cow) and the Kalpavriksha (the celestial tree) and will fulfil all human desires and aspirations'. Speaking thus, Siddha Yogi led Namdharak to the holy Aswatha tree on the banks of the Bhima-Amaraja

Sangam. Siddha Yogi seated himself at the foot of the tree and asked Namdharak also to be seated in front of him. Namdharak pleaded with Siddha Yogi to narrate the Guru Charitra *and said, 'One great doubt troubles me much, and you must first clear it for me. Why should the one, who is beyond all* gunas *and qualities, who is formless, take form at all and especially the human form, and come down to earth? I am unable to reason out and understand why, while men strive all their lives to conquer and transcend their* gunas *and take to severest penances, with the sole objective of getting freedom from the thraldom of the body and to merge in the formless God, God himself assumes human form and incarnates on earth? What was the reason for* Nirguna *to become* Saguna? *Please make it clear to me.'*

The Siddha Yogi then began to narrate as follows:

Whenever earth is overpowered by evil and the gentle and pious folks are harassed and troubled by *asuras*, i.e., by the demonic-natured people, and whenever righteousness is on the decline, God incarnates on earth to restore dharma, to punish the wicked and to reform them, and to protect the pious and the good (see endnote). The devotees especially will be ever protected by God; God brooks no harm to be done to his ardent and faithful devotees by anyone or being. Let me tell you the anecdote of Ambareesha, which will explain to you clearly the mystery of the avatars.

King Ambareesha was a very righteous ruler and was also a great devotee of Lord Sri Hari. He was a scrupulous follower of all shastric injunctions. Once, after observing the *Ekadasi* fast, on the following morning he was about to break his fast. Just at that time, Sage Durvasa arrived. The king offered his obeisance to the sage and prayed that he should accept his hospitality. The sage agreed and went to bathe in the river telling that he would return soon. But hours passed by and yet the sage did not return. It was nearing midday and the *Dwadasi* hours were passing away. Unless Ambareesha broke the fast before the *Dwadasi* hours passed away, the fruits of the *Ekadasi* fast would be lost altogether. Consulting his priests, he sipped a little water, taking the Lord's name. The fast was thereby symbolically broken, yet without actually any food being taken. The sage returned after midday. He was furious that the king had taken something, though it be just water, without having offered him any food. In his fury, he was about to curse the king. Just at this juncture, as Ambareesha was all the time praying and was totally absorbed in the thought of Lord Sri Hari, the latter appeared and told Durvasa, that he might curse him (Sri Hari) instead of cursing Ambareesha, his devotee. Durvasa foresaw how immensely the curse was going to benefit the world, and pronounced the curse upon Sri Hari that he would have to be born again and again in the world, beginning with the life of a fish and further in one of the avatars; that he would have no steady place to live in and would be continuously wandering and be for ever on the move from place to place, thus indicating the Dattavatara too.

The curse of Durvasa thus became a blessing to the world. The Lord had to take incarnations on earth. Besides the ten principal incarnations, he took many other incarnations, which are all described in Srimad Bhagavata. One of the most glorious incarnations was that of Sri Dattatreya.

THUS ENDS THE THIRD CHAPTER OF SRI *GURU CHARITRA* DESCRIBING SAGE DURVASA'S CURSE ON SRI HARI, WHICH HAD LED TO THE LORD'S INCARNATIONS ON EARTH.

Glory to the all-merciful, the omnipresent and the ever-responsive Guru Nath!

Note

Each of the incarnations (avatars) has a profound and eternal message.

Matsya (Fish)	:	recover the treasure of wisdom from the deluge of doubt.
Kurma (Tortoise)	:	live unattached as master of here and hereafter.
Varaha (Boar)	:	carry the burden of duty on the twin tusks of discipline and devotion.
Narasimha (Mab-lion form)	:	let not your ego hide the glory of God.
Vamana	:	offer yourself at the feet of the Lord and gain the feet.
Parasurama	:	learn the lesson of surrender or suffer.
Sri Rama	:	what one meets in life is destiny and how one meets it is self effort.
Sri Krishna	:	strive to become an instrument in my hand.
Buddha	:	perfect yourself so that you may aid others to perfect themselves.
Kalki	:	build the mansion of life on truth, morality, peace, love and non-violence (*sathya*, dharma, *shanti*, *prema* and ahimsa).

4

Sri Dattavatar

This chapter describes the advent of Sri Dattatreya as the son of Anasuya and Atri. This chapter illustrates the power of chastity, i.e., purity as exemplified in the life of Anasuya. Her purity could transform the great Trinity (the *Durlabhya*, i.e., the unattainable) into mere babes in her arms and make them *Saulabhya* (bringing within one's easy and close reach).

The name Atri means one who has transcended the three *gunas*. Anasuya is one who is bereft of human frailties such as jealousy, etc., and is spotlessly pure. Where 'Atri' and 'Anasuya' co-habit, the Lord himself is also sure to abide.

*N*amdharak asked Siddha Yogi how the three great gods—Bramha, Vishnu and Maheshwara, were born as a single manifestation, as Datta. His heart was yearning to know the whole Guru Charitra *from its very beginnings and origin.*

Siddha Yogi began describing the origin of creation.

In the timeless beginning, there was no earth, no sky, no planet, no universe and no being. It was all an infinite expanse of water. On it was resting Lord Sri Narayana. Actually that primal water itself was God. Out of the water was born Hiranyagarbha and out of Hiranyagarbha emerged Bramhanda. Bramhanda split into two and one became the sky and the other the earth. The Lord then created the four-faced Bramha and entrusted him with the task of creation of both the animate and the inanimate beings. Bramha, out of his Manas, created the seven sages, known as 'Manasa Putras'. Atri Rishi was one of those seven sons of Bramha.

Atri practised severe penance for countless number of years and attained *Bramha-Jnana*. Later, at the insistance of Bramha, he married Anasuya, the daughter of Kardama Prajapati. Anasuya was the embodiment of perfection and was entirely blemishless and as her name itself indicates. She had no malice against anyone and had overwhelming and motherly love for all beings. She was an embodiment of chastity, who worshipped and considered her husband alone as God. She is reckoned foremost among the *Pativratas*. Her fame and glory spread far and wide, all over the three worlds.

Indra, the Lord of Heaven, felt all his power waning out into insignificance like that of an oil lamp before the dazzling and splendorous sunshine of the rising glory and powers of Anasuya, and was afraid of losing his supremacy. He approached the three gods—Bramha, Vishnu and Maheshwara, and entreated them to arrest the ever-increasing powers and glory of Anasuya by somehow casting a blemish on her chastity. He said Anasuya's name and fame had been already outshining and eclipsing that of the three divine consorts, Lakshmi, Saraswati and Parvati, who were till then ranked as the foremost amongst the women in all the worlds.

The gods wanted to put Anasuya's purity and power to test. They transformed themselves into mendicants and approached the hermitage of Atri Rishi. They begged for alms. At that time, Atri Rishi had gone to the river to offer his daily oblations. Anasuya came out and welcomed them and extended hospitality to them. They made a strange request that the food prepared be served to them by Anasuya without wearing any garment. Anasuya, though perplexed at such a strange, embarrassing and impossible condition, however, thought for a while as to what she should do. '*Atithis* cannot be turned away under any circumstances; *Atithis* are aspects of God himself,' she thought. 'But … yes!' it flashed in her mind. 'If only the guests were her babies and she their mother, she could feed them without donning a garment!' she concluded. Her thoughts—the thoughts of a pure and chaste mind instantly became a reality; the elderly guests turned into babies. She then fed them with all the motherly solicitude and love, sang lullabies for them and put them to sleep in a cradle.

When Atri Rishi returned home, to his amazement, he found Anasuya fondling the three babies and singing to them lullabies on Upanishadic truths. Anasuya rose and offered the children at the feet of her husband and said, 'These children are the gift (*datta*) of God to us.' Atri Rishi was overwhelmed with joy.

Atri Rishi, through his *Divyadrushti*, realised who the children really were. He prayed to them, 'Oh, Supreme gods— Bramha, Vishnu and Maheshwara—it is all your inscrutable divine *leela*. You, the infinite beings, chose to become babes in our humble home so as to delight us who have been childless and have been praying to you in our heart of hearts to bestow on us a child. How blessed are we to fondle you!' Tears of joy started welling out from the sage's eyes, bathing the babes, so to say.

The babes now assumed their real forms and made their appearance before the couple, as the Trinity — Bramha, Vishnu and Maheshwara. They said, 'We are pleased with you both. You ask for whatever boons you wish.' The couple prayed, 'Let the joy you gave us as babies in our home a little while ago, become permanent and a lasting reality. Make this humble cottage of ours your own home, and give us the blessed opportunity to fondle you as our own children.' The gods said, 'Your wish will surely be fulfilled. Let us also, who have never known what a mother's and a father's love is like, experience and enjoy it as children in your home. That is in truth, what we have been seeking for and why we came here, under the pretext of *bhiksha.*'

To Anasuya, Bramha was born as Chandra, Vishnu as Datta and Maheshwara as Durvasa. The children grew up under the fondling care of their parents. Atri Rishi performed their *Upanayana Samskara.* After this, Chandra sought permission of his parents to take his place in the skies and to make it his abode. Durvasa also sought permission of the parents to leave home for his pilgrimages and penance. Both of them merged their divine selves and power in their brother Datta before their departure from home. Thus, in Datta were merged all the divine aspects and powers of the great Trinity, which became symbolised in his three faces and six hands and because of which, he came to be called as Dattatreya (Datta Thraya). The name also bears another meaning— 'the one who gifted himself as son to Atri'.

Dattatreya, from his very early years itself, took to the task of redemption of the world as the Supreme Guru and Protector. He is a *Purna Jnanavatar*, incarnated to dispel darkness of ignorance in the world and to bestow spiritual knowledge and wisdom on all the aspirants.

THUS ENDS THE FOURTH CHAPTER OF SRI
GURU CHARITRA DESCRIBING THE GLORIOUS
ADVENT OF THE DATTAVATAR ON EARTH.

Glory to the all-merciful, the omnipresent and the ever-responsive Guru Nath!

5

Incarnation of Sripada Sri Vallabha

This chapter describes the reincarnation of Sri Dattatreya in the *Kali Yuga* as Sripada Sri Vallabha, in Peethapuram, as a son to Sumata. Sripada Sri Vallabha sets out on his divine mission at a very early age, after curing his lame and blind brothers and blessing the household with endless prosperity.

Siddha Yogi again referred to the curse of Durvasa Rishi on Lord Vishnu. Due to this curse, Lord Vishnu had reincarnated himself several times. Each of the incarnations subdued evil, reestablished dharma, *destroyed the wicked people, and helped and protected the good.*

Like the incarnations of Vishnu in the earlier Yugas, *in* Kali Yuga, *Lord Dattatreya too had to incarnate to promote righteousness, to dispel spiritual ignorance which had overtaken the world due to the influence of* Kali, *and to light the lamp of wisdom among people. Lord Dattatreya was born as Sripada Sri Vallabha. The Siddha Yogi narrated about this avatar to Namdharak.*

There is a place called Peethapuram * on the eastern coast of southern India. There lived a pious Brahmin couple in this place; the husband's name was Appalaraju and the wife's name was Sumata. While managing the household on one hand, Sumata used to devotedly assist her husband in religious rituals on the

---

* This place is identified as the present Pithapuram town near Kakinada in the east Godavari district of Andhra Pradesh, and at this place in recent times, a Dattatreya Temple has also been built.

other. She was very hospitable and used to serve guests with great veneration.

On one *Amavasya*, there was a *shradh* ceremony in the house. All the food preparations were ready, but the priests had still to take the sacramental food. At this juncture, a *sanyasi* came near the back door and asked for food. How to offer food to this strange guest before the priests were fed, was a dilemma for Sumata. On *shradh* days to feed anyone before the priests (who symbolise and represent the departed souls, the *pitridevatas*) are fed is prohibited; if anyone else is fed, it is supposed to nullify the merit and the purpose of the *shradh* ceremony. In her dilemma, Sumata looked with embarrassment at the face of the *sanyasi*. She instantaneously felt that 'the guest' was no ordinary being.

Has God himself come to test me? she felt. She forgot everything as to what was right and what was wrong, and she rushed to serve him food. Lo! the mendicant was Guru Dattatreya himself. Dattatreya was extremely pleased with Sumata for her goodness of heart, and said, 'Mother! I am very much pleased with you. Ask for whatever boon you may wish.' At this, Sumata was overjoyed. In that ecstasy, she spoke out, 'Maharaj! Let the word "mother" (Amma), as you addressed me, now become true and real (i.e., may you be born to me). That is all what I beseech you.' The Lord said, 'So, be it!' and instantly disappeared.

In course of time, Sumata became a mother and Sripada Sri Vallabha, the incarnation of Lord Dattatreya, was born to her as her son. In truth, it was not a birth in the normal sense. It was the manifestation of the Lord as a child in the house. How blessed is the mother that bore the Lord as her child! The child was named Sripada, as advised by the priests of the place, as the child's feet bore all the auspicious and holy marks and signs like the conch, chakra, etc.

Sripada's thread ceremony *(Upanayana Samskara)* was performed at the age of seven. Just as the initiation ceremony commenced, Sripada shone like *Jnana-Bhaskara* (Sun of Wisdom), and started reciting Vedic mantras with great mastery. All the pandits and scholars were dazed at Sripada's self-manifested knowledge and wisdom, and bowed down to him.

When Sripada attained marriageable age, and his parents had found a suitable match for him, they told him about it. Sripada smilingly said, 'Renunciation *(Vairagya)* alone is my companion in life and every woman in the world is none else but my mother.' As he said that the *Vairagya Stree* (Yoga Stree) would be his life's companion, he came to be known as Sri Vallabha (Sripada Sri Vallabha). Sripada further said, 'My mission is to go out into the world, to give initiation to and guide the sadhus.' Saying thus, he sought permission from his parents to take to *sanyasa* and leave the home. But it was too much for the parents to give their consent. How could they forego such a son? The situation was all the more poignant because among the other two children they had, one was dumb and deaf and the other was blind, and both were invalids and mentally retarded. If Sripada Sri Vallabha forsook them, who would look after them in their old age? What would be the plight of the family? That was the anxiety and anguish of the parents.

Sripada understood their worry and anxiety. He called his brothers near him, cast a divine and benevolent glance at them with overflowing love, and what a wonder! Instantly their physical and mental disabilities disappeared. They became perfectly normal and also gained instantaneously the knowledge of all the Vedas and scriptures. All were overwhelmed with joy. Sripada then blessed all of them saying that they would have a healthy and prosperous life. He enjoined on his brothers to serve the parents with love and devotion and assured them all, liberation in that birth itself.

Sripada Sri Vallabha then decided to set out on his mission. He bade goodbye to his parents. To his mother he said, 'Mother, don't be sorry that I am leaving you now. I have got a divine mission to fulfil. I have to redeem the world from the ignorance it is steeped in. I have taken this birth as your son only to redeem humanity. I have to instill into all people faith in God and reveal to them the divine glory.' He consoled all his relatives with his kindly advice and loving words and went out of sight in a trice. Using his yogic power, he travelled with the speed of mind, and reached the holy Varanasi (Kasi) instantly. There he remained incognito. He then went to Badarikasram on a pilgrimage, worshipped the deity there and then went to the south. He arrived at Gokarna-Mahabaleswar*. Gokarna is a hallowed place; it is the seat of Mahabaleswar Sivalinga. Sripada Sri Vallabha stayed there for three years and with his presence made it even a holier place.

THUS ENDS THE FIFTH CHAPTER OF SRI *GURU CHARITRA* DESCRIBING THE REINCARNATION OF LORD DATTATREYA AS SRIPADA SRI VALLABHA.

Glory to the all-merciful, the omnipresent and the ever-responsive Guru Nath!

---

* This place is in the present state of Karnataka.

6

Gokarna Mahabaleswar

This chapter describes the birth of Gokarna Mahakshetra. Ravana, by the merit of his great penance, earns the Atma Linga from Lord Siva. How the Atma Linga happened to get grounded at Gokarna is described in this chapter.

Namdharak prayed to Siddha Yogi to tell him about the Gokarna Mahatmya. He said it must have had great significance as it was a place chosen by Sripada Sri Vallabha, in preference to all other holy places in Bharat, for his sojourn and stay.

Siddha Yogi began the narration of the birth of Gokarna Atma Linga, as originally related by Lord Ganesa.

In the most ancient times in the *Treta Yuga*, there was a great Brahmin sage, Pulasthya, in the kingdom of Lanka. His wife's name was Kaikasi. They had a son named Ravana, who was the ruler of the kingdom. Ravana had ten heads and twenty arms and he was unusually mighty and strong. Kaikasi was a great devotee of Lord Sankara, and she offered worship to a Sivalinga every morning. She would not take food until she finished her worship. For her worship, she would find a new and original Sivalinga every day. If she failed in finding a new Sivalinga she would fast for the day and for that day, she would prepare a Mrithika Linga (the linga form moulded out of clay) and would do her worship to it.

One day, as Kaikasi did not get an original Sivalinga, she was doing her worship to a Mrithika Linga which she had prepared. Ravana saw this and felt in his pride and conceit that it did not befit her, the mother of a mighty person like him, to have to do worship to a mere Mrithika Linga, instead of the original Sivalinga. He said he would bring down the Kailash itself along with Sankara into Lanka for his mother's worship. He made a vow to this effect and set out for Kailash. Reaching there, he tried to pull out the Kailash mountain, for taking it to Lanka. The mountain began to totter; the *Deva-Ganas* and even Goddess Parvati were being tossed about. Even the heavens and netherworlds became shaky and extremely panicky. Goddess Parvati asked Siva what was happening and Sankara told her that Ravana, the son of his great devotee Kaikasi, was trying to pull out the Kailash to take it away to Lanka for his mother's worship. He said that Ravana was a great devotee of his, and hence he was refraining from doing anything in the matter. But with further pleadings of Parvati, Sankara intervened and pressed down merely with the toe of his right foot, which nearly crushed Ravana under the mountain. Ravana realised his folly and started praying to Sankara for his mercy and grace. In his rich musical voice, he began singing Sama Vedic hymns in the praise of the Lord. He undertook penance; he made a new musical instrument (*Yantra Karkamalika*—Rudra Veena) with his head, veins and nerves and started playing on it a rich and enrapturing music to please the Lord. He was cutting off his heads and offering as sacrifice in oblation to the Lord. It was a penance unprecedented and never undertaken by anyone ever before. Sankara was very much moved by the devotion and austerities of Ravana. He appeared before Ravana and told him that he would give him whatever boon he would wish for. Ravana prayed he wanted Kailash itself for his mother's worship.

Sankara said that it was an impossible wish; but he would, instead, give him his Atma Linga which is the divine core of

Lord Siva himself. He said the Atma Linga embodied in itself the highest divinity, and whoever worshipped it for just three years, would himself become almost like Sankara. He, however, warned and cautioned that the Linga should not touch the ground till it reached Lanka and was enshrined there.

Ravana was elated at winning the Atma Linga, but all the gods were frightened because the new power which Ravana won through the possession of the Atma Linga would make him the mightiest person and unconquerable even by gods and unconquerable even by the Trinity. Ravana had already subdued and enslaved the Five Elements and the *Navagrahas*. Now his pride and power would have no bounds and restraints. The gods started shuddering in fright and prayed to Lord Vishnu to save them and the worlds from the impending doom. Lord Vishnu approached Ganesa and together with Narada, they planned out how to deprive Ravana of the Atma Linga. The plan was that Vishnu would create an artificial dusk by covering the orb of the sun with his Sudarsana Chakra. Ravana would then break his journey, wherever he be, to perform his *Sayam Sandhya*. Ganesa would then appear there as a rustic boy. Ravana would request Ganesa to hold the Atma Linga in his hands till he (Ravana) would finish his *Sandhya Vandana*. Narada would then appear there and draw Ravana into conversation and delay the latter in completing his *Sandhya Vandana*. In the meanwhile Ganesa would ground the Atma Linga.

Ravana was still midway to Lanka, proudly carrying the Atma Linga. The sun suddenly dimmed down due to the contrivance of Vishnu, and giving the impression that it was already nearing dusk. Ravana was a meticulous observer of the daily rituals and therefore, was keen on doing his *Sandhya Vandana* before sunset was over. But what to do with the Sivalinga while doing the *Sandhya Vandana*? Siva told him that it should not be kept on the ground till he reached Lanka. While he was in this dilemma, there appeared nearby a shepherd-boy playing around and who looked so guileless and innocent. It was Lord Ganesa himself in that guise. Ravana called out to the boy and pleaded with him to hold the Sivalinga for him till he finished his evening oblations to the sun deity. The boy pretended that he was in a hurry to get back home as it was getting dark. On Ravana's further pleading, the boy said the Sivalinga seemed to be too heavy for him, and anyway he would hold it but Ravana should return soon. He said, 'If you delay I shall lay it on the ground and go away.' He added, 'However, I shall call out to you thrice before putting it on the ground and leaving.'

Ravana, placing the Sivalinga in the hands of the boy, hurried to the river. There he was accosted by Narada, who went on complementing and congratulating him for winning the Atma Linga which is the most powerful linga in the whole world. He said, 'It will make you the mightiest person in the world, and you will forever rule over all the gods.' Narada thus delayed Ravana, engaging him in conversation. Before Ravana could finish his *Sandhya Vandana*, he heard the boy calling out to him. Ravana took it easy, but nevertheless completed the *Sandhya Vandana* fast and hurried back. Lo! By the time he reached back, the boy had already grounded the Sivalinga. Ravana was furious with the boy, but the boy pleaded, 'It was too heavy for me, I called out for you thrice. As you did not return I couldn't help laying it on the ground.'

Ravana tried with all his might to pull out the Sivalinga, the more he pulled the more firmly it was getting stuck in the ground. However, with the pull of Ravana, the linga got twisted and elongated into the shape of a cow's ear (*Go-Karna*). As it withstood the mighty strength of Ravana, the Sivalinga came to be known as Gokarna Mahabaleswar, and the place also came to be called Gokarna Mahabaleswar and is deemed most holy, as the Sivalinga was installed there by Lord Ganesa, the foremost of the deities and further more, the installation was done at the instance of Lord Vishnu himself.

It is said that Ravana did the severest of penances at this place only, and attained all the boons from Lord Siva. All the gods also are said to have done great penances at this holy place.

The power of this place has been described in detail in the Skandha Purana.

THUS ENDS THE SIXTH CHAPTER OF SRI
GURU CHARITRA DESCRIBING HOW THE
ATMA LINGA OF SIVA FOUND ITS HABITATION AT
GOKARNA AND MADE IT ONE OF THE HOLIEST
SPOTS IN THE LAND.

Glory to the all-merciful, the omnipresent and the ever-responsive Guru Nath!

7

Gokarna Sthala Mahatmya

This chapter describes the Gokarna Kshetra Mahatmya. Gokarna had so much sanctity that Sripada Sri Vallabha chose to visit and spend some years there. A visit to this holy place burns off all sins however much grievous they be and earns for the person *Kailasha-pada*. Gautama Rishi narrates to King Mitrasahu who was under a curse, how a Chandala woman, with sins galore on her head, earns *Kailasha-pada* by the mere coincidence of her dying at the holy Gokarna.

*N*amdharak was thrilled with joy listening to the origin of *Gokarna Mahabaleswar*. He said to Siddha Yogi, 'From what you have said, I believe that the place must be spiritually very powerful, and it should have been conferring immense benefits materially, morally and spiritually on all the pilgrims visiting there. I am eager to hear of any instance in which anyone had derived such benefits from making a pilgrimage to the place.' In reply to this, Siddha Yogi narrated the following anecdote.

In the Ikshwaku race, there was once a king by name Mitrasahu. He was a very pious, noble and kind-hearted king. He treated his subjects as his own children and was ever engaged in promoting their welfare. Vasishta Maharishi was his family guru and priest. The king, however, had one weakness (vice), viz., his craze and overfondness for hunting.

The king once went out for hunting and killed many wild animals. Thereafter, he confronted a wicked *Rakshasa* and wounded him mortally. The *Rakshasa*, before falling down dead, told his brother that he should take revenge of his death. The brother *Rakshasa* took the guise of a human form, went to the king's place and managed to become the palace-cook. One day there was a *shradh* ceremony in the royal family. Meat is forbidden on such a day. As the Brahmin priests and *rishis* would come to partake of the food, the vicious *Rakshasa* surreptitiously cooked human flesh on that day, and taking everyone unawares, served it to the Brahmin priests, instead of the vegetarian food which was supposed to be served. The priests got enraged and were furious, and on the spur of the moment, without waiting to know the truth, cursed the king that he would become a *Bramha Rakshasa*. The king was about to curse the priests in revenge taking water in his palm for the purpose, when the queen restrained him saying it was not proper for anyone to curse the priests. The king then let the water from his palm drop on his own feet. The feet got charred and because of this, he came to be known as *Kalmashapada*. Vasishta Maharishi, realising that the king was really innocent, felt sorry for the curse uttered, and told the king that he was blessing him that the curse would last only for twelve years, at the end of which, he would get back his normal form.

The king, because of the curse, became a *Bramha Rakshasa*, and made the forest his habitation. He used to kill and eat whichever or whoever came by that way, whether they be animals, beasts or human beings. One day, a Brahmin couple happened to be passing through the forest. The *Bramha Rakshasa* caught hold of the Brahmin, and ignoring the requests and plaintive pleadings of the wife, who was imploring him to consider her as his own daughter and spare her husband's life, mercilessly killed the Brahmin and devoured him. At this the wife of the Brahmin, who was then suddenly widowed because of the blood-thirstiness of the *Rakshasa*, cursed him saying, 'Although after the expiry of twelve years you are going to get back your human form, if you try to court the pleasure of your wife, you will instantly drop down dead and your queen would become a widow like me'. Thereafter, the woman, along with the bones of her dead husband did *Sahagamana* and ended her life.

The king, after the expiry of the curse period of twelve years, was rid of the form of *Bramha Rakshasa*. Having become normal again, he returned to his kingdom. He confided to the queen the curse of the Brahmin woman. Hearing so the queen was heart-broken as the prospect of her getting a son was now doomed. Seeing the grief of the queen, the king consulted the wise men of the court and the priests, to find out whether they could suggest him any way to escape from the curse. They advised him, that if the royal couple could make pilgrimages to holy places and do their offerings to the gods, the power of the curse would at least get mitigated and with divine grace, it could perhaps even be overcome altogether.

The king and the queen set out on pilgrimage to most of the holy places of the land, doing severe penances at those places. They came to Mithilapur at last. They were very exhausted and sat down under the shade of a tree to rest. At this juncture, the king saw the illustrious Sage Gautama passing by, along with a group of other *rishis*. The king ran towards him and fell prostrate at the sage's feet and prayed that he should save him from the curse of the Brahmin woman and show him the way to expiate the sin of *Bramhahatya*.

Sage Gautama told the king that he should visit the holy Gokarna; his pilgrimage to the holy place would expiate his sin for certain. The sage said that all the gods, even all the celestial beings make pilgrimage to Gokarna for expiating their sins and to earn merit. He said that even Bramha and Vishnu visited the holy place and did penances for a long time in order to earn merit.

The sage cited instances of the incomparable redeeming power of the holy place. The greatest sins like killing or causing the death of a Brahmin, a cow, etc., could be expiated by pilgrimage to and worship at Gokarna. He narrated the following incident, which he himself had witnessed just a few days ago.

The sage saw a low caste woman at Gokarna; she was blind and was suffering from a dreadful disease. She was very exhausted and was very hungry. She begged for food, but could not manage to get anything. Due to exhaustion and hunger, she died. As soon as she died, messengers of Siva came near her in a celestial *Vimana* to take her to Kailash. But, at the same time, the messengers of Yama also arrived there. Both the groups were laying their claims on the *jiva* of the dead woman. Gautama inquired of them as to why this conflict and confrontation should arise between them. The *Yamadootas* said that the woman was a very sinful person; the sins she committed in her life were gravest and what she deserved were only the tortures and fires of hell. But the *Sivadootas* said that although she had committed many sins yet as she had died at the holy Gokarna, Lord Siva had granted her *Kailasha-Pada* and had sent them to fetch for her.

Her past story was as follows:

The woman, in her previous birth, was born in a Brahmin family. Her name was Saudamini. She was very beautiful and charming. When she was ten years old, she was married, but her husband died only after a few years of the marriage. In course of time, unable to control her sensuous desires and passions of youth, she yielded to and started living with a *Wani* from her neighbourhood. She also got addicted to drink and other evil habits. Once after drinking wine, in her intoxication, she killed a calf for food, mistaking it for a goat. At that time the *Wani* was away. When she came to her senses, it was time for milking the cow and she went for milking. But the cow, not finding its calf nearby, did not yield any milk. The woman felt dead scared as to how her husband and neighbours would react when they would come to know what she had done. She pretended to weep, and told that a tiger had come killed the calf and run away with it. Everyone believed it to be true. After some years, the woman died and she was taken to hell. She was put to great torture there.

This woman was later reborn as a Chandali. She was very ugly. As she grew up, she lost her sight and became blind. She was overtaken by leprosy. As long as her parents were alive, they took care of her and looked after her. After she lost her parents, there was none to take care of her; she never had enough food to eat. She was suffering great misery.

In the holy month of *Magha*, she decided to travel to Gokarna, along with a group of pilgrims, for the festival of Sivaratri. She thought if she accompanied them, they would give her also something to eat during the journey, but the pilgrims did not take to her kindly. On the day of the festival too she had to fast as none too, had given her anything to eat. She received a few *bilwa* leaves instead, which was being distributed among the pilgrims. In anger, she flung them away. Lo! The *bilwa* leaves, although she never intended it, fell right on the Sivalinga. In a few moments after this, the woman who was famished and exhausted, died.

Even the least worship, either done with devotion or without devotion, knowingly or unknowingly is enough to please Siva. Thus the Chandali earned the favour and grace of Siva*. The merit earned by her was all the more because it happened to be done at *Gokarna*, the abode of Siva's Atma Linga, and besides, that day was the holy *Sivaratri* day. Therefore, no sooner did the woman died, than Lord Sankara sent his messengers to bring her to Kailash. Hearing the narrative of the *Sivadootas*, the men of Yama beat a retreat, leaving the woman in the hands of the *Sivadootas*.

Such being the glory and power of Gokarna, Gautama Rishi advised the king to go to Gokarna and do penance there, and assured him that he would be thereby freed from the curse. The king as advised by Gautama Rishi, made a pilgrimage to Gokarna, did penance there, and thereby got rid of the curse. Thereafter, he lived happily with his wife, was blessed with sons and lived for a long time.

THUS ENDS THE SEVENTH CHAPTER OF SRI
GURU CHARITRA DESCRIBING THE REDEEMING
POWER OF THE HOLY GOKARNA KSHETRA.

Glory to the all-merciful, the omnipresent and the ever-responsive Guru Nath!

---

* The term Chandala, in a sense, is our *Deha-buddhi*, i.e., obsession with the idea that 'I am the body'. Sivalinga signifies the *Atma-buddhi* or *Sivoham-Bhavana* i.e., the understanding that one is not the body but the Spirit. From *Deha-buddhi*, we have to raise ourselves to *Atma-buddhi*, to earn the *Kailasha-pada*.

8

Sani Pradosha Vrata Mahatmya

In this chapter, Sripada Sri Vallabha teaches about the *Sani Pradosha Puja Mahima* to Ambika, who in a state of desperation, came to the river with the intention of drowning herself along with her blockheaded son. He narrates how a shepherd-woman was born as Yasoda in her next life through the merit earned by her by merely watching the Sani Pradosha Puja, and becoming the (foster) mother of Lord Sri Krishna.

Sripada Sri Vallabha also blessed the blockheaded son of Ambika and endowed him with all shastric knowledge and wisdom.

In this chapter is also described the emergence of the Mahakaleswar Jyotirlinga as a result of the Sani Pradosha Puja done with deep devotion by the shepherd-boy.

Siddha Yogi continued with the narrative of Sri Vallabha.
From Gokarna, Sripada Sri Vallabha went to Sri Sailam and did the *Chaturmasya** there. From there, he went to Navratti (Nivruthi) Sangam. After spending some time there, he finally came to Kuravpur (near the present Raichur). His spiritual fame spread far and wide, and devotees used to pour in for his darshan all the time. His spiritual power was such that with his mere darshan, people used to be relieved from all distress. He always

---
* The four-month stay at a fixed place during the rainy season, performed by the monks who otherwise are forbidden from staying at any fixed place for more than five days.

radiated peace and love. The ailing used to be cured instantly; spiritual seekers coming to him used to feel highly uplifted. His mere glance would transport people to higher realms of consciousness and fill their hearts with supernal joy and transcendental peace.

At that time, there lived in Kuravpur a learned Brahmin. His wife's name was Ambika. She gave birth to many children but except the last one, none of the others survived. Unfortunately that boy who survived was dull-headed. All efforts of his father to teach him were of no avail as the boy had no grasping power at all. This was a cause of frustration and anxiety to the parents. The father died in dejection. Having no support, the son and the mother were thrown into penury and had no means of livelihood. They had to take to begging and had to live a very hard and miserable life. They were disgusted with their lives, and both of them decided to end their lives by throwing themselves into the river. As they approached the river bank with the object of putting an end to their lives, the woman saw Sripada Sri Vallabha who came there for his bath. Seeing the halo around his face and the divinity in his looks, her aching heart was soothened, and her desperation overcome by a new-born peace, hope and joy in her heart. The compassion and love in Sripada's looks charged new life in her depressed and broken heart. She fell at his feet and vented out the anguish in her heart, and said, 'How I wish to have a son like you in my next birth at least.' 'So be it, mother!' said Sri Vallabha. He added, 'But you will have to observe a particular *vrata*; you will have to worship Lord Maheshwara in the evenings on *Trayodasi Tithi* days coinciding with and coming on Saturdays, and is called the Sani Pradosha Puja. It is a powerful *vrata*, and if dutifully performed, it will certainly endow you a son like Lord Krishna himself.' He then narrated the following anecdote.

Once upon a time, there lived a king named Chandrasena in Ujjain. He had a friend by name

Manibhadra, an ascetic and who was deeply devoted to Lord
Maheshwara. Lord Maheshwara, very much pleased with
Manibhadra's devotion, gave him the celestial gem in the
shape of Marakatha Linga. This gem, by its mere touch,
could turn iron into gold, and fulfil any wish of the person
who wore it. Manibhadra gifted the gem to Chandrasena,
which brought great prosperity to his people and the
kingdom. All the kings and people of other regions came to
know about the gem. Some of the neighbouring kings
wanted to get possession of the gem, and they plotted and
invaded Ujjain. That day happened to be Sani Trayodasi day,
and the king, as was his wont, was engaged in worship in the
Siva Temple. Although he was told about the invasion of his
kingdom by the enemy kings, he remained unperturbed and
unmoved, and did not leave from his place of worship. One
of the cowherd-boys saw the king's worship, and he also was
seized with a desire to worship. He picked up a round stone,
and started worshipping it as a Sivalinga. It was getting late
in the night but the boy remained totally absorbed in the
puja. As the boy did not return home while all his
companions returned back, his mother felt worried. She
came searching for him and found him doing his worship.
She asked him to stop the puja and return home along with
her instantly. But the boy refused to move from there. The
mother got furious and threw out 'the stone' which he was
worshipping as the Sivalinga. The boy felt very unhappy and
distressed at the sacrilege committed by his mother in her
anger. He thought he should atone for it by giving up his
life. Lord Siva was very much moved by the anguish and the
sincere and deep devotion of the boy, and appeared before
him in linga form, dazzling with a million suns' effulgence.
It was the manifestation of the Jyotirlinga. Along with the
Jyotirlinga, emerged by itself a magnificent temple—the

Mahakaleswar Temple. The boy prayed Siva to pardon his mother for the sacrilege she had committed. Lord Siva said that the (boy's) mother had already earned great merit as she had witnessed the puja which he (the boy) was doing with such great devotion, and because of that she would be having God himself as her child in her next birth. Meanwhile the brilliance of the light, emanating from the Jyotirlinga was spreading far and wide, far up to the horizon and in all directions. The kings who attacked Ujjain saw the marvel and realised that Ujjain and its king were in divine hands, and that it would be suicidal on their part to enter into a fight against such a king. They made peace with the king and returned to their kingdoms. Thus Ujjain remained safe, the king and the people remaining unscathed by the enemies' attack, and all this was possible due to the power of Sani Pradosha Puja.

The king made the shepherd-boy the ruler of the shepherd community and gifted him with many villages to rule. The shepherd boy's mother felt very penitent for the sacrilege she had committed by casting away the 'stone', which her son was worshipping with such great devotion. Having witnessed the emergence of the Jyotirlinga as a fruition and reward for the worship done by her child, she also was filled with great devotion. In her next birth she was born as Yasoda. As foretold by Lord Siva, she became the foster-mother of Lord Sri Krishna. This was the merit she earned by merely witnessing the Sani Pradosha Puja being done by her son. Had she done the puja herself, Lord Krishna would have been born to herself, as her own son.

Sripada Sri Vallabha finally said to Ambika, 'If you do the Sani Pradosha Puja devotedly and regularly, you will certainly bear God himself as your own child in your next life.'

Sripada Sri Vallabha then blessed Ambika's son. With the mere touch of Sripada, the boy became fully enlightened. Wisdom and knowledge dawned on him. He became proficient in all the scriptures, making the mother happy in all measures.

THUS ENDS THE EIGHTH CHAPTER OF SRI
GURU CHARITRA DESCRIBING THE SANI PRADOSHA
PUJA MAHATMYA.

Glory to the all-merciful, the omnipresent and the ever-responsive Guru Nath!

9

Sripada Sri Vallabha
Blesses the Washer-man

In this chapter, Sripada Sri Vallabha gives a boon to his devotee, a *rajak*, that he would be born in a Nawab family and would be a ruler in his next birth and would also have his darshan but in his new avatar (i.e., when he would reappear as Sri Narasimha Saraswati).

Siddha Yogi narrated another incident which took place during Sripada's stay at Kuravpur.

Every day—morning, midday and evening—Sripada used to come for his bath to the Sangam (confluence) of Krishna and Venya rivers. A *rajak* also used to come there daily with loads of clothes for washing. Thus he used to have Sripada's darshan three times daily. He used to wash Sripada's clothes daily, dry them and thus used to serve him. Deep devotion grew in him for Sripada.

One day it so happened that a Muslim Sultan was camping on the banks of the river (near the confluence). As usual, when the washer-man went to the river with his bundles of clothes for washing, he saw the Muslim king and his wives bathing in the river. The women were wearing rich ornaments and precious jewellery. There were many guards keeping watch around the camp. The *rajak's* eyes were dazzled seeing the glory and pomp of the king. He thought how lowly and miserable his own life was,

and felt that a life like that of the Nawab alone was worth living.
He started thinking how happy he would be if he also were to be
born in a royal family and be a king. His mind was brooding thus.

Later in the day, when the *rajak* met Sripada, the latter asked
him what was plaguing him. Sripada knew what was going on in
the *rajak's* mind, and he had love for him because of his devotion
and the services he was doing to him (Sripada). Sripada told him
that he was blessing him to be born in a royal family in his next
life and to have all his heart's desires fulfilled. He further said, 'If
you so desire, I will make you a king even in this life, why even
now itself.'

The *rajak* was overwhelmed with the joy for Guru Nath's
solicitude for him. He said, 'Lord, I am now too old for any
pleasures of the world. Whatever blessings you want to confer
on me, please defer them for my next birth. But please, do not
ever forsake me. How can I live without your darshan?'

Sripada then said, 'Let it be so. In your next birth you will be
born in the Nawab's family at Vaiduryapura (Bidar). You will
enjoy all royal luxuries and pleasure to your heart's content. You
will have my darshan too, but not in my present form, but in the
form of my new incarnation then as Sri Narasimha Saraswati. But
remember, that it is not earthly pleasures and indulgence of the
senses one should covet in life, but one should ever aspire for the
grace of God alone, which is far above all the earthly enjoyments
and achievements.* Anyway, because of your devotion to me, I
will grant you liberation too, in your next life.'

---

*   The *Kalpavriksha* grants whatever we ask for. If we seek 'Sreyas' from it, it will readily
      grant it to us, if we seek 'Preyas' that also will be readily granted to us by the same
      celestial tree. It all depends on what we yearn for. The *rajak* symbolises our (i.e., the
      normal man's) state with sensuous cravings and worldly longings. Sage Patanjali says
      that Iswara is the one who, by his mere *Sankalpa* can grant the *Kaivalya-pada* (the
      highest spiritual state) to the aspirant. Most of us do not know what to seek from Iswara.
      We ask him to grant us the trinket-joys of the world, but we do not ask for the eternal
      and divine bliss which he is ever ready to grant to us even now and here itself.

      Just as his devotion to the Guru redeemed the *rajak* eventually and granted him
      liberation in his next life, may we too cultivate devotion and earn our own redemption
      too.

Sripada Sri Vallabha decided a little later, that he should now end his sojourn on earth in the present avatar of his. He had lighted up the lamp of wisdom. He had helped many yearning souls on the spiritual path. He had relieved the sufferings of many. He had revived that Sampradaya—of attaining liberation through devotion and service to the Guru and through the practice of renunciation and observance of the moral codes of life. On the *Aswiyujasuddha Dwadasi* (twelfth day of the bright fortnight in the month of *Aswiyuja*) Sripada Sri Vallabha walked into the waters of the confluence of the rivers and disappeared just as Lord Sri Rama had ended his avatar in the *Treta Yuga*, by merging himself in the waters of the Srayu River of Ayodhya. Thus ended another one of the most glorious avatars of the Lord.

Although Sripada Sri Vallabha had withdrawn his avatar, yet it is known that he did appear countless number of times and still continues to do so, in his very physical form, to all those who have set their hearts on that holy form and offer their devotion to that form in all sincerity and earnestness.

THUS ENDS THE NINTH CHAPTER OF SRI
GURU CHARITRA DESCRIBING RAJAK
VARA PRADANAM.

Glory to the all-merciful, the omnipresent and the ever-responsive Guru Nath!

10

Sripada Sri Vallabha's Blessings after His Mahaprasthan*

In this chapter, an account is given of how Sripada Sri Vallabha, even after the withdrawal of his avatar (i.e., even after *Mahaprasthan*), continues to manifest and shower his grace on his devotees. An illustration is given how Sripada Sri Vallabha protected a Brahmin devotee by bringing him back to life after he was killed by dacoits. The same grace continues to be showered even now, on whosoever seeks it.

*N*amdharak entreated Siddhamuni to enlighten him further on the leelas *and* mahimas *of Sripada Sri Vallabha, which are said to be occurring even after the withdrawal of his physical form as avatar.*

Siddha Yogi narrated the following anecdote which is just one among the countless such occurrences.

There was one Brahmin called Vallabhesh. He used to earn his livelihood in some small trade. He was an ardent devotee of Sripada and used to visit Kuravpur every year for the darshan and worship of the *Guru padukas* enshrined there. Once he was planning to take up a new business venture, which was fraught with considerable risk. He took a vow that in case he would

---

* Reading should not be broken after reading this chapter. Chapters 10 to 21 are to be completed in one session, i.e., in one day's sitting or duration.

succeed in the venture through Sripada's grace, he would feed a thousand Brahmins at Kuravpur. To his joy, he succeeded in the venture and earned a handsome profit.

In order to fulfil his vow, Vallabhesh set out to Kuravpur, taking along with him quite a sum of money for spending for the proposed feast. A group of thieves learnt of his journey and followed him. They told the Brahmin that they also were devotees of Guru Nath and visited Kuravpur every year for the darshan and worship of the *padukas*. Vallabhesh believed them and felt happy that he had good company for the journey. They halted in the forest for rest in the night. The Brahmin fell fast asleep. While the Brahmin was sleeping the thieves got a huge stick and knocked a heavy blow on the head of the Brahmin. The Brahmin opened his eyes wreathing in great pain, and felt aghast to see his companions trying to kill him. He closed his eyes and prayed to Sripada mentally uttering *'Digambara, Digambara, Sripada Sri Vallabha Digambara'* (Oh like the all-expansive sky, like the all-expansive sky, Oh the omnipresent Lord Sripada Sri Vallabha!). As the thieves hit him further, also inflicting knife injuries in his neck, he fell unconscious and died. The thieves seized the bag of money from the Brahmin and started to run away from there. But they were aghast to find a person with matted hair, body smeared with ashes, holding a trident in his hand, looking fiercely at them, and blocking their way. The strange *sanyasi* pierced the thieves with his trident, who died instantly. However, one escaped his wrath as he fell at the feet of the *sanyasi* and pleaded in mortal fright. 'Oh divine one! Please spare my life. I was actually not in that group but just accompanying them. I pray to you to pardon me.' The *sanyasi* relented and giving *vibhuti* to him said, 'Apply this *vibhuti* over the injuries of the Brahmin and keep strict watch for the safety of the body till day-break.' Saying thus the *sanyasi* disappeared just as instantaneously as he had appeared. The thief who was

spared his life, did as commanded by the *sanyasi*. Lo! in the early
hours of dawn, and as the darkness was melting away giving way
to the light of sunrise, the Brahmin came back to life, just as if he
was waking up from a sound sleep. There were no marks of
injuries even on his head and body. The thief who had survived
narrated to the Brahmin all that had happened, and begged his
pardon. The Brahmin, seeing also the dead bodies of the other
thieves, realised that it was none else but Sripada Sri Vallabha
Deva who had come to his rescue. With tears of gratitude
welling out from his heart, he sang of his glory. The thief who
had survived, completely reformed now, handed over the money
bag safely to him.

The Brahmin safely reached Kuravpur, and gave a rich and
sumptuous feast to more than four thousand people, and
fulfilled his vow in a much bigger way.*

*The Siddha Yogi commented at the end, 'Sripada Sri Vallabha
Deva is ever present, and is everywhere, giving succour and
protection to whosoever prays and offers his devotion to him.'*

THUS ENDS THE TENTH CHAPTER OF SRI
GURU CHARITRA WHICH DESCRIBES BHAKTA
SANKATA HARANAM.

Glory to the all-merciful, the omnipresent and the ever-responsive Guru Nath!

---

* The three thieves who figure in this chapter are symbolic of our *gunas*, viz., tamas, rajas
and sattva. *Tamas* and *Rajas* try to obscure our Self. *Sattva* is relatively harmless and is
a silent spectator. By contemplation on Guru, one must destroy and get rid of *tamas* and
rajas first. *Sattva*, when separated away from *tamas* and *rajas*, cannot be of any harm to
us. Actually it can really be of much help to us in our initial Sadhana, although it also
needs to be transcended eventually.

11

Birth of Sri Narasimha Saraswati

This chapter describes the advent of Sri Narasimha Saraswati. He was born as a son to Amba in Karanjapuri as per the promise made to her in her previous life by Sripada Sri Vallabha. At birth, he could chant the *Omkar*. He was otherwise 'dumb' till his *Upanayana* was performed. After Upanayana, he bursts into the recital of Vedic mantras and begins to glow with knowledge and wisdom.

In an earlier chapter, it has been said how Sripada Sri Vallabha blessed the destitute woman Ambika, advising her to observe Sani Pradosha Vrata and worship Maheshwara. Ambika had prayed to him that, at least in her next birth, she should have a son like him. Sripada Sri Vallabha told her that her desire would be fulfilled if she faithfully observed Sani Pradosha Vrata and win the grace of Maheshwara. Siddha Yogi narrated to Narasimha Saraswati what happened to Amba (Ambika) in her next birth.

As per Sri Vallabha's advice, Ambika strictly observed the Vrata till her death. In her next birth, Ambika was born in a Brahmin family, in Karanjanagar (a town near Akola, in the former state of Berar. She was named by the parents as Amba Bhavani. When she came of age, she was married to a young man named Madhav, who was very pious and deeply devoted to Lord Siva. Both of them used to observe Sani Pradosha Vrata regularly.

A few years after the marriage, a boy was born to Amba (in AD 1458). During her pregnancy, she was having divine visions and experiences. Her mind was always dwelling on holy ideas and auspicious thoughts. There was a divine lustre spreading over her body and also radiating forth from her face. And on one auspicious day, a son was born to her. Strangely, instead of the normal crying, *Pranava Nada*, the chant of *Omkar*, was emanating from the mouth of the infant. The wise men of the village said that astrologically the boy was going to be a Mahapurusha and a great saviour of the world. He had all the auspicious insignia of God himself. On the tenth day, the boy was named as Narahari. His eyes bespoke of omniscience and his face seemed to reflect all the wisdom to the worlds. The infant was an attraction for all the people of the town.

Narahari's mother did not seem to have sufficient breast-milk to nurse the child. She expressed this to her husband and suggested that he should purchase a cow to provide milk for the child. The child seemed to have heard it, and touched with his tiny hands the nipples of the breasts of the mother. Lo, the breasts were full of milk! The infant was manifesting many divine miracles. Nevertheless, the child seemed to be dumb. Except the *Pranava Nada* that emanated from his lips at the time of the birth, the child never uttered any sound. The parents were afraid and were worried that the child would be dumb for ever! The mother used to weep saying, 'Are we not destined to enjoy the prattle of the child?' The child used to however make little gestures which seemed to indicate that, after his thread-ceremony, he would be quite normal in speech. Yet the parents were not relieved of their anxiety. To assure and comfort them, Narahari once took hold of an iron piece lying in the house and, through his mere touch, changed it into gold.

When Narahari was seven years old, his thread-ceremony was performed, and, to the wonder of all, the miracle of miracles happened. All the assembled Brahmins were amazed to see 'the dumb Narahari' chanting Vedic mantras. The joy of the parents knew no bounds and they shed profuse tears of joy.

The mother asked Narahari to beg alms, according to the tradition of the thread-ceremony. Narahari said, 'Mother can I now take it that I have your permission to take to *sanyasa* which I very much desire? You asked me to beg alms. That implies you have sanctioned my heart's desire to take to an ascetic's life.' The mother was aghast at these words of Narahari. What she only meant was that he should ask for the *bhiksha* of the Vatu from the mother as mere formality as per the tradition of the thread-ceremony. She broke down into tears and pleaded as to how he could think of forsaking her and the home and taking to an ascetic life. He was her only child and the only hope. She pleaded that all should follow the *Asramadharma* and should take *sanyas* only after going through the householder's life *Grihasthasrama* and that alone would be the proper way. One should not skip one's responsibilities, duties and obligations. She was inconsolable. Narahari said, 'Mother, understand me and see the truth.' Saying thus, he placed his right palm on her head. As soon as he did this, the memory of her previous life was revived. She remembered the boon Sripada Sri Vallabha gave her. She understood then that it was the divine Sripada Sri Vallabha who was born to her as her son now, as she had prayed to him in her former life. She realised it would not be possible to hold back the divine being in the confines of her home for long. But nevertheless, she pleaded with him whom she now realised as none else but the illustrious Dattatreya, to stay in the home for at least a few more years.

THUS ENDS THE ELEVENTH CHAPTER OF SRI
GURU CHARITRA DESCRIBING SRIPADA
SRI VALLABHA'S REINCARNATION AND THE NEW
INCARNATION'S CHILDHOOD.

Glory to the all-merciful, the omnipresent and the ever-responsive Guru Nath!

12

Narahari Taking to Sanyasa

In this chapter Narahari, Amba's son, gives spiritual instruction to his mother; he blesses her that she would have two more sons within a year, and one more son and daughter later. After the birth of the two sons (twins), Narahari leaves home for Kasi. He was hardly nine years old at that time. At Kasi, he took initiation into *Sanyasasrama* from Krishna Saraswati and took the name of Narasimha Saraswati. After that he went to *Badarikasrama* and visited many holy places.

Siddha Yogi continued the narration.

Narahari explained to his mother the higher philosophy of life. She had tried to tell him earlier that one should not skip the responsibilities of the household; one should pass through the prescribed stages of life in sequential order, the *Asramadharmas.* After *Grihasthasrama* only, which mellows man, his senses having been appeased, should one take to *Vanasprasta* or *sanyasa*, and not before that. Narahari revealed to his mother that he was not a normal mortal being who has to necessarily go through all the stages of life. Everyone has his own *adhikara* and one has to decide for himself his course of life, using his discrimination properly.

He continued with his observations sayings, 'Life is like a bubble. Death might knock at any time and snatch us away. Every moment of human life is precious and is the god-gifted opportunity for man to regenerate himself spiritually and speed up to the blessed state of self-realisation. In the earlier *Yugas*, man's life was long. The stages of life prescribed by the shastras were all right for them. But in the *Kali Yuga*, men have only a short span of life and do not have the longevity of the earlier *Yugas*. If one goes through life slowly, without taking to the pursuit of higher purposes of life, and if his life is cut short early, isn't this birth futile? One should cultivate *Vairagya* towards worldly pleasures from early stages of life. One should not fritter away his energies in human foibles. The world is illusory. If one does'nt use discrimination and does not cultivate *vairagya,* he would sink into the mire of *samsara* and will let go the precious life to waste. One should set his mind on the goal of life and strive to achieve it from the early stages of life, because who knows when he will be snatched away by death. Losing this life without realisation of God will be the greatest tragedy for man …'

The mother realised that the spiritual fire raging in her son cannot be smothered and that her motherly love and attachment should not be let to hold him back from his quest for the Infinite. However, she pleaded with him to stay at home for at least a few years more, still she had another child. Narahari agreed to it and said that she would have four more children, three sons and one daughter.

A year later Amba Bhavani had twins, two sons were born to her and then she yielded to let Narahari leave the home. While bidding farewell, touched by the tears of the parents, Narahari said, 'Whenever you think of me and want me to be with you, wherever I may be, you will have my darshan.' He told them again that they would have one more son and also a daughter. With these consoling words to his parents, young Narahari— who was hardly in his ninth year at that time—left his home and set out on his spiritual quest. The entire village bade a tearful farewell just as it happened to Krishna and Balarama, when they left Brindavan for Mathura.

Narahari came to Varanasi, the spiritual centre of Bharat. Every day after taking his bath in the sacred waters of the Ganges, he used to worship Kasi Visweswara three times a day. At Kasi he came in contact with Sri Krishna Saraswati, a highly advanced *yogi* and a fully realised soul. Narahari requested Sri Krishna Saraswati to initiate him into the *Sanyasasrama*. Sri Krishna Saraswati was pleased at the devotion, the austere discipline and earnestness of Narahari and much more so with his intellectual brilliance and scriptural knowledge. Krishna Saraswati recognised in him a future savant of the spiritual culture of the country, and especially one who was going to glorify the supremacy of the *Sanyasasrama* again, as was earlier done by Sri Adi Sankaracharya of Kaladi. He was immensely happy to have Narahari as his disciple and to initiate him into *sanyasa*. Narahari was given by him the new name of Narasimha Saraswati.

Namdharak interrupted Siddha Yogi and asked why Narahari, God Incarnate Himself, needed a Guru and why should he go through the formality of Initiation? Siddhamuni said, 'Guru is the link between God and the embodied being, even though the latter may have been a divine incarnation. Sri Rama had Vasishta Rishi as Guru and Sri Krishna has Sandeepani Rishi as his Guru'. He gave a glorious account of the Guru parampara, originating with Lord Sankara Himself. 'Sankara-Vishnu-Bramha-Vasishta-Sakti-Parasara-Vyasa-Suka-Gaudapada-Govindacharya-Sankara Bhagavatpada … thus flows the glorious Guru parampara,' said Siddha Yogi.

Siddha Yogi explained that for spreading true knowledge, for the enlightenment and welfare of all, Sri Narasimha Saraswati conducted a number of Jnana Yagnas by discoursing and giving sermons, going from place to place around Varanasi. Hundreds of people were guided on the spiritual path by him. A number of them became his disciples.

From Varanasi, Narasimha Saraswati went to Badarikashram forest with his disciples. Then, he moved from place to place and arrived at Ganga Sagar near Calcutta. Travelling along the banks of the holy river, he reached Prayaga (Triveni), the holy confluence of the sacred rivers— Ganga, Yamuna and the subterranean Saraswati. He initiated one Madhava Saraswati into sanyasa *at the holy Prayaga.*

THUS ENDS THE TWELFTH CHAPTER OF SRI *GURU CHARITRA* DESCRIBING THE GLORIOUS GURU PARAMPARA THAT NOURISHED AND SUSTAINED THE PERENNIAL FLOW OF SPIRITUAL WISDOM (JNANA GANGA) IN THE HOLY AND BLESSED LAND OF BHARAT* DESA.

Glory to the all-merciful, the omnipresent and the ever-responsive Guru Nath!

---

* The land which honours and lives by the principle of Bharati, i.e., Goddess Saraswati (the goddess of knowledge)

Narasimha Saraswati's Healing Touch

This chapter describes the visit of Guru Nath along with his disciples to his parents at Karanjapuri. From there he again sets out on his itinerary. At Vasar Brahmeshwar, Guru Nath cures the chronic stomach-ulcer of a Brahmin, who was about to kill himself, being unable to bear the excruciating pain of the ulcer.

Namdharak said to Siddha Yogi that listening to the Guru's lifestory, he felt that it was like drinking nectar. He pleaded with the Siddha not to stop the narration but to continue with it. He said he was particularly eager to know any incident relating to Sri Narasimha Saraswati during his stay at the holy Prayaga, and where he went thereafter. Siddha then continued his narration.

Many more disciples flocked to Narasimha Saraswati at Prayaga. Some of them were Bala Saraswati, Krishna Saraswati, Upendra Saraswati, Madhav Saraswati, Sadanand Saraswati, Dhyan Jyoti Saraswati and also Siddha himself. He was day in and day out engaged in giving spiritual discourses and *upadesa* to people and drawing them and guiding them on the spiritual path. Just as during infancy he changed a piece of iron into a block of gold, now he was transforming men of clay into spiritual gems. To the common people and laity, he was preaching moral laws and religious disciplines. To *Jijnasu*, he was imparting Vedic wisdom. To *sadhakas*, he was giving yogic instruction and guidance and spiritual enlightenment. He was himself an example unto all. His life itself, in truth, was his message. His darshan itself uplifted man ethically and spiritually.

It was nearly 36 years since Sri Narasimha Saraswati left his parental home and his parents were anxious and pining to see him. As per the promise he made to them, he thought he should give them the joy of seeing him. He came to Karanjanagar along with his disciples. The joy of the parents knew no bounds. His mother now vividly remembered her previous life's incidents. How Sripada Sri Vallabha blessed her, taught her about the Sani Pradosha Puja, the performance of which found its fruition in her becoming the mother of Sri Narasimha Saraswati, who was none else but the reincarnation of Sripada Sri Vallabha Deva. She realised how blessed she was.

Sri Narasimha Saraswati told his mother that she might not have been happy about his having taken to *Sanyasasrama* because of her love for him. He explained to her the unique merits of *Sanyasasrama*. He said it is the spiritual acme of life. It would besides liberate not only the one who has taken to *sanyasa*, but also all his ancestors for several generations. He blessed the parents saying that they would spend their last days at the holy Kasi and would certainly attain salvation and liberation from re-birth. He further indicated that his own taking to *Sanyasasrama* had a very special purpose, the purpose of revivifying the glory of *Sanyasasrama*, the significance of which was getting missed by people because of the growing materialistic outlook and way of life.

Narahari's mother, Amba Bhavani had a daughter born to her after Narahari left home. Her name was Ratnai (Ratnabai). After her marriage she approached Narasimha Saraswati and prayed that she be saved; she said the problems of life were almost crushing her. Narasimha Saraswati told her that the duty of a woman was to serve her husband, considering him as God. That alone is sufficient for a woman to attain salvation, he said. He also foretold that her husband would be taking to *sanyasa* (but very much late in life, after both of them had become fairly old). He further said that because of some of the sins committed by her in her previous life, she was destined to suffer in this life from a dreadful skin-disease but that also will be late in life. He told her that she could however, overcome it if she made a pilgrimage to the holy *Papavinasini Theertha* near Gandharvapura (Ganagapur). He assured her that she would have his darshan at the time of her death and she would attain salvation.

As almost everyone in the town wanted Sri Narasimha Saraswati to visit their homes for *bhiksha*, it is said he took many forms and blessed each house, by accepting *bhiksha*, in the span of few days he stayed in the town. Sri Narasimha Saraswati, after visiting his parents, went on pilgrimage to Trayambak and Nasik. He narrated to his disciples there the *Gautami-Mahima*; what severe penance Gautama Rishi did to bring Ganga (Godavari River) to the earth. River Godavari is an aspect of the holy Ganga itself and it was Gautama Rishi's penances that made Godavari to descend and come down for the purification of the land and its people.

During his pilgrimages, Narasimha Saraswati came to a certain place called Manjarika on the banks of River Godavari. He met one very learned pandit there by the name Madhavaranya. Madhavaranya was overjoyed at meeting Sri Narasimha Saraswati and sang many songs in praise of him. He sought his blessings and grace. Guru Nath revealed to him *Viswarupa* and then advised him to always do the Manasa Puja to Lord Narasimha (the man-lion incarnation of Lord Vishnu). He said that all his earthly needs would be fulfilled by the grace of Lord Narasimha, and that he would attain *Bramhaloka* after his death.

Siddha Yogi continued narrating about the healing powers of Sri Narasimha Saraswati that could free human beings from all ailments.

From Manjarika, Sri Narasimha Saraswati came to Vasar Brahmeswara (Brahmeswara Kshetra), which is also on the banks of River Godavari. There he saw one Brahmin near the river. The Brahmin was suffering from severe stomach-ache for several years. He used to get unbearable pain and it was difficult for him to take food. He was fed up with his life and decided to end his life and for that purpose came to the river to drown himself by tying a heavy boulder around his neck. The all-knowing and omniscient Narasimha Saraswati came near him and asked him what his trouble was. The Brahmin told him about his misery, and said that he would not be able to bear and put up with it any longer. Sri Narasimha Saraswati comforted him by saying that he had a panacea, a unique remedy for him and he would be free from the ailment soon and he was not to worry himself about it any longer. Just at the juncture, the *gramadhipati* of the place, a Brahmin of *Kaundinya Gotra* and by the name Sayamdeo, had come to the river for his bath. Seeing Sri Narasimha Saraswati, Sayamdeo was overjoyed and he prostrated at Guru Nath's feet, and started singing praises of him. When Sayamdeo requested him to come to his house for food, Guru Nath told him to invite the ailing Brahmin also for food.

Sayamdeo said he was afraid that the Brahmin might die if he fed him and he would then incur the *Bramhahatya dosha*. 'He has hardly taken food yesterday, and he is almost in death pangs now. Any food is almost like poison for that poor Brahmin,' commented Sayamdeo thus expressing his apprehensions for inviting the Brahmin also for food. Guru Nath told him that he need not have such apprehensions any longer.

Guru Nath graced the house of Sayamdeo for the *bhiksha* along with his disciples and the ulcer-patient. The Brahmin who had not been able to eat even a morsel of food normally was now able to eat at Sayamdeo's house most sumptuously and with great gusto and relish. His chronic ailment, plaguing him for years on end, had now disappeared totally. Sayamdeo and everyone wondered at this, and realised that Sri Narasimha Saraswati was none other than Bhagawan Dhanvantari himself who had come in human form.

THUS ENDS THE THIRTEENTH CHAPTER OF SRI
GURU CHARITRA DESCRIBING THE MIRACLE OF
THE STOMACH-CURE OF THE BRAHMIN BY
SRI NARASIMHA SARASWATI.

Glory to the all-merciful, the omnipresent and the ever-responsive Guru Nath!

14

Sri Narasimha Saraswati
Rescues Sayamdeo

This chapter narrates how Sayamdeo, the village-officer of Vasar Brahmeswara, was protected by Guru Nath from being killed by the Muslim Nawab.

Siddhamuni continued with the narration while Namdharak excitedly listened.

Sayamdeo was very happy at the darshan of Sri Narasimha Saraswati. He was even more happy that Sri Narasimha Saraswati graced his home and sanctified it. His wife Jakhai also was very happy that Guru Nath had accepted *bhiksha* at their house.

At that time a great worry was weighing on Sayamdeo's mind. He told his problem to Sri Narasimha Saraswati and prayed for his guidance and help.

Siddha Yogi narrates further how Sri Narasimha solves Sayamdeo's problem.

The Muslim ruler of the region was not well disposed towards Hindus and especially Brahmins. Every year he used to call a Brahmin-pandit to his durbar and kill him, secretly. He found great pleasure in this demonic act. That year the turn seemed to have fallen on Sayamdeo; Sayamdeo was summoned to visit the durbar. He knew fully well what fate awaited him there. He would never again have the pleasure and fortune of the darshan of Guru Nath in this life. Alas! there can be no escape for him from the summons of the Nawab.

Sri Narasimha Saraswati told Sayamdeo that he need not entertain any fright about his visiting the Nawab, that the latter would not be able to do him any harm at all and that he (Sayamdeo) would be returning home safely and happily too. He further told him that he (Guru Nath) would be staying on (at Vasar Brahmeswara) till his return. He thus sent him with his blessings.

Sayamdeo reached that court of the Nawab. The Nawab felt greatly elated at the sight of Sayamdeo and the prospect of the fulfilment of his vicious scheme. But alas! as soon as these vicious thoughts started rising in his mind, he saw an apparition. He felt that a fierce-looking Brahmin with fiery looks and holding heavy weapons was attacking him and showering blows mercilessly on him. His body started seething with torturous pain. He prayed to the apparition for forgiveness and said he would never in future commit the crime of killing or causing injury to anyone. The apparition disappeared and in its place was standing Sayamdeo, the meek Brahmin. The Nawab treated Sayamdeo with great respect and honoured him by giving him many rich gifts. Sayamdeo returned home most happily and with his heart overflowing with gratitude towards Sri Narasimha Saraswati. After reaching his place, he rushed for the darshan of Guru Nath and fell at his feet, praying him to remain there for ever and never leave him. Sri Narasimha Saraswati said it was not possible for him to stay at that place any longer. Many devotees from other places were calling on him and he had to move out. He added that his grace and blessings, however, will be ever with him and his family and said that after 16 years he (Sayamdeo) would have his darshan again, at the holy Ganagapur.

From there Sri Narasimha Saraswati went to Vaijnath (Vaidyanath), famed as the abode of Arogya Bhavani Parameswari. He remained there for a year in his invisible form.

THUS ENDS THE FOURTEENTH CHAPTER OF SRI *GURU CHARITRA* WHICH DESCRIBES GURU NATH'S PROTECTION OF SAYAMDEO FROM DEATH.

Glory to the all-merciful, the omnipresent and the ever-responsive Guru Nath!

15

Holy Places of Bharat

In this chapter Guru Nath's instructions to his disciples regarding the merits of doing pilgrimages and the places which they should unfailingly visit is described. After sending most of his disciples on pilgrimage, Guru Nath lives in seclusion (invisible to others) at Vaijnath. The Siddha Yogi was the only disciple who was retained by Guru Nath with him at Vaijnath. (The mere study of this chapter with faith and devotion, is believed to confer on the reader the very merit of doing the pilgrimages himself).

Namdharak asked Siddhamuni why Sri Narasimha Saraswati chose to remain in an invisible (unseen) form for a year at Vaijnath. There must have been a divine purpose for every single act of Guru Nath and Namdharak wanted to be enlightened on this.

Siddhamuni continued his narration.

Sri Narasimha Saraswati was exceedingly compassionate to one and all. He used to shower his blessings and grace on anyone, often without any consideration whether the person deserved them or not. People of all sorts, good, bad and indifferent used to come to him. Some were, of course, genuine seekers of the spirit. Some used to come to seek redress for their afflictions. But many used to come seeking his grace and blessings for the fulfilment of their worldly desires and ambitions, and some for the success of their vicious schemes. Sri Narasimha Saraswati was distressed about it; what a unique opportunity they were misusing, he thought. He had come down like a *Kalpavriksha* for the moral and spiritual regeneration and uplift of people, but unfortunately, most people were not able to realise this and use his presence and grace and blessings for that high purpose. Further, he felt that although he himself was beyond all bounds of karma and all laws of Nature, yet his relieving all kinds of people of their afflictions, superseding the operation of the laws of karma would not be congenial to the ultimate good, and might weaken the moral order even more. Thinking thus, Sri Narasimha Saraswati decided that he should withdraw himself from people for some time at least, and accordingly, took to an invisible form for his stay at Vaijnath. But before taking to an invisible form (*Guptarupa*) Guru Nath called all his disciples and told them that they should go out on pilgrimage and visit all the holy places, bathe in all the sacred rivers of the land and should reach Sri Sailam by the year Bahudanya and join him back there. They were not happy to leave the presence of Guru Nath, even if it be for visiting the holy places of the land. Guru Nath told them, 'It is not necessary for the disciples to be always in the physical presence of the Guru. Constant chanting of Guru's *upadesa*, Guru-mantra and worshipping of the Guru's form in the shrine of one's own heart, is real Guru *Sannidhana*, i.e., living close to the Guru. I have got to be alone for some time. But I am indeed ever with you. Try to feel my constant presence wherever you will be and wherever you go. Further for the *yatis* (*sanyasis*), pilgrimages constitute the most beneficial and necessary discipline; the mind gets purified and steadied thereby and one will experience a higher state of consciousness and divine awareness. I bless you all that you will have the most rewarding experiences. And surely you will all meet me at Sri Sailam.'

The disciples had no other option but to abide by Guru Nath's command. They however sought his instructions as to which holy places they should visit. Guru Nath then explained the significance of the various holy places and of the sacred rivers of the land, and the special merits each one of these would confer on the pilgrims. Visits to these holy places and doing the appropriate ceremonies and rites there—as prescribed according to their respective *asramas* in life, would wash off all sins, purify the body and mind, and in the end confer liberation not only to them, but also to 21 generations of their ancestors as well as 21 generations of their descendants.

Siddha Yogi then narrates the particular pilgrim-centres Guru Nath had advised his disciples to visit and the specific deeds that they should perform during their stay.

Kasi is the foremost of the pilgrim-centres. One should have a bath in the holy Bhagirathi (Ganges River) there. From Kasi, one should go to Ganga Dwara and Triveni (Prayaga). Yamuna, Saraswati, Varuna, Kusavarta, Satadruvu, Vipakasa, Saravati, Vitasta, Asikni, Marudhvrudha, Madhumati, Dhrutavati are the most sacred rivers and a bath in them will be most purifying. So also are the rivers Chandrabhaga, Revati, Gomati, Vedika, Kausiki, Sahasravakta, Purna, Bahuda, etc. Bath in these rivers is equivalent to several folds of *chandrayanam* and other *vratas* and austerities. Wherever there is confluence of any two or more rivers, they are as sacred as the Triveni Sangam. Vairacharu Pushkara Theertha, Kurukshetra, Sri Sailam, Sri Rangam, Rameshwaram, Anantasayanam, Mahalaya Theertha, Namisaranya, Badari, Kedar, Narmada, Kakamukha, Gokarna, Ayodhya, Mathura, Dwaraka— are all Muktikshetras. Godavari Bheemeswaram and Vajhara are as sacred as Prayaga. Kusatarpan, Godavari Sagara Sangam, the rivers Purna, Krishnaveni and Tungabhadra and the Pampa Sarovar are all very sacred. Hariharakshetra and Pandaripur, burn away all sins of the pilgrims. Bhima-Amarja Sangam at Ganagapur is very sacred. There are *Koti theerthas* there. The Aswatha tree at Ganagapur is as powerful as the *Kalpavriksha*. Near the Aswatha tree is *Narasimha Theertha*, and northwards to it are the *Papavinasini Theertha, Varanasi Theertha, Rudrapada Theertha,*

Chakra Theertha, Koti Theertha, Manmadha Theertha, etc. There is the Kalleswara Temple there. It is as holy as Gokarna.

When Brihaspati enters Simha Rasi, the subterranean current of Ganga enters Godavari, this is known as Godavari-Pushkara. This takes place in 12-year cycles. Likewise when Brihaspati enters Kanya rasi, it is Krishna Pushkara, and so also in case of all the other southern rivers, each having its Pushkara in its own cycle. A bath in the respective rivers at the Pushkara time is most auspicious. Man gains his spiritual evolution thereby. Whoever bathes in the rivers Bhima-Krishna confluence, becomes purified and will be born as a Brahmin or as a *yogi,* i.e., as a pure *sattvic* person in his next life. Whoever bathes in the Patala Ganga will have Lord Mallikarjuna's Jyotirlinga darshan at Sri Sailam and will attain liberation. Krishna Sagara Sangam and Kaveri Sagara Sangam are annihilators of all sins. Seshadri (Tirupati Venkateswara Kshetra), Kumbhakonam, Kanyakumari, *Matsya-Theertha, Pakshi-Theertha,* Rameswaram, Dhanushkoti, Kolhapur (the seat of Mahalakshmi) are sacred places.

On banks of River Krishna is Bhillawadi, the place of Bhuvaneswari Devi. At Amarapur, on the banks of River Krishna there is the confluence of five rivers (Panchanadi Kshetra). There are also *Yugalaya-Theertha, Surpalaya-Theertha,* etc. Where River Malapaha joins River Krishna, is the place where Sage Viswamitra did penance. At Kapila Kshetra, River Krishna flows as Uttara Vahini (i.e., in northern direction). Whatever penance is done there, it gains million-fold potency. Pithapur is Dattatreya-kshetra. Manigiri is the place where the seven sages did their penance. Darshan of Ahobila-kshetra earns the merit of 60 *yajnas.* At the onset of the rainy season, the river waters get polluted and should be avoided by pilgrims for varying periods of time. (For the residents there however this prohibition does not apply).

Pilgrimage is the means whereby all past sins are washed off, and immense spiritual merit is earned. All these places are resonant with spiritual vibrations and they enrich and speed up the men on their spiritual evolution, for certain.

Advising the disciples thus and giving many more detailed instructions, Guru Nath sent all the disciples on long pilgrimages. He especially told them about doing *nadi-pradakshinas* and what immense benefit they confer. With one *nadi-pradakshina*, one would have lived away and exhausted all his karmic lives and attain liberation.

'While all other disciples thereafter, left to do the long pilgrimage with Guru Nath's blessings, I was allowed to remain with Guru Nath and serve him,' thus concluded Siddhamuni.

HERE ENDS THE FIFTEENTH CHAPTER OF SRI *GURU CHARITRA* CALLED THE THEERTHA-YATRA PRAKARANA.

Glory to the all-merciful, the omnipresent and the ever-responsive Guru Nath!

Note

The Holy Places of Lord Dattatraya

Girnar (Saurashtra, Gujrat)   : main abode of Lord Dattatreya.

Kuravpur (Raichur, Karnataka)   : Sripada Sri Vallabha's site of penance.

Gangapur (Gulbarga, Karnataka) : abode of Sri Narasimha Saraswati.

Narsobachi Wadi   : Sri Narasimha Saraswati's site of penance.

Sri Sailya   : samadhi site of Sri Narasimha Saraswati.

Fruits of Devotion to the Guru

In this chapter, Guru Nath narrates to a Brahmin about the necessity of single-pointed devotion to the Guru and the merit of Guru seva, by way of illustration of the anecdote of Dhaumya Rishi and his disciples namely Aruni, Baid and Upamanyu. Unless the Guru is pleased, the doors of knowledge will not be opened to the student/aspirant.

Guru Nath now comes to Bhillawadi (Bhuvaneshwari Kshetra) on the eastern bank of River Krishna. He stays there for four months (*Chaturmasya* — four months of the monsoon season), under the Audambar tree on the western side of River Krishna.

Siddhamuni told Namdharak that Guru Nath stayed at Vaijnath for a year, where Siddhamuni alone attended him. From Vaijnath, Sri Narasimha Saraswati, accompanied by Siddhamuni, visited Amba Bhavani Kshetra and lived there for a few days. Siddhamuni now continued his narrative.

At this place, a Brahmin *yogi* came to Sri Narasimha Saraswati and prayed to him for guidance and help in his *sadhana*. He said that this mind was very restless and he was unsuccessful to concentrate. He said that he had one Guru earlier, who initiated him to a mantra but it did not seem to help him at all. He said he had left off that Guru as he had no respect nor liking for him any longer, and that he was now seeking out another Guru. He requested Sri Narasimha Saraswati to accept him as his disciple.

Sri Narasimha Saraswati told him that it is never proper to talk disrespectfully of one's Guru, and that he had committed a very great mistake in forsaking his Guru. He said that it is not for the student to judge the merits or demerits of the Guru. One should have implicit faith in the Guru. Guru is the treasure-house and abode of all knowledge and wisdom. Guru is even superior to God; the student must ungrudgingly, selflessly, dedicatedly and lovingly serve the Guru, whatever be the hardships of service. There is nothing comparable to the service rendered to the Guru. Only if the Guru is pleased will the gods be pleased. If the Guru is not pleased, all the gods even cannot help him a wee bit. Guru bhakti and Guru seva form the foundation of spiritual *sadhana*, and the winning of Guru's grace alone is the fruition of all *sadhana*. Sri Narasimha Saraswati narrated the stories of Dhaumya Rishi's disciples as example and illustration of this truth.*

Dhaumya Rishi had three disciples, one was Aruni Panchal, the second was Baid and the third was Upamanyu. Aruni was asked by the Guru to water his field so that the cereal crop would grow well. The water had to be brought into the field through a canal from a tank which was little far away. The tank was shallow. Aruni dug the canal deep and put up the bunds of the canal, and water started flowing into the field. Then, unfortunately, a breach developed in one of the bunds of the canal and the water started draining out and escaping away through the breach, thus stopping the flow of water into the field. Aruni tried his best to fill up the breach by piling up stones, putting sand, etc., over there, but could not succeed. The water was going waste and he was worried as to how to get the field filled with water. Then he got an idea; he lay down at the site of the breach, thus blocking it.

---

* Anecdote from Mahabharata

The water thereby, started flowing into the field. He remained there in the same position so that the field would get the water fully.

It was quite late in the night and as the boy did not return home, the Guru was worried as to what could have happened to him, and he came to the field searching for him. He was surprised and felt glad to find the field full with water, which was never the case any time ever before, but at the same time, he was worried as Aruni was nowhere in sight. He called out loudly, 'Aruni! Aruni!' From the waters of the canal Aruni replied in a feeble voice, 'Gurudeo! I am here.' The Guru reached to him and pulled him out. Aruni fell prostrate at the Guru's feet and offered his obeisance to him. The Guru was touched by the boy's unselfish devotion to him and placing his hand on the boy's head, blessed him saying, 'May you become proficient and gain mastery in all the Vedas and shastras.' No sooner than the Guru said this, Aruni became fully enlightened and all knowledge dawned on him in a flash.

'Such will be the result of Guru seva,' said Sri Narasimha Saraswati to the Brahmin. Sri Narasimha Saraswati continued further with his narration. 'Now listen to the Guru seva of Baid'.

Baid was asked by the Guru to till the land, sow the seeds, raise the crop and to take care till harvesting was completed and the grains were safely brought home. Baid was working on the field, day in and day out, without wasting a single moment, and sparing no pains. Due to all the labour exerted and pains taken by him, the crop came out very well and yielded a very rich harvest. Baid loaded the grains on the cart and started to drive the cart to the Guru's house. The load was too heavy and the bullock was unable

to draw the cart. Baid was also trying to pull the cart along
with the bullock. Unfortunately, the bullock got stuck up in
the mire on the way and the cart-wheels also sank deep down
into the mud. The bullock was not able to pull out the cart.
Baid was struggling with all his strength to push the cart-
wheels and make the cart move. In the process, he almost
lost his breath and was about to collapse. Dhaumya Rishi
was coming himself to see how Baid was faring with the
collection of the harvest. On the way itself he saw the
heavily-loaded cart and Baid. But alas, he found Baid
tottering on his feet and collapsing almost on the verge of
death. The Guru was very much moved with the selfless and
steadfast devotion of Baid. He pulled Baid out of the mire
and placed his right hand on his head, which immediately
revived him. Not only that, Baid received total illumination
and enlightenment, and all knowledge dawned on him with
the blessing touch of the Guru.

Sri Narasimha Saraswati then gave the account of Upamanyu's
Guru seva and bhakti.

Upamanyu was also a very devoted disciple, but he had
the habit of overeating. The Guru wanted to curb this habit
of his over-indulgence with food. The Guru gave
Upamanyu the task of looking after his herd of cattle.
Upamanyu used to leave home very early in the morning
along with the herd, after eating the little food the Guru
gave him. The grazing grounds were far away, and he used to
return along with the herd only very late in the evening. In
the afternoons, he used to beg alms from the houses which
were nearby and had his afternoon food. The Guru finding
the boy still fat, asked him what he was eating in the
afternoons. The boy told the Guru, that he was begging
bhiksha from the houses near the grazing grounds and was

eating whatever food he obtained thus. The Guru said he should not eat the food he got as *bhiksha*, but should bring it and give it to him and eat only whatever he (the Guru) gave him. Upamanya started doing as the Guru said, but as he was feeling very hungry in the afternoons, he started drinking the remnants of the milk that continued to drip from the cow's udders, after the calves had drunk their fill. The Guru prohibited that even. Upamanyu became very much emaciated for lack of food. Unable to bear the hunger, one day, seeing some milk exude from some wild leaves, he drank that milk. That exudation was poisonous and it effected his eye-nerves and made him blind. In the evening, trying to drive the cattle home and being unable to find the way due to his lost sight, he fell into a well. As he did not reach home, the Guru came searching for him. Dhaumyamuni saw his disciple fallen in the well. He pulled him out, and moved much by the boy's truthful and implicit obedience to the word of Guru, touched his eyes with his hand, chanting the invocation mantra to the Aswini Devatas. Upamanyu instantly regained his sight. Not only that, the Guru, through his blessings, endowed him with all the scriptural knowledge and wisdom. Upamanyu became a most renowned rishi. It was his *sishya* by name Udanka who presided over the great serpent-sacrifice of Janamejaya, which brought even Indra down from the heaven, along with his throne, towards the sacrificial fire. It is also said that Udanka, soon after completing his discipleship, obtained from Adisesha in Patala, the latter's ear-*kundalas*, and brought and offered them as *Guru dakshina* to his Guru Upamanyu.

Sri Narasimha Saraswati, by these examples, taught the Brahmin the supreme importance and necessity of Guru seva for acquiring spiritual knowledge and wisdom.* The Brahmin now realised his great error in not discharging his duty to his Guru, and in speaking ill of him. He felt very sad and felt he should atone for it by ending his life. Sri Narasimha Saraswati was touched by the sincere repentance of the Brahmin and told him, 'Your repentance has absolved you of all your sin.' He then placed his hand on the Brahmin's head. Lo! the Brahmin got enlightened with all knowledge and wisdom. Sri Narasimha Saraswati told the Brahmin that he should go immediately to his Guru, fall at his feet and pray for his forgiveness. He said that it is only then that the enlightenment he got now by his grace would become secure and lasting.

Sri Narasimha Saraswati then left the Amba Bhavani Kshetra and went to Bhillawadi where there is the ancient temple of Sri Bhuvaneswari Devi. There on the western bank of River Krishna under the banyan tree, Sri Narasimha Saraswati made his abode, and stayed there for four months.

THUS ENDS THE SIXTEENTH CHAPTER OF SRI *GURU CHARITRA* DESCRIBING GURU BHAKTI PRABHAV.

Glory to the all-merciful, the omnipresent and the ever-responsive Guru Nath!

---

* The three disciples in the above illustration represent the three graded *gunas, tamas, rajas* and *sattva*. Devotion to Guru will unfailingly take us beyond the *gunas*. *Gunas* transcended, *Atma Jnana* will shine forth in us. While the Guru's grace helps us in finally transcending the *gunas*, transcending of each one of the three *gunas* will take its own time. Each aspirant progresses at his own place, which is largely dependent upon the characteristics of nature of his predominant *guna*. Upamanyu symbolises *tamo-guna* predominantly, and the latter takes longer duration of time to get transcended and sublimated. Baid symbolises *Rajo-guna*, which could be transcended in a Lesser time. Aruni symbolises *sattva-guna* and it could be transcended but in one day. With devotion, dedication and surrender to the Guru, one becomes *gunatheeta*, i.e., one who goes beyond the trammels of *Maya*, which alone will enable him to experience his true inner self.

17

Metamorphosis of the
Blockheaded Youth

This chapter describes how Guru Nath transforms a blockheaded Brahmin youth into a great pandit, who was directed to him by Goddess Bhuvaneswari Devi herself.

Siddha Yogi says to Namdharak that the purpose of Sri Narasimha Saraswati's advent is for bringing about the moral and spiritual regeneration of the people of the whole land, not merely of people of a particular area or region of his birth. He was a Parivrajaka, *a constant itinerant, never staying normally at one place for more than five days at the most. Like clouds moving in all the directions and to even the farthest corners, only for the purpose of showering rain and to provide the life-giving waters to all, so also Sri Narasimha Saraswati, wandering all over the land, visiting all the pilgrim-places, was bestowing his grace on all people, of different places and different regions and of all types. He used to alleviate the afflictions of the people by his divine powers; for the spiritual aspirants, he was* Jnana-Bhaskara, *dispelling their doubts, illumining their intellect, and uplifting and enriching their spirit. Every word of his, whenever and to whomsoever he uttered, had a deep spiritual truth in simple and easily understood language and illustrating through the most apt examples and anecdotes.*

Siddha Yogi then begins narrating the story of the blockheaded youth.

During Guru Nath's stay at Audambar on the western banks of River Krishna, in the vicinity of Bhillawadi, one Brahmin youth from Karavir Nagar came for his darshan. The visitor narrated his story to Guru Nath. His father was a learned scholar in all the shastras and was a strict and meticulous observer of all religious rites. His mother also was a very pious lady. In his seventh year, his thread-ceremony was performed and he was initiated into Vedic studies. Alas! he was too dull to make any progress. To add to his misfortune, he lost both his parents when he was barely ten years of age. He was advancing in age but without making any progress in studies. He became a butt of ridicule in the town. Even his near relations were showing nothing but contempt towards him. A few well-wishers of his advised him that he should still try and pick up learning. They stressed the importance of learning in life. Through learning only comes wealth, happiness, respectability and fame. They told him that only a learned man will be welcomed anywhere and will be received with respect by others. He will be honoured in royal courts, in assemblies of the pandits and the wise. A man without learning is given no recognition and will receive no respect anywhere.

The youth felt greatly frustrated and desperate. He felt his life was a waste. He felt that death would be far better than his living a life of humiliation. He left his village and went out wandering. In his wanderings he came across the temple of Bhuvaneswari in Bhillawadi on the eastern bank of River Krishna. He sat before the idol in the temple and started on a fast, praying that unless the deity blessed him with learning and knowledge, he would continue his fast and cut off his tongue and even his head. Moved with compassion, the goddess appeared before him in a dream and said, 'Go to the other side of the bank. Sri Narasimha Saraswati, the embodiment of all learning and wisdom, is on sojourn there. Pray to him, he will fulfil your desire.'

The youth went to Sri Narasimha Saraswati to receive his blessings. Sri Narasimha Saraswati placed his hand on the head of the youth. The blockheaded youth became enlightened with all scriptural learning and knowledge instantly!

THUS ENDS THE SEVENTEENTH CHAPTER OF SRI *GURU CHARITRA* DESCRIBING BRAHMIN YOUTH'S UDDHARANA.

Glory to the all-merciful, the omnipresent and the ever-responsive Guru Nath!

18

Poor Brahmin Finds Treasure*

This chapter describes how Guru Nath comes to the Panchaganga Kshetra, the holy confluence of the Panchaganga and River Krishna, near Amarapur. Guru Nath relieves the poverty of a Brahmin of Amarapur by making him discover a treasure pot in his own yard.

*S*iddhamuni told Namdharak that Sri Narasimha Saraswati's sojourn on the banks of River Krishna was to sanctify the places around and to regenerate the people morally and spiritually. Sri Narasimha Saraswati visited the Panchaganga Sagar, the confluence of the five holy rivers—Siva, Bhadra, Kumbhi, Bhagawati and Saraswati, where they all meet and merge in River Krishna. The temple of Amareswar was located there and hence the place was called Amarapur. Nearby was the Sakti Theertha, where resided sixty-four Yogini-Saktis, serving and worshipping Amareswara, but unseen by others. Nearby was Papavinasini and other holy theerthas too. Sri Narasimha Saraswati stayed at Amarapur for 12 years. This place came to be later known as Narsobawadi, after Sri Narasimha Saraswati.

To avoid crowd, Sri Narasimha Saraswati lived here in seclusion. In the afternoons, however, he used to go out in the guise of bhikshu into the town and ask for alms at just one or two houses.

---

* Study of this chapter is believed to earn for one the grace of Goddess Mahalakshmi.

Siddha Yogi narrates to Namdharak about an incident that took place during Sri Narasimha Saraswati's stay at Amarapur.

In that town lived a poor Brahmin. Added to his poverty he had a large number of children. He used to live by alms. But when he could not get enough alms, his wife used to cook the leaves of the *ghevada** creeper which was growing on their front yard. Thus the creeper turned out to be the main source of sustenance for the family most of the days.

One day Sri Narasimha Saraswati came to the door of the poor Brahmin and asked for *bhiksha*. The Brahmin welcomed him and offered him worship duly. But as they had nothing in home that day, the wife cooked *ghevada* leaves and served Guru Nath. Guru Nath ate it with great satisfaction. He blessed the couple saying, '*Mahalakshmi prasada Siddhirastu*' (may the great goddess of wealth shower her full grace on you). Then he left.

But while leaving the house, he did a strange thing. He pulled to the ground the *ghevada* creeper and threw it aside. The Brahmin's wife and children were very angry and furious that the stranger, ungratefully, destroyed the creeper, which was their main sustenance. The wife began to weep, and the children too, as they all loved and looked after the creeper with great concern and solicitude. They were all worried how they would be able to sustain themselves on the days when the Brahmin would return home without receiving any alms.

The Brahmin tried to comfort his wife by saying, 'God is there to feed and protect if we have but faith in him. Is he not sustaining the frog in the cavity of the stone? How does the

---

* The *ghevada* creeper symbolises the growth and proliferation of our desires. When they are fulfilled one attains some temporary satiation but not lasting peace. The Guru pulls down the creeper above the ground. The Brahmin (*sadhaka*) strives to pull out the roots also (the embedded *vasanas* — impulses). The heart and mind thus purified, rid of all desires together with their root impulses also, are the very treasure-chest, the reservoir of unending Divine joy and bliss. We will have then gained the possession of Atmic Treasury — the only real treasure, which puts an end to all our miseries is for ever ...

mother get milk from her breasts to feed the child, if it is not the doing of God? Are not birds and animals in the forest provided with their food? When God is there, the Provider and Providence for all, why should we bother our heads with unnecessary worries and anxieties? Without praying to him, why wail over a tiny creeper? We can as well plant a branch again, and it will grow up in a few days. Everything will have a divine purpose and everything is for our good; we should take things in that spirit. I am sure our guest certainly would not have intended any harm to us, let us face things as they come, but with full faith in the Lord and in his doings.'

The wife was now reconciled and calmed down. Both of them went into the yard. The Brahmin pulled out the roots of the *ghevada* creeper also and started digging there to make place to plant a branch-creeper there. Lo! as he was digging with the iron crowbar, he heard a clinging sound as if the crowbar was hitting against a hard surface. As they dug out and looked in, they found a vessel full of gold coins lying buried there. They took it out and were overjoyed that the guest's blessing '*Sri Mahalakshmi Prasada Siddhirastu*' turned true so soon. They immediately ran after the strange *bhikshu*. They found him at the Audambar tree and fell at his feet, pouring out their gratitude. Thereafter they remained staunch devotees of Guru Nath.

THUS ENDS THE EIGHTEENTH CHAPTER OF SRI
GURU CHARITRA DESCRIBING VIPRADAINYA
HARANAM — REMOVAL OF THE MISERY
OF THE BRAHMIN.

Glory to the all-merciful, the omnipresent and the ever-responsive Guru Nath!

19

Guru Nath's Grace on the Yogini-Ganas

This chapter describes the *Audambar Vriksha Mahima*. It also narrates about the special worship which was being done by the *Yogini-Ganas* to Guru Nath every day. Guru Nath shows Prayaga, Kasi and Gaya to Ganganuja and makes him complete the whole pilgrimage within just a single day. Sri Narasimha Saraswati later announces that he was leaving from there. He comforts the *Yogini-Ganas* that he would continue to be present there only in his subtle form (grace-body) and will be answering the prayers of all his devotees.

Namdharak asked Siddhamuni why Sri Narasimha Saraswati was always more fond of the Audambar tree and why was it so significant. Siddhamuni explained as follows.

Due to the curse of Sage Durvasa, Lord Vishnu had to take ten incarnations on the earth. The curse was, of course, a boon to the world.

When Lord Vishnu manifested himself as Narasimha in Narasimhavatara to protect Prahlada and for destroying Hiranyakasyapa, he had to make use of his nails (claws) to kill him. He tore open the belly of Hiranyakasyapa with his claws. In the stomach of Hiranyakasyapa, there was the Kalakoota poison. The nails of Narasimha were drenched with the poison when he tore the stomach and entrails of the demon. As a result, Narasimha's nails were seething with great heat and pain. Goddess Lakshmi, seeing the suffering of her Lord, plucked some fruits of the Audambar tree which she happened to find nearby. The Lord stuck his nails into the fruit deep into its pulp. The Lord's pain was assuaged instantly by this. The Lord was immensely pleased and blessed the Audambar tree, and said it would from then onwards be as powerful on earth as the *Kalpavriksha* in the heavens. He said that whosoever would worship the Audambar tree, would get all desires and wishes fulfilled.

Thus, the Audambar tree had become a wish-fulfilling tree, from very ancient times. Sri Narasimha Saraswati wanted to make it holier. Therefore, he chose to be always seated under the Audambar tree. Seated under it, apart from granting the fulfilment of the worldly desires of his devotees, he used to shower spiritual grace and uplift them spiritually. Thus the Audambar tree had come to acquire heightened spiritual powers too.

As already said earlier, near Amareswar on the bank of River Krishna, there was the *Sakti-Theertha* wherein lived many *yoginis*, numbering about sixty-four. Every day, by noon, they all used to come to the Audambar tree to worship Sri Narasimha Saraswati and then return to their place, unseen by any.

Some people were curious to know all about Sri Narasimha Saraswati, as to what he ate, how he got his food, what he did and who all came to him, etc. One by name Ganganuja (a poor farmer) was asked to keep a secret watch upon Sri Narasimha Saraswati and find out the facts. Ganganuja was a very guileless, simple-hearted and devout person. As Ganganuja was watching clandestinely, to his amazement he saw the *yoginis* coming and offering worship and doing *aarti* to Guru Nath. He also saw that after the *aarti*, Sri Narasimha Saraswati and the *yoginis* stepped down into the river. Lo! the waters of the river started receding, making a pathway for Sri Narasimha Saraswati and the *yoginis** to walk along. Ganganuja also followed them surreptitiously. As they reached the middle of the streambed, Ganganuja following behind, saw them entering into a golden-splendoured city. The residents of the city, men and women, looking like angels and gods, dressed in silken and shining garments, welcomed Guru Nath with *mangala aarti*. Sri Narasimha Saraswati looking back towards Ganganuja, asked him why he followed them. Ganganuja fell at Guru Nath's feet and prayed to be forgiven. Sri Narasimha Saraswati told him he should not reveal to anybody what he had seen. Goddess Lakshmi also favoured him and he was relieved of his drudgerous life. He used to come for Guru Nath's darshan, every morning, afternoon and evening and serve him for most part of the day, with great love.

As it was going on thus, on one *Magha Purnima* early morning, Ganganuja while serving Guru Nath said, 'Gurudeva! It is said that in the month of *Magha*, a bath at the holy Triveni Sangam at Prayaga is most meritorious. I heard only, but know nothing of Prayaga and Kasi, etc.' Guru Nath then said to Ganganuja, 'This Panchaganga Sangam here is as holy as the Prayaga and Kolhapur is as meritorious as Gaya. In and around here also exists Kasi. All the merits of Kasi, Gaya and Prayaga can be found and gained here itself. Nevertheless, as you seem to be very desirous of seeing northern Kasi, etc., I will show them to you today itself.' Guru Nath stood up on the tiger skin on which he was seated; he told Ganganuja to catch his feet and *padukas* firmly. Instantly they were at Prayaga. After taking bath there in the morning, by afternoon, they were at Kasi. After bathing in the holy Ganges and having Lord Visweswara's darshan, by evening they were at Gaya. By sunset, they were back at Amarapur!

---

* The *yoginis* symbolise the *Yogic Saktis* (powers). They are ever at the will and command of a realised *yogi*. There are said to be 16 *vidyas* and 64 *kalas* which a *yogi* is supposed to acquire and attain. The 64 *yoginis* described in the above narrative are symbolic of the 64 *kalas*. These are ever at the service of one, who is a master of his body, mind and senses.

Sri Narasimha Saraswati stayed under the Audambar tree at the Panchaganga Kshetra for quite a long time—12 years. Now he decided to leave from there. Everyone was sorrowful and unhappy that Guru Nath would be leaving from there, much more so were the *yoginis*. Sri Narasimha Saraswati comforted them and said, 'I am leaving my *padukas* here. I will be ever present where my *padukas* are worshipped. Whatever wishes be prayed for, by offering worship to the *padukas*, they will be granted and fulfilled'.

Sri Narasimha Saraswati, comforting them all, moved out from that place in the direction of Ganagapur, which is in the vicinity of the holy rivers—Bhima and Amaraja.

Even after Guru Nath left for Ganagapur, the Audambar tree and *Guru padukas* enshrined there continued to manifest Guru Nath's power and grace in the same manner as when he used to physically live there.

THUS ENDS THE NINETEENTH CHAPTER OF
SRI *GURU CHARITRA* DESCRIBING THE HOLY
SIGNIFICANCE OF THE AUDAMBAR TREE,
THE SPECIAL GRACE WHICH GURU NATH
SHOWERED ON THE YOGINI-GANAS,
AND ALSO OF GANGANUJA'S KASI YATRA.

Glory to the all-merciful, the omnipresent and the ever-responsive Guru Nath!

20

Guru Nath's Blessings on the Brahmin's Wife

The chapter describes that even after Guru Nath left the Panchaganga Kshetra (Narsobawadi), his *padukas* which had been left under the Audamber Tree continued to respond to the prayers of devotees as per the assurance given to the *Yogini-Ganas* by Guru Nath. A woman was freed from a *Bramha Rakshasa*, who had caused death to all the five children born to her. With the grace of Guru Nath, two sons were born to her again. But one of the sons, just when the parents were planning to do his *Upanayana* ceremony, dies. Guru Nath in the guise of a *yogi*, appears before her and imparts philosophical teaching about the inevitability of death. He tries to reconcile her with the event, but the woman remains inconsolable.

In this chapter, Siddhamuni described to Namdharak the Audambarsthan Mahima, which remained undiminished and ever full, even after Guru Nath's departure from there to Ganagapur.

Guru Nath continued to reside there, but in his invisible form, and continued to shower his grace on whoever offered worship to the *Guru padukas* at the foot of the Audambar tree on the confluence of the *Panchaganga* at Amarapur.

In a village called Shrirolgrem, there lived a Brahmin couple. The woman gave birth to five sons, but unfortunately none survived. The woman was plunged in grief at the loss of all her sons. She started praying to Guru Nath that he should expiate her from her previous lives' sins and save her.

One night Guru Nath appeared in her dream, in the guise of a Brahmin. He comforted and consoled her. He said that none can escape destiny—the consequences of deeds whether done knowingly or unknowingly. He told her further, 'In your previous life, there was one Brahmin of *Saunaka Gotra*. You borrowed one hundred rupees (sovereigns) from him which you did not repay. He was greatly upset about your non-payment and, in desperation, committed suicide. He became a ghost after his death and has been haunting you with vengeance in your present life. He has been the cause of the death of all your sons.'

The woman prayed to the Brahmin who was talking to her in the dream to tell her how she could atone for it and get freed from the ghost. The Brahmin told her, 'When the Brahmin died, he had none to perform his funeral rites. It is now past 16 years since his death. You now arrange for his funeral rites and give the hundred rupees you owed him in charity in the dead man's name, to any Brahmin belonging to his *gotra* (i.e., the same *Saunaka Gotra*). After doing this, you will have to do penance for a month as follows. You take your bath at the confluence of *Panchaganga* and Krishna rivers and do seven *pradakshinas* around the Audambar tree there, observing fast; you do the same again after bathing in the *Papavinasini Theertha* and *Kamya Theertha*. You do *abhisheka* to the *Guru padukas* and offer your worship with all sincerity and devotion. If you do accordingly, all the sins of your past lives will be washed off and you will bear a noble and good son and your desires will be fulfilled.'

To this, the woman replied, 'Oh Mahatma! I can do all the fasts and worship, but how can I repay the hundred rupees. I am too poor to do that.' After saying thus, she began sobbing. The Brahmin then said, 'Have faith in the Audambar, it is none else but the celestial *Kalpavriksha*. Through your worship to it, all good will accrue to you.'

The next morning after the dream, she started on her one-month penance. She was fasting, and after taking bath in the holy confluence and other *theerthas—Papavinasini* and *Kamya Theertha*, she was making *pradakshinas* (circumbulations) around the holy Audambar tree and was doing *abhisheka* and worship to the *Guru padukas*. The third night after she started her penance, the Brahmin-ghost appeared in her dream and demanded from her immediate repayment of the hundred rupees. He was threatening he would throttle her neck if she did not pay him. In mortal fright, she started running towards the Audambar tree. She found Guru Nath standing there. The ghost who was chasing her stopped suddenly seeing Guru Nath. The woman fell at Guru Nath's feet praying to be saved. Guru Nath looked at the ghost and said, 'Do not trouble her any longer. She took refuge at my feet and no harm would ever come to her hereafter. If you give up your ill-will against her, I will rescue you also. I will tell her to do atonement-rites to you with whatever money she could manage, and relieve you from your present state. I bless you to attain better state of life.' The ghost was reconciled. Guru Nath told the woman, 'You start the atonement rites from tomorrow itself. You will be freed from the sin of causing the Brahmin's death. After that, every day for a week, make seven *pradakshinas* around the Audambar tree. You will have a son who will live long.' At this the woman suddenly woke up from her sleep and felt greatly relieved.

She observed the instructions of Guru Nath meticulously and was freed from the persecution by the ghost for ever.

Thereafter, one night, the woman had a dream in which Guru Nath gave her two coconuts and said, 'My child! you take these two coconuts... You will have offspring and will have all happiness.'

After the woman finished her worship as told by Guru Nath, she returned to her village. In the course of the year, she gave birth to two sons. The woman and her husband were very happy.

The children grew up. As they attained the *Upanayana* age, the parents were planning the celebration with great enthusiasm. But alas, the elder boy, just in his eighth year, suddenly died after a very brief illness. The woman broke down in grief and was wailing. Her relatives tried to console her and were preparing to take the body for cremation as it was nearing sunset. But the woman did not allow them to remove the body. She was blaming Guru Nath that although he gave her two sons, he had snatched away one of them without showing any mercy. She said, 'Is this the repayment you do to me, after all my vigils, fasts and worship? What is the use of all worship? It is all nothing but madness on my part. I will end my life and join my dead son.' At this juncture, a *Bramhachari* came over; he was trying to comfort and console her, talking to her about the immortality of the spirit, and the evanescence of the body. Can you guess who this visitor was? He was none else but Sri Guru Nath himself!

THUS ENDS THE TWENTIETH CHAPTER OF SRI *GURU CHARITRA* DESCRIBING THE BRAMHA SAMANDH PARIHAR.

Glory to the all-merciful, the omnipresent and the ever-responsive Guru Nath!

21

Gurusthan Mahima

This chapter describes how Sri Guru Nath, moved by pity at the sorrow of the woman, brings back the dead child to life.

Siddha Yogi continued with the narrative.

The Bramhachari consoled and comforted and said, 'No one has come into the world to live and stay permanently. Death is inevitable to whoever is born. This body is perishable and cannot last indefinitely. The body is constituted of the five elements. When the elements mutually combine and take a form, it is called body. Man is enveloped by the covering of illusion, called *Avidya*, and he forgets his eternal nature. The body is just a vesture which the soul dons in its earthly sojourn. As the body wears out, the soul discards it, as we discard old and worn-out clothes, and dons a new body just as we wear new clothes. Man is really the soul which is immortal and he has no death in reality. It is the physical body that dies and drops off, but the core personality, the Atman, is deathless.'

The Bramhachari continued his advice to the woman as follows. 'Everything is pre-determined by destiny, by the deeds of one's past life or lives. We have to accept events as they come and should try to understand and experience the higher truths. Though we cannot alter much the course of the *Prarabhda Karma*, yet we should try by righteous living, to refrain from evil and to build a brighter and happier future for the next life. But the ultimate purpose of life is to realise the eternal Self and gain freedom from the cycle of birth and death for ever. That is the real *Sadgathi*.

'What a false attachment you are suffering from for this son of yours! You weren't his mother in his previous life. You will not be his mother again in his next birth. That you were his mother this birth of his is just incidental. Why mourn over this transient kinship, forgetting eternal truths? Life is like a bubble. It will burst off at any time. How long it will last has been pre-determinded by destiny. It is futile crying over death. Now let your relatives take the dead body away for the cremation and thereby help to speed up the *jiva's* ascent to higher births (*Sadgathi*). Don't bind it down here.' But the woman was inconsolable. She said she did all the worship bid by Guru Nath. The sons were the gift to her by Guru Nath. How could God snatch away the gift he himself had given? She had been betrayed by Guru Nath. She complained, 'I will take the body of my child to the *Guru padukas* and end my life there.'

The *Bramhachari* then told her, if her heart was so much set on her dead son's life, if she was feeling she could not live without him, she might take the body of the child to the *Gurusthan* and place it near the *padukas* and do whatever she wanted thereafter.

The woman and her husband came to *Gurusthan* along with the body of the dead child. She placed the body near the *Guru padukas* and again broke into sobs. They sat down there. Meanwhile, as it was nearing sunset and as the woman remained so obstinate, the relatives and people who came to do the death rites of the child left. It was night and the couple exhausted by the strain they went through the whole day, fell asleep at that spot only. In the night the woman got a dream. She saw Guru

Nath coming near her and telling her, 'Mother! Do not grieve. Nobody will ever get disappointed who repose their faith in me. See! I am reviving your dead child. I am giving him longevity.' The woman suddenly woke up. She was doubting whether it could be true. But lo! as she looked at the child, the child was opening his eyes. She put her hand on the body. The body was warming up. Thinking she was perhaps still dreaming, to make sure, she woke up her husband. He was also wondering unable to believe anything. The boy cried saying, 'Mother! I am feeling very hungry. Give me milk at least.' Wonder of wonders! The woman's dry breasts started overflowing with milk. The woman hugged her son to her bosoms and suckled him with milk. The child became quite normal and healthy and was playful as he used to be.

The couple fell prostrate at the *Guru padukas*, shedding tears of gratitude to Guru Nath. At daybreak when the relatives and other people came there, hoping that the woman would have been reconciled by then and would hand over the body of the dead son for the rites, to their wonder, they saw the boy fully alive and playing and the parents fondling him with joy! They exclaimed, 'What a mighty power is Guru Nath and how merciful and compassionate he is!'

THUS ENDS THE TWENTY-FIRST CHAPTER OF SRI
GURU CHARITRA DESCRIBING THE EPISODE
OF THE REVIVAL OF THE DEAD CHILD.

Glory to the all-merciful, the omnipresent and the ever-responsive Guru Nath!

Note

The body is said to be a vesture (garment) which the *jiva* wears. When the vesture, is worn out, the *jiva* discards the worn out, old vesture, in order to don a new one. That is how death and birth are explained. But then the question may arise: a new born baby's body is not like an old worn out cloth, yet we see some new-born babies dying. We see children and young dying much before they become old and ripe in age and bodies becoming decrepit in the natural course without living their full span of life. If we stitch a new garment from very old material which has not been stored properly and has been already worn out, then the garment will not last long! The body is like the temple of God. It has to be kept pure and unpolluted. If such a god-gifted body is misused by entertaining vices, the damage done to the body could persist in its subtler state even in the later birth/s of the *jiva*. The new body of the *jiva* may be very young, but the subtle body-material out of which it has been made may not be strong enough to last the full span of life. The damages and ravages of the body in the previous life of the *jiva*, will perhaps to some extent and in a subtler way, be carried forward to and is inherited by the new body, and especially so when one has died with excessive body-attachment and obsession. As a result, the new body may not be able to last long. It may break down and fall off prematurely.

Let us try to keep the body pure. Let us not bind the *jiva* with more and more births... Let us strive to earn for it freedom from the thraldom of unending cycle of births and deaths, by leading it back to its divine source, through moral rectitude, spiritual *Sadhana*, and more than anything else, by our total surrender at the feet of the Guru.

22

*Guru Nath's Advent at Ganagapur**

From this chapter onwards begins the glorious saga of
Ganagapur. It begins with the narrative of Guru Nath making
the old, dry buffalo yielding milk copiously and thus relieving
the poverty of a Brahmin couple of Ganagapur.

Implicit obedience to the Guru, and unquestioning faith in
his words are needed both in worldly matters as well as in
spiritual *sadhana*. There is nothing that cannot be achieved.
'*Sraddhaavaan labhate Jnanam,*' says the Bhagwad Gita.

*N*amdharak told Siddhamuni that his listening to the sacred
Guru Charitra *had very much awakened his spiritual
yearning and had illumined many higher and spiritual truths for
him. He vociferously expressed his gratitude to Siddhamuni. He
said he was keen to know about Guru Nath's stay and* leelas *at
Ganagapur; Siddhamuni resumed the narrative.*

Sri Narasimha Saraswati made Ganagapur more or less his
permanent abode, after coming from Amarapur. He lived there
in his visible form continuously for 24 years. In the beginning,
however, he did not allow himself to be seen by many and rather
lived more in seclusion. Most of the time he used to remain at
the Bhima-Amaraja Sangam. However, as days passed on he
chose to allow himself to be seen by more and more people.

---

* ˙ Study of this chapter is believed to grant cattle-wealth and prosperity.

At Ganagapur, there lived a poor Brahmin couple. The Brahmin used to eke out his livelihood by seeking alms in the village. He had one buffalo which was very old and had gone dry long back. He was, however, keeping the buffalo, because some grocers used to hire it for carrying salt bags and thus used it to fetch the Brahmin a little money now and then.

One day Guru Nath came to the house of the Brahmin asking for *bhiksha*. At that time, the Brahmin was away, having gone out for alms into the town. The Brahmin's wife welcomed Guru Nath and requested him to wait for the *bhiksha* till her husband returned home with alms. But Guru Nath told her that he would not be able to wait that long. He said that a little milk would do for him for the *bhiksha*. The woman said she was very sorry that there was no milk at all in the house. Guru Nath, then pointing to the buffalo in the yard said, 'You have a buffalo there, how then do you say there is no milk in the house?' The woman said the buffalo had been dry since many years now and it was kept by them because they got a little money from it now and then when people took it on hire for carrying salt-bags. Guru Nath said, 'I can't believe it. I would like you to milk it and show me whether it is really dry.' The woman, as the guest was insisting, took a small tumbler, went near the buffalo and started to milk it. Lo! milk was flowing out from the udders of the buffalo profusely. The tumbler was too small and she had to fetch bigger vessels from the house to collect the milk. The woman could not believe it at all. She was overjoyed and fell at Guru Nath's feet, pouring out her gratitude for relieving their poverty by making the buffalo wet. She gave the milk as *bhiksha* to Guru Nath.

The news of the miracle which Guru Nath performed in the poor Brahmin's house spread among all the people of the town and around. It also reached the ears of the king. Veneration and devotion to Guru Nath started growing in people's hearts.

The Brahmin couple, thereafter, frequently used to go to Amaraja Sangam to offer their prayers and worship to Guru Nath.

THUS ENDS THE TWENTY-SECOND CHAPTER OF
SRI *GURU CHARITRA* DESCRIBING
VANDHYA MAHISHI DOHANAM.

Glory to the all-merciful, the omnipresent and the ever-responsive Guru Nath!

23

*Bramha Rakshasa Attains Liberation by Guru's Grace**

> This chapter describes Guru Nath's settling down at Ganagapur *Math* at the request of the king of that place. Guru Nath blesses a *Bramha Rakshasa* and restores it to human form and grants him *Sadgathi.*

Siddhamuni continues the narrative.

As the news of Guru Nath's miracle of making the decrepit and dry buffalo yield plenty of milk and making it wet again and thus relieving the poverty of the Brahmin spread, people started flocking to the Brahmin's house to see the buffalo, especially when it was being milked. Hitherto Sri Narasimha Saraswati was remaining almost incognito at Amaraja Sangam, not revealing himself to many. How long can the light hide itself under the bushel? The news about the divine sage spread all around. The king also came to the Sangam to pay his respects and obeisance to Sri Narasimha Saraswati. Seeing Guru Nath, the king realised that this was none else but the Supreme Divinity, the Supreme Being which the Vedas tried their utmost to discover but could not succeed at all, and for whose vision (darshan) all the gods, angels and sages do the severest penances and austerities. He is

---

* Study of this chapter is believed to remove *vaastu-doshas* and to protect against afflictions from *grahas,* i.e., from evil effects of planets.

the Omniscient, the Omnipotent and the Omnipresent being, who is the creator, the sustainer and destroyer of the universe, and the abode of all wisdom, auspiciousness and divine virtues. He realised how blessed he, his kingdom and his people were that the intangible, infinite and the supreme being has chosen to appear before them in a visible and embodied form. The king fell at his feet and prayed that he should continue to stay in his kingdom only and should not leave the place and forsake them. He begged him to step into his palace and sanctify it.

Sri Narasimha Saraswati felt that the time had now come for him to come out of his secluded life and to reveal himself freely to all, and to carry out his divine mission in wider and fuller measure; he was also touched by the devotion of the king and felt that Ganagapur, with the holy Sangam in its vicinity, is a merited place for his stay and for carrying out his mission. He gave his consent to the king telling him that he would accede to his prayer and would stay at Ganagapur. The king was overwhelmed with joy at this and realised how blessed he and his people were.

Sri Narasimha Saraswati accompanied the king from Sangam to Ganagapur. He was received in the palace in all grandeur. All the people came out to welcome him, throwing and offering flowers at his feet and waving lights and doing *aarti*. There was one big house in the palace grounds, which was vacant and unoccupied. There was a Aswatha tree by the side of the house. It was spacious. But it was believed to be a haunted house, a place haunted by a *Bramha Rakshasa* and hence was not considered by the king to be an apt place for Sri Narasimha Saraswati to reside. But Sri Narasimha Saraswati said that the place would suit him. As soon as he entered the house, the *Bramha Rakshasa* came out in a fury with the object of assailing 'the intruder'. But seeing Sri Narasimha Saraswati, the *Bramha Rakshasa* realised that it was 'no intruder' but 'the Redeemer' who had come to bless all and him too. He fell prostrate at Guru Nath's feet, begging to be forgiven for all his sins and to be saved by his grace. Sri Narasimha Saraswati, in great compassion, told the *Bramha Rakshasa* that he had already been blessed by him and that he should go to the Bhima-Amaraja Sangam and bathe in the holy waters of the confluence there, and all his sins would be expiated once and for all, and he would be released from rebirth also forever.

The king built a *Math* at Ganagapur, at the place, for the divine guest to stay. Early morning Guru Nath used to leave the *Math* for the Sangam, which was a couple of miles away from the *Math*. He used to have his bath there and perform all religious rites and then return to the *Math* by midday. The king used to come every day by noon for the sage's darshan and for offering him his worship.

The name and fame of Sri Narasimha Saraswati and of his divine miracles spread by now far and wide, and thousands of devotees used to pour in for Guru Nath's darshan, for redress of afflictions of their body, mind and spirit.

THUS ENDS THE TWENTY-THIRD CHAPTER OF
SRI *GURU CHARITRA* DESCRIBING
BRAMHA RAKSHASA MUKTAKARANAM.

Glory to the all-merciful, the omnipresent and the ever-responsive Guru Nath!

24

Sri Narasimha Saraswati's
Viswarupa Darshan

This chapter describes Guru Nath vouchsafing Viswarupa darshan to Trivikrama Bharati.

Trivikrama Bharati is taken to the very threshold of *Jnana* and he is able to gain a glimpse of the all-pervading divinity. 'One sees the Self in all and all in the Self' in the state of *Jnana*.

Siddhamuni continued his narrative of the leelas of Guru Nath, which an enraptured Namdharak was listening to.

At Kumasi village which was not far away from Ganagapur, there lived an ascetic named Trivikrama Bharati. He was well versed in all the scriptures, and was an *upasaka* of Lord Sri Narasimha, the fourth among the ten avatars of Lord Vishnu. He was doing severe austerities to win the grace of the Lord.

Trivikrama Bharati heard of Sri Narasimha Saraswati, and how all were flocking to him for his darshan. He heard also that the king himself walked barefooted, along with all his royal retinue, attending upon Sri Narasimha Saraswati while the latter was being borne in a royal palanquin in all pompous splendour and to the accompaniment of music and play of drums, bugles, etc. It was said to be an everyday regal procession for Narasimha Saraswati, as he proceeded every morning to Sangam for his bath and while he returned to the *Math* at Ganagapur from Sangam after his worship *(Anushtana)* was over. Trivikrama Bharati did not feel it proper at all for an ascetic to be living in such pomp. He thought that all this was certainly not befitting a true and genuine *sanyasi* and Narasimha Saraswati must have beguiled the king through hypnotism or by some other dubious means. He began speaking derogatorily about Guru Nath.

Whatever be the happenings anywhere, whichever be the thoughts passing in anybody's mind however far away the person be, nothing ever escapes the notice of the omniscient and omnipresent Guru Nath. How can anything escape, his notice when he indeed is the inner resident *(antaryamin)* in the hearts of all beings and the witness of all happenings? He pitied Trivikrama Bharati for the wrong and erroneous notions he was holding and wanted to correct him and teach him the truth. He was himself like the lotus which though resting in water, yet remains unwetted by it. The worldly paraphernalia, etc., around him, had least attraction for him. He just let his devotees to have their way, just for their joy, pleasure and satisfaction. In his true nature, he is the supreme renunciate Lord Siva Himself. He wanted to reveal his true nature *(Swaswarupa)* to Trivikrama Bharati.

Guru Nath set out in palanquin, with the usual pomp and paraphernalia, towards Kumasi village. The king arranged for his cavalry, caparisoned elephants, horses, etc., to head the procession. It looked as if an emperor was going on his *Digvijaya yatra*.

Trivikrama Bharati, that morning also, as usual, began 'manasika puja' to his Ishta Devata, Lord Sri Narasimha. But strangely, despite his best efforts, he was unable to concentrate on his Lord's form. He was an adept *yogi*, and every day his mind used to get instantly fixed on the Lord's Form in the chamber of his heart, no sooner than he seated himself for the meditation. He was feeling worried as to what was happening to him that day, and why all his long number of years of practice of Yoga was failing him suddenly. He prayed to Lord Narasimha to forgive him for any lapse he had committed knowingly or unknowingly. As he started his prayers thus, lo, in his heart, he began seeing the form of Sri Narasimha Saraswati in place of his Lord Narasimha, who was shining in the same splendour as the latter. The vision and experience was vivid, and remained persisting however much he tried to draw away his mind from it.

Just at this juncture, Sri Narasimha Saraswati's procession reached near his place. Lo, what a unique wonder! It appeared before Trivikrama Bharati that everyone of the retinue, without exception, was shining in divine splendour. The vision was spreading, even beyond the horizon. Lo, wherever he glanced, it was all myriad forms of Sri Narasimha Saraswati alone. Trivikrama Bharati was overwhelmed with wonder; he fell prostrate on the ground and started praying to Sri Narasimha Saraswati to forgive him for all his impertinent and ignorant prattle before, not knowing that he, Sri Narasimha Saraswati, was none but the Supreme Lord who had come on earth. He prayed to be accepted as his disciple and be blessed.

As he prayed thus, Sri Narasimha Saraswati withdrew the Viswarupa vision, and Trivikrama Bharati could now see things in the normal way. He ran to the palanquin and fell prostrate at the feet of Guru Nath, pouring out his new-born devotion to him, in adulation. 'You are my Lord Narasimha, you are Trivikrama and Vamana. You are Bramha, Vishnu and Maheshwara ... you are all ... forgive me for my ignorance and ego, and light up the flame of wisdom in me,' he prayed.

Sri Narasimha Saraswati drew him near and said, 'Spiritual aspirants should rid themselves of all ego and be free from malice towards others. They should try to see the same Atma/Spirit as inherent in all. They should abstain from reviling others. *Sarva jiva Tiraskaram Iswaram Prati gacchati.* If you slander any one, it is tantamount to slandering God himself. The same supreme spirit is embodied in all. Try to see the divine in all. Fill your heart with love …' Guru Nath gave him much more advice and instruction. Trivikrama Bharati became a staunch disciple and devotee of Guru Nath hence onwards.

THUS ENDS THE TWENTY-FOURTH CHAPTER OF SRI *GURU CHARITRA* DESCRIBING THE GURU'S VISWARUPA DARSHAN TO TRIVIKRAMA BHARATI. WITH THIS CHAPTER ENDS THE JNANAYOGA SECTION OF THE *GURU CHARITRA*.

Glory to the all-merciful, the omnipresent and the ever-responsive Guru Nath!

25

*Pride of the Foolish Pandits**

This chapter describes how two boastful Brahmins who, so to say, were trading in the Vedas, were brought by Trivikrama Bharati before Guru Nath.

This chapter commences the Karma Kanda section of Sri *Guru Charitra.*

*N*amdharak was rapturously listening to the glorious narration of Guru leelas *being narrated by Siddhamuni, the blessed disciple of Guru Nath. Siddhamuni continued his narrative as under.*

There was a Muslim Nawab ruling Vidur Nagar at that time. He had no respect or tolerance for the Hindu religion. He used to tempt Brahmins to come to his court by offering money and gifts, and make them recite the Vedas and explain the meaning. Public recital of the Vedas before anybody and everybody, and especially before the non-believers and who have no reverence, is against Vedic injunctions. After making them recite and explain, he used to ignore the deeper and more sublime meaning of the words, and drawing perverse and distorted meanings of the Vedic words and hymns, he used to taunt the Brahmins, deride the Hindu religion and gloat over it. But most of the Brahmins never used to come forward, however

---

* The Karma Kanda section ends with chapter 37.

much the Nawab tempted and pressed them. Veda is our very
Mother. It is profound. It is divine. How can any self-respecting
person bear the sacred text being taunted by shallow-minded
persons?

However, there were two Brahmins who came forward to be
used as pawns in the hands of the Nawab. No doubt they were
very scholarly persons. They knew the Vedas by rote but had not
imbibed even a grain of true wisdom from the Vedic study.

The two Brahmin pandits impressed upon the Nawab, that
there was none in the land who had knowledge more than them.
They said that the Nawab should arrange for a debate in
scriptural and Vedic subjects in his court, and that they would be
able to defeat anyone and establish the supremacy and
superiority of their scholarship and knowledge over all others.
But none of the pandits agreed to come to the Nawab's court for
the contest, because the Vedic subjects were sacred and were
meant for *pathana* (chanting and contemplation), and not for
vada (i.e., acrimonious debates). The pandits said they would go
out into the country and seek out contest in different villages
and towns. If anyone ever dared to contest against them, they
were confident to defeat him. And in case nobody came
forward, that meant an open acknowledgement by all of the two
pandits' supremacy, and therefore, the ruler should recognise it
and honour them befittingly. The Nawab encouraged them in
this, only with the object of enjoying watching the pandits
disputing amongst themselves acrimoniously.

The pandits set out on their challenging campaign, puffed
up with pride of the patronage and backing of the Yawan ruler.
They came to Kumasi and they were told that Trivikrama
Bharati was the most scholarly pandit of the area, and if he was
defeated, it would establish their unchallengeability. When the
pandits proposed to Trivikrama Bharati that he should enter into
contest against them, the latter declined, saying it did not befit

him, a renunciate and *sanyasi*, to enter into discussions and debates for winning name and fame. The pandits said, if he did not want to contest against them, he should acknowledge them as unchallengeable and should accede *Jaya-Patra* to them. Trivikrama Bharati saw their conceit and ambition and thought that they should be taught a fitting lesson. He took them to Sri Narasimha Saraswati at Ganagapur. As soon as they entered into the presence of Guru Nath, Trivikrama Bharati fell down prostrate at Guru Nath's feet, offering his obeisance. The pandits, however, did not show any respect and they showed off their pride and arrogance.

Sri Narasimha Saraswati enquired as if he was not aware of what had brought them to him. Trivikrama Bharati narrated about the campaign on which the pandits had set out. The pandits demanded that Sri Narasimha Saraswati should enter into debate with them or should acknowledge their unchallengeability and give them the *Jaya-Patra*.

Sri Narasimha Saraswati chided them saying what benefit would accrue to them by showing off their intellectual scholarship. The knowledge of Vedas* and scriptures need to be imbibed and digested into integrated wisdom, into intuitive experience, fructifying in the realisation of the self, the spiritual reality. He cited the instances of Ravana, Banasura, etc., who were all well versed and proficient in Vedic lore, but which made them highly conceited and egoistic. And what was the result? It led only to their total ruin and destruction, along with all their clan. The Vedic knowledge is not for earthly conquests and for winning applause from people. The knowledge should be put to

---

* The Vedas are meant for *Buddhi-yoga*, but are not meant for *Buddhi-Vada*. Rationalism (especially, materialist rationalism) cannot reach us beyond *Buddhi-Vada*. It is only the *Buddhi-Yoga* that can reach us beyond the mind and the intellect and into the realms of the spirit, which is the sole and true (ultimate) purpose and aim of the Hindu scriptures, and for that matter, of all the religious scriptures of the world. From the plane of intelligence, into the realm of intuition, they want men to rise.

use for the conquest of one's senses and ego, and to realise the all-pervading divine and spiritual reality. All the loving well-meant advice of Guru Nath fell on deaf ears. It did not change the minds of the pandits, whose hearts were deeply set on winning worldly acclaim for 'their scholarship'.

THUS ENDS THE TWENTY-FIFTH CHAPTER OF
SRI *GURU CHARITRA* DESCRIBING
THE VAIN-GLORIOUS AND CONCEITED PANDITS.

Glory to the all-merciful, the omnipresent and the ever-responsive Guru Nath!

26

Infinite Glory of the Vedas
and Their True Purpose

This chapter describes Sri Narasimha Saraswati explaining
to the two vain-glorious pandits about the sanctity of Vedic
lore and that Vedas are not meant for *vada* and polemics.
Vedas are verily the mother; they are to be treated with
reverence and veneration. They are meant to illumine our
intellect and to help us discover our true self, and are not
intended for bartering them for self-aggrandisement. They are
not for *jeevanopadhi* but for *Jeevana-Paramavadhi.* They are
meant for Bhakti and Mukti and not for Bhukti. They are
meant for nurturing and enriching the spirit but not for filling
and pampering one's being.

Siddhamuni continued with the narrative.
Sri Narasimha Saraswati told the pandits that it was wrong,
presumptuous and childish on their part to believe that they had
mastered all the Vedas and gained all knowledge. It is indeed
beyond the ken and capacity of anybody, even of gods, to have
full and proper understanding of the Vedas.

The Vedas are indeed countless and endless—'*Ananta Vai
Vedah*', it is said. Even Bramhadeva could not gauge the extent of
the Vedas. The Lord himself had to incarnate on earth as
Badarayana, i.e., Vyasa, and he collated a small portion of them
into the four Vedas, which we have heard of. It was indeed a very

tiny portion of the original Vedic lore abstracted for the purpose of making a beginning and for paving the way for dharmic life. Even Badarayana, in truth, could not find the beginning and end of the Vedas. As even these four Vedas, tiny portions from the original which is limitless, cannot all be studied and understood by anyone, even if he be allotted aeons of life. Vyasa Bhagavan taught each one of the Vedas (some little portion from each) to one student, each of whom was specially blessed with the full extent of a *Kalpa* his lifespan. Thus spending a full *Kalpa* for their study, Paila learnt a small portion which goes under the name of *Rig Veda*, Vaisampayana learnt another small portion which goes under the name of *Yajur Veda*; Jaimini learnt another small portion which goes under the name of *SamaVeda* and Sumanta learnt another small portion which goes by the name of *Atharva Veda*. These at least, they could learn, only because of the special grace of their Guru, Vyasa Bhagavan. That being the case, how ridiculous it was for any man, whose lifespan was so short to claim and boast that he had mastered the Vedas!

In ancient times, Bharadwaja Rishi had resolved that he would learn and master all the Vedas. As he proceeded with his study, he found that although decades and centuries were rolling by, the progress he could make was too little. He undertook penance to propitiate Bramha and when Bramha appeared before him, he prayed, 'Grant me as much lifespan as would suffice for my completing the study of the Vedas'. Bramhadeva smiled, as if in derision, and said, 'My child! I can make you *Chiranjeevi*, but alas, it is beyond all my powers to help you to make a complete study of all the Vedas. See there the infinite heights of the Vedas'. As he said this, Bharadwaja Rishi could see the splendorous mountains of the Vedas, their peaks hardly visible, and penetrating into the highest skies. Their effulgence was like that of a million suns. Bharadwaja instantly realised his folly in hoping that he could master all the Vedas, which would never be possible even if he be granted millions and millions of aeons as his lifespan. He was crestfallen and fell at the feet of Bramha, that he should somehow bless him with the Vedic wisdom. Bramha gave him three handfuls of material from the infinite mountain peaks and told him, 'If you can study and understand this much, you will be most blessed indeed'. Bharadwaja strove for all his life and he could not complete even that much study, of the three handfuls of material that Bramhadeva gave him. Guru Nath again said, that being the case, how fallacious it is for a mere mortal of the *Kali Yuga* to claim that he has mastered all the Vedas, alas!

Guru Nath now started speaking of the glory of the Vedas and their structure, which was unheard of before by any. Guru Nath said that this was what had been told by Vyasa Bhagavan to each of his disciples regarding the respective Vedas he taught them. Briefly, it is as under:

'*Rig Veda* has as its auxiliary *Ayurveda*, the science of life. Its presiding deity is Bramha. Its *gotra* is Atreyasa. Its *chandas* is Gayatri. The *Rig Veda Purusha* has red lotus-like broad eyes, and a three-feet-long shapely neck. He has beautiful flowing locks of hair. *Rig Veda* has in all 12 sections or divisions. Its systematic recital, with the correct intonation, endows greatest merit. Much of the portion of *Rig Veda* is not known to any in the *Kali Yuga*.

'*Yajur Veda* has as its auxiliary the *Dhanurveda* (the science of archery and weapons). Its presiding deity is Rudra. Its *gotra* is Bharadwaja. Its *chandas* is Tristup. The *Yajur Veda Purusha* has bright lotus-like eyes, with an effulgent body and majestic stature.

'*Yajur Veda* has 86 *bedhas* (sections or divisions). It is humanly impossible to explain every section of this Veda. Each section has many sub-sections, chapters and branches which are dealt with in great detail, but are not easily comprehensible. They have profound meanings and implications. They deal with sacrifices, *Achara-Vidhis*, the detailed instructions governing the performance of sacrifices, the mantras for the purpose and the strict discipline to be observed by the Brahmin, especially by the priests officiating at such sacrifices. This Veda broadly consists of mantras, *bramhanas, samhitas* and *aranyakas.*

'This Veda has eight *Upangas,* viz., *Pratipada, Anupada, Chandas, Bhasha,* dharma, *Mimansa, Nyaya* and *Tarka.* It has also six *Angas* (limbs) namely, *Siksha, Kalpaka, Vyakarana, Nirukta, Chandas* and *Jyotisha.*

'*Sama Veda* has as its *Upaveda, Gandharva Vidya/Veda.* Its presiding deity is Vishnu. Its *chandas* is Jagati. Its *gotra* is Kasyapasa. *Sama Veda* has a thousand *sakhas* (sections). The *Sama Veda Purusha* dons on his neck a beautiful flower garland and wears a white waist cloth. He has all the virtues like *sama* and *dama,* i.e., total mastery over senses and mind. He has radiant eyes, a most fair complexioned golden-splendoured body and is nine feet tall in height.

'*Atharva Veda* is full of mantra shastra. Its *Upaveda* is *Astra Vidya/Veda.* Its presiding deity is Indra. Its *gotra* is Vaijanasa. Its *chandas* is Tristup. The *Atharva Veda Purusha* is of fierce form and of dark complexion. He is not as austere as the other three *Veda Purushas.* Atharvana mantras can be used for malevolent purpose also and thus misused. The Veda has chiefly nine *bedhas* and five *Kalpas.*'

Sri Narasimha Saraswati told the pandits that the Vedas are most profound. They are the sole protection for mankind both in the world here and world hereafter. They are to be worshipped as mother. Humility is the true mark of scholarship. He again emphasised that knowledge, if at all anyone can gain and profess about the Veda, will be just no more than a grain of sand while the Vedic lore is like the unending stretch of the sandy shores of all the seas of the earth.

The pandits, in their pride, could not grasp the wise counsel of Sri Narasimha Saraswati and still kept up their air of arrogance.

THUS ENDS THE TWENTY-SIXTH CHAPTER OF
SRI *GURU CHARITRA* GIVING A BRIEF ACCOUNT
OF THE FOUR VEDAS AND THEIR INFINITE GLORY.

Glory to the all-merciful, the omnipresent and the ever-responsive Guru Nath!

27

Humbling the Pride of the Pandits

This chapter describes how the two vain-glorious pandits
were humbled, and had brought upon themselves a curse
which turned them into *Bramha Rakshasas*.

*Siddhamuni tells Namdharak how Sri Narasimha Saraswati
lovingly counselled the pandits to desist from discussion and
arguing (doing* vada*) about the sacred truths of the Vedas in public,
for gaining personal aggrandisement. And especially a* sanyasi *like
Guru Nath himself was not the kind of person who would enter
into debate with any, on the sacred lore. Their duty was to
contemplate on the Vedic and Upanishadic truths in seclusion and
solitude. He warned and told them that if they still persisted in
their challenge and insisted on debate, it was tantamount to
courting their own ruin like the* patang *(glow-worms) hovering
around the lamp and playing with fire, to meet their self-
destruction. As the pandits were still unheeding, Sri Narasimha
Saraswati decided to humble their pride and punish them.*

*Siddha Yogi then begins to narrate how Guru Nath teaches
the pandits a lesson.*

Sri Narasimha Saraswati beckoned to one of the disciples,
asked him to go out into the street, and call the man who was
just passing by. The man was brought in. The man bowed to

Guru Nath in all humility* showing great respect and veneration. He was however feeling perplexed as he belonged to a low caste and was at a loss to understand why he was called into the august presence of Guru Nath.

Sri Narasimha Saraswati asked him what caste he belonged to. The man told him he was a Matanga (Harijan). Sri Narasimha Saraswati glanced at him with his look of grace and pouring out his nectarine love. That was enough to metamorphose instantly the Matanga completely. Sri Narasimha Saraswati gave his *danda* (yogic staff), to one of his disciples standing by. He asked him to draw seven lines, one after the other on the ground in front of the Matanga. After that, he asked the Matanga to step forward and cross the first line. When the Matanga did so, Guru Nath asked him to what caste he belonged. The man replied he belonged to Kirat Vamsa (the hunter-caste) and his name was Van Rakha. He then asked him to cross line after line. After the second line was crossed he asked him again the same question as before. The man replied he was then Ganga Putra (i.e., belonging to the fishermen's community). After the next line, he said he belonged to the Sudra caste. After the fifth line, he said he belonged to the Vaisya caste (i.e., to the merchant community). After the sixth line, he said he belonged to the Kshatriya caste (i.e., to the warrior community). After crossing the seventh line, he said he belonged to the Brahmin caste and devoted to Vedic *adhyayan*.

Sri Narasimha Saraswati then gave sacred ash (after charging it with mantra) to be besmeared all over the body of the Matanga—now turned into Brahmin. He then told the pandits that they can do the *vada* with the stranger and seek the *Vijaya-Patra* from him if they can win over him in the contest. Their pride was humbled witnessing the instantaneous transformation

---

* Humility is the true mark of learning. *Vidya* is not for earning money, i.e., not for *bhukthi*, but for *bhakti* which will earn for us no less than the vision of God himself— the supreme reality.

of the low-caste Matanga into a Brahmin of high Vedic learning, by the mere look of grace from Guru Nath. And as the debate started, the Brahmin-turned Matanga was arguing and reciting Vedic mantras as Brihaspati or Bramhadeva himself. The foolish pandits' tongues were parched, they were perspiring profusely and their limbs were shaking. They fell at Guru Nath's feet and begged to be forgiven for their pride and arrogance in not heeding to his advice, in their ignorance and foolishness.

Sri Narasimha Saraswati said with compassion, 'I cannot help you much now. By your greedy desire to trade in Vedas, you have drawn the Veda Mata's curse upon yourselves. For a period of 12 years you will be turned into *Bramha Rakshasa* but I bless that you will be released from the curse then as you will happen to hear the recital of *Narayana Sukta* from a pious Brahmin, and then you will turn into Brahmins again.' He asked them to go to Sangam and take their bath. The pandits fell down dead the same day.

THUS ENDS THE TWENTY-SEVENTH CHAPTER OF
SRI *GURU CHARITRA* DESCRIBING THE HUMBLING
OF THE PRIDE OF THE PANDITS.

Glory to the all-merciful, the omnipresent and the ever-responsive Guru Nath!

28

Actions and Consequences (Law of Cause and Effect)

This chapter* narrates the story of the Harijan-turned Brahmin who was first unwilling to go back to his home but soon sank back into delusion again, when the holy ash (*bhasma*) was washed off his body. He went back home along with his wife and children merrily, forgetting all that had happened just a little earlier.

*S*iddhamuni told Namdharak that the Matanga, now blessed with Bramhanic knowledge, asked Sri Narasimha Saraswati to let him know why he was born as a Chandala in this birth, while he was a Brahmin in his former life.

Guru Nath explained in great detail the rules governing Karma and its consequences (fruits as well as retribution). While Trivikrama Bharati and all present listened with rapt attention. Siddhamuni begins narrating Guru Nath's explanations.

The caste in which one is born is determined by his past karmas (actions and conduct). Good actions lead to higher birth, births in higher castes; and sinful and bad actions lead to births in lower castes or even in sub-human species.

---

* The views expressed in this chapter is not relevant in modern times and is strongly condemned by all. One needs to understand such customs in the context of the time when they were practised.

Brahmin is predominantly of *sattvic* (of pure, serene and tranquil) temperament; he has a special duty and role in the society. He is the spiritual custodian of the people of all communities. He has the great responsibility of looking after the spiritual wellbeing of all, just as it devolves on the eldest son in the family, to take all care and responsibility for the material and general wellbeing of all his younger brothers and sisters in the family. He has to observe strict discipline; perform all the prescribed rituals as per Vedic injunctions and his conduct should be a model and example to all others. His daily rituals are for the wellbeing of all. For that high purpose, the Brahmin has to consecrate his entire life. That was why Brahmins of yore were ranked as equal to Gods, and even the rulers (kings) used to honour them as such.

If a Brahmin fails in the discharge of his ordained duties, he will slide down to birth in the lower caste(s). Apart from the duties ordained, there are also actions prohibited. If a Brahmin indulges in any of the prohibited actions, he gets born in the lowest caste(s) or even as an animal or may be even as a lowly creature. Guru Nath listed many acts of omissions and commissions which cause a Brahmin to be born as a Chandala. He told the Matanga that because he ill-treated his parents in his previous life, he was born as a Chandala in this life. Among the many sins listed which cause the downfall of men (*Durgathi* in contrast to *Sadgathi*), especially of the Brahmins, the following are some—

   (a)   forsaking the Guru and the parents and ill-treating them;

   (b)   forsaking the wife and the children;

   (c)   committing adultery, theft, etc., (even sensuous thoughts about other women are as much a sin);

   (d)   killing animals or inflicting the least suffering upon them;

   (e)   separating away the calf from its mother;

(f) non-observance of injunctions regarding food;

(g) failure to perform the *shradh* ceremony to the departed souls (ancestors) and forbears of the family;

(h) indulging in slanderous talk, especially blasphemy against the Vedas, deities and gods;

(i) turning away guests and not offering them food;

(j) refusing to give drinking water to thirsty persons;

(k) indulging in iconoclasm (breaking of idols) and causing damage to temples and places of worship, or fouling tanks, wells and rivers;

(l) non-observance of the *Nitya-Vidhis*, the daily obligatory duties enjoined on one.

Guru Nath lists many types of sins and their consequences such as after-life in hell, birth involving congenital infirmities like blindness, lameness, etc., and birth as an animal, reptile or a worm, etc.

Trivikrama Bharati asked Sri Narasimha Saraswati as to what are the *Prayashchitta* rites (atonement rites) or methods by means of which one can absolve himself of the sins he committed. Guru Nath then explains the *Prayashchitta-Vidhis* (methods of atonement) for the sins committed. He says as follows—

'Sincere and heartfelt repentance, prayer to the Almighty God who is the *Karmaphaladata* (dispenser of the results of karma) for forgiveness, and abstinence from further sinful conduct, will mitigate to a large extent the retributive effect of the sins. To absolve oneself completely from the consequences of the sins, *Prayashchitta* rites are prescribed in the shastras, but they will be effective only where they are performed in true spirit of repentance and with reformation and rectitude in the conduct of the person doing the *Prayashchitta*.'

Guru Nath explained various *Prayashchitta* rites, some of which are—

(a) penitence, fasting and prayers;

(b) pilgrimages to holy places and bathing in holy rivers;

(c) giving gifts in charity like cow, gold, money, etc.;

(d) *Kruchra* and *Chandrayana vratas* (observances);

(e) chanting of Gayatri Mantra (ten thousand times or chanting of Pavamana/Suthra, etc., as many times); and

(f) rendering of service to others and especially to the Guru.

Observance of *Kruchra* includes fasting for three days, followed by sustaining oneself on milk, for the next three days, on ghee for further three days, etc. Those who are weak are permitted to eat gingley seeds; otherwise what is prescribed is water in which is soaked either Ashwatha or banyan leaves or lotus flowers or Darbha grass, etc.

The *Chandrayana Vrata* begins with fast on new moon day, taking one morsel of food the next day, and increasing one by one morsel of food every day afterwards; from full moon day onwards again decreasing one by one morsel of food every day and with total fast again on the new moon day.

Through *Gayatri Homa* and *Veda Parayana* also, as much merit is earned as by doing these *vratas*.

With stay at Kasi for a month, all sins are absolved. A bath at Setu-Bandhan absolves the sin of causing death of a Brahmin and the like. Sustaining oneself with one single and limited meal a day and reciting of *Purushasukta* for six months, will absolve one of all his sins. The recital of *Narayanopanishad*, *Vishnu Sukta*, etc., will absolve one of all the sins committed in countless former lives.

Before starting to do the *Prayashchitta*, one should begin by sipping *Panchagavya*, after fasting on the previous night.

Panchagavya is a mixture of the cow's milk, urine, dung, ghee, curds and water in which is dipped the Kusa grass. It is sanctified by the chant of the mantras and preferably also blessed by the Guru/priest.

All the above rites are very potent means by which one can absolve his sins done knowingly or in ignorance.

Guru Nath, after explaining the implications of Karma and the consequences, told the Matanga again, that as he, in his previous life, ill-treated his parents, he was born as a Chandala in the present life. He then advised him to go to the Bhima-Amaraja Sangam and take the purificatory bath there, by which his sins would be expiated and he would be born as a Brahmin in his next birth.

The Matanga prayed that as he had already been transformed into a Brahmin through the grace of Guru Nath and was also endowed with scriptural knowledge, whereby he was able to win in the contest with the pandits, Guru Nath should recognise and confer on him Brahminhood permanently and that he would not like to wait for the next birth for becoming a Brahmin. Sri Narasimha Saraswati tried to explain to him that as he was born in this birth from the womb of a Chandal woman, even though he had been now endowed with scriptural knowledge, he could not get recognition as a true Brahmin. True Brahminhood, besides birth in a Brahmin family, needs certain *samskaras* to be gone through and also certain disciplines and upbringing. Both are as much necessary, and that he would be merited for them in his next birth with his blessing. Sri Narasimha Saraswati further gave the illustration of Viswamitra, who was born as a Kshatriya, and though through austerities and penance attained spiritual power and eminence, could not get recognition as a Brahmin, because of his birth. However, on the advice of Vasishta Rishi, when he virtually burnt down his body by the hot rays of the sun and grew a new skin and body, he got recognition as Bramharishi.

The Matanga was however not reconciled and was still pestering Guru Nath that he should get the recognition as Brahmin then and there itself.

At that juncture, the Matanga's wife, along with the children came over. She saw him and went close to him. The Matanga wanted to drive her away and started beating her. The woman started weeping and crying and prayed to Sri Narasimha Saraswati to make her husband stop beating. Sri Narasimha Saraswati asked one of the disciples to call one *Lubdhak*, a Brahmin but without any Vedic learning, and who earned his livelihood by doing all sorts of lowly tasks. Sri Narasimha Saraswati asked him to pour water over the body of Matanga and give him a full bath. When the water was poured on the Matanga, it washed out all the *bhasma* applied on his body earlier. Along with the *bhasma*, the scriptural knowledge which the Matanga obtained earlier also disappeared and was lost totally from his memory. The Matanga became as he was before, the same unregenerate being. He was seized with *moha* and delusion and, seeing his wife and children, ran to them, totally forgetting whatever had happened earlier.

THUS ENDS THE TWENTY-EIGHTH CHAPTER OF
SRI *GURU CHARITRA* DESCRIBING
KARMA VIPAKA AKHYANARM.

Glory to the all-merciful, the omnipresent and the ever-responsive Guru Nath!

29

Significance and Power of Vibhuti

In this chapter the great power of the holy ashes is further explained. The mere touch of holy ash on the body of Sage Vamadeva, the *Maha Rakshasa*, got him liberated.

Veepudhi (*vibhuti*) **Dharana Mantra**

Trayambakam yajamahe sugandhim pushti vardhanam
Urvarukamiva bandhanaat mrutyor muksheeya maamrutat

> *The one who spreads a fragrance (of vibhuti) around himself and all around,*
>
> *Who fosters the worldly wellbeing, as well as the spiritual wellbeing of all,*
>
> *That three-eyed Lord, him I worship ...*
>
> *Oh, you the supreme one!*
>
> *Like the ripened cucumber which severs itself from the creeper and drops off,*
>
> *Grant release for me from death,*
>
> *(from the unending cycle of births and deaths),*
>
> *But, pray, never cause severance for me from immortality* (amritatwa)
>
> *And may I ever abide in awareness of thee ...*

Siddha Yogi continued the narrative to Namdharak as follows.
Trivikrama Bharati requested Sri Narasimha Saraswati to
enlighten them about *Bhasma-Mahima** and how it posseses
such great power as they just witnessed in the Matanga episode.
Sri Narasimha Saraswati then narrated the following anecdote.

There used to be one *yogi* called Vamadeva. He used to
smear his body always with *bhasma*. His hair was matted
and he used to wear the bark of trees for his garment. He was
a very exalted *yogi*. He had won over all the human frailties,
sublimated his senses and conquered the six inner enemies—
Shadripus (likes, dislikes, greed, delusion, ego and pride,
envy and jealousy)—which enslave man. He was a fully-
realised soul and a *Bramha-Jnani*. He used to be always
wandering, visiting holy places. One day he came to the
Krouncharanya (forest). This forest was full of wild beast;
there were also ghosts and *Bramha Rakshasas* inhabiting the
forest. One *Bramha Rakshasa* noticed Vamadeva entering
the forest, and he was very happy that he would be having a
good feast with the body of the *yogi*. He fell upon him with
a view to eating him up. But Vamadeva was least perturbed,
and remained steady and calm. The contact with the *bhasma*
on the body of Vamadeva wrought an instant and total
transformation of the *Bramha Rakshasa*. He was totally
changed, rid of his demonic nature by the contact with the
bhasma. He prayed to Vamadeva to free him from the cycle
of birth and death. He told Vamadeva that by the mere
contact with *bhasma*, he gained the memory of all his past
twenty-five births. He started recounting them to
Vamadeva.

The *Bramha Rakshasa* said he was actually a king of
Yavandesh. But he had a very vicious and lustful nature. He

---

*   In the metaphysical sense, *bhasma* means destruction of the *deha-buddhi* or the *deha-
bhranti*, i.e., overcoming the idea and obsession that 'one is the body and nothing
beyond that'. One who have transcended this *deha-bhavana*, as exemplified in the
person of Vamadeva, will have nothing to fear from. He is indeed one with Lord Siva
himself.

led a very sensuous life, running after women always, without any decency, compunction and consideration. His sins crossed all bounds and limits. In an encounter with an enemy king, he was killed. He was dragged to the court of Yama. He was subjected to great torture in hell, and later he had to take several births only because of all his sins. He was born as a tiger in one birth, as a wolf in the second birth, as a dog in the third birth, as a camel in the fourth, as a monkey in the fifth, then as a cat, thereafter as a tortoise, then as a frog, and so on. He had suffered much, all of his own making though. Now the mere touch with *bhasma* had so much soothened his soul, and never before had he felt such peace. He further said that his hunger, which never got satiated normally, however many animals or persons he might eat, was now totally appeased, and that he was feeling a great sense of peace and happiness. He prayed that he should be enlightened as to how the *bhasma* came to possess such great redeeming power.

Vamadeva told the *Rakshasa* that the power of *bhasma* is beyond all description, and it is beyond the comprehension of any, except of Lord Siva. Siva only knows; he alone knows fully the glorious power of *bhasma*. That is why he (Siva) smears his whole body always with *bhasma*.

Vamadeva told that there lived once a Brahmin in Dravidadesa. He took to bad ways of life. He took to theft. Once when he was committing a theft, he was caught and beaten up. He died and his body was thrown in the cemetery. In the cemetery, at that time, a dog was sitting on *chitabhasma* (ashes of a burnt corpse). That dog saw the body of the dead Brahmin, and came and sat on the body sniffing it all over. As it was doing so, the *chitabhasma* from its body fell over the body of the corpse. No sooner did the *chitabhasma* fall over the body of the corpse, than the *Sivadootas* appeared over there, stopping the *Yamadootas* who had already come there to take away the *jiva* of the evil man. A dispute arose between the servants of Yama and Siva. The guards of Yama were claiming the *jiva*, because the sins committed by the man were countless, and the place he deserved was nowhere else but hell. But the *Sivadootas* said that with the touch of *bhasma* on the body, all his sins, however heinous they might have been, had been burnt off and expiated. It is Lord Sankara's command that whenever they see a dead person's body with *bhasma* smeared on the forehead or even on any part of the body, they should fetch that *jiva* to Kailash. Thus saying, the *Sivadootas* snatched away the *jiva* from the *Yamadootas'* hands and took it away to Kailash. When this was reported by *Yamadootas* to Lord Yama, the latter went to Siva in anger, and complained to him about the intrusion, high-handedness and interference of *Sivadootas* preventing his servants from discharging their duties and carrying out justice. He complained how could dharma be protected and the rule of law enforced by him in the world under such circumstances. Siva then told Yama that *bhasma dharma* is the highest dharma and it annuls and supersedes all other codes and injunctions of dharma. He told Yama Dharma Raja to tell his servants that they should abstain from approaching the bodies of the dead, smeared with or wearing the marks of *bhasma*.

'Such was the *mahima* of *bhasma*,' said Vamadeva to the *Bramha Rakshasa*. The *Rakshasa* requested Vamadeva to teach and explain to him the *Bhasma Dharana Vidhi*. Vamadeva explained the same through another anecdote.

Once Lord Siva and Parvati went to the Mandara Mountain. All the gods, *rishis, apsaras, gandharvas, yakshas, kinnaras, rudragan, Sivadootas,* came and assembled over there. Lord Siva was seated on his throne. By his side was seated Mother Parvati. Golden in complexion, and bedecked in the richest jewellery and adorned with beautiful flowers, she was radiating all splendour. All were absorbed in the ecstacy of the darshan of the divine couple, the mother and father of the universe.

Sanatkumara Rishi prayed to Siva to teach them the one *Dharma Vidhi* which will be simple to be observed by all and yet will confer all the four *Purusharthas*—the four chief aims of life, dharma, *artha, kama* and *moksha* and which will destroy all the sins, endow bodily and mental purity and also intellectual illumination.

Lord Siva said there is one *Dharma Vidhi* which is simple and can be followed by each and everyone and which will confer all good and save men from all the ills of the world. This *vidhi* is called the *Tripundra Bhasma Dharana Vidhi*. The *bhasma* is symbolic of the ultimate truth of all matter. It has a spiritual significance in that it is changeless, immutable like Godhead. It is colourless or white, so to say, indicating purity. In *Jabalopanishad, Bhasma Vidhi* is described in great detail.

Agani is the presiding deity for *bhasma*. The ash from the sacrificial fire is most sacred. In the absence of it, ash prepared from cow-dung is to be used. A little of ash is to be taken, reciting the *Sadyojata* ... mantra. While reciting the *Manasthoka* ... *mantra,* a little water is to be added and mixed in it with the aid of the thumb. Then chanting the *Thrayambakam Yajamahe* ... mantra, it has to be taken near the forehead and while reciting the *Thrayayusham Jamadagne* ... mantra, the same is to be applied in three lines, i.e., *tripundra dharana*. First, with the aid of the middle and ring fingers two lines are to be applied, the top one and the bottom are from left to the right, then with the aid of the thumb, the middle line is to be applied, drawing it from right to the left. The marks are not to extend beyond the sides of the eyebrows. With devotion, these marks are to be always worn on the forehead.

The first line mark is Bramha Devata and is symbolic of Rig Veda. It is denoted by 'अ' (A). It endows 'Kriya Sakti'.

The second line is Vishnu Devata, and is symbolic of Yajur Veda. It is denoted by "ऊ" (U). It endows 'Icha Sakti'.

The third line is Maheshwara himself and is symbolic of Sama Veda. It is denoted by 'म' (M). It endows 'Jnana Sakti'.

Bhasma Dharana can be done by one and all, and during all the stages of life. It will cure all the ills of the body, mind and spirit. It ensures mental purity, intellectual illumination and spiritual enlightenment in their life, and in the life beyond it opens up the gates of Kailash for him, which is the eternal abode of supreme peace and beatitude *(Prasanthi)*.

Lord Siva finally said that for destroying one's sins, there is nothing comparable to doing *Bhasma Dharana,* but it should be done with full faith and devotion. For one who applies ashes on his forehead and wears the *rudraksha mala* on his neck, there will be nothing wanting for him either in this life or in the life beyond.

That was what Lord Siva explained to Sanatkumara Rishi and all the assembled sages.

Hearing the divine glory of *bhasma,* the *Rakshasa* sought the *bhasma* from Vamadeva and applied it upon himself. His *Rakshasa* form totally changed and he got a new splendorous body. A divine vehicle came and took him away to Kailash.

THUS ENDS THE TWENTY-NINTH CHAPTER OF
SRI *GURU CHARITRA* DESCRIBING
THE BHASMA MAHIMA.

Glory to the all-merciful, the omnipresent and the ever-responsive Guru Nath!

30

*Vairagyabodha**

This chapter describes the story of the young woman Savitri and the death of her sick husband whom she brought all the way from her far away home, for Guru Nath's darshan with great hopes of his recovery.

Siddhamuni continued the narrative to Namdharak describing the glorious account of the leelas *of Guru Nath.*

Guru Nath's name and fame was increasing day by day and it started spreading over the whole country. People from all regions, even from the farthest parts of India, started visiting Ganagapur for Guru Nath's darshan and for seeking his blessings. Whoever came, went back with their hearts filled with great satisfaction and a sense of fulfilment in life and with peace and joy. Everyone returned with a deep conviction that Guru Nath, though physically staying at Ganagapur, is ever with them wherever they be living and is ever providing his protection. Without his call, none can ever think of going to Ganagapur for his darshan and without his will none will be able to visit the place and have the audience with him. His love is like the love of a thousand mothers. Whoever visits there will have all his aspirations fulfilled and his grievances redressed although he might put these people to much test during the process.

---

* Chapters 30 to 35 are to be completed in one session, i.e., one-day's sitting or duration.

There lived in the town of Mahur, a Brahmin who was quite well-to-do and rich. His name was Gopinath. His wife gave birth to many children but none of them survived. They prayed fervently to Lord Dattatreya that they may have at least one son. In response to their faith and prayers, they had a son born again, whom they named as Datta, i.e., after the name of Lord Dattatreya with whose blessings he was born. The boy was very healthy and free from any ailment. The parents were very happy. When the boy was five years of age, his thread ceremony was performed. When he was sixteen years of age, he was married to a girl whose name was Savitri, and who was very beautiful. The young couple were leading a very happy life.

After four years of happy married life, the young man unfortunately fell seriously ill. The parents consulted many *Vaidyas* and tried various treatments bearing a lot of expenses. But there was no improvement in his condition; in fact, it was deteriorating day by day. The young wife thought that if she could take her husband to Ganagapur and pray to Sri Narasimha Saraswati, his life could be saved. She felt that was the only hope for her. She expressed the same to her parents-in-law. They did not want to stand in her way. They were very distressed and worried that the boy's condition was becoming more and more critical, all the medical treatment proving of no avail. They also felt that only divine grace, if at all anything, could save their son and that they should let their daughter-in-law do whatever she felt was the best course.

The young wife told her husband that she would like to take him on pilgrimage to Ganagapur for Sri Narasimha Saraswati's darshan and that would certainly restore his health. The young man with tears in his eyes, started saying how distressed he was, not for his illness, but considering that he had not been able to give her any happiness and had to see her toiling all the time looking after him and his needs. Savitri reassured her husband that she was very happy in doing service to him, and was prepared to make any sacrifice so that he recovered soon from his ailment. She said that troubles do come in life as per one's karma; no one can escape it altogether, but with divine grace it should be possible to overcome it. She said she had all hopes that Sri Narasimha Saraswati would rid him of his illness by his grace, and would shower his blessings on them.

Comforting the parents-in-law, telling them not to worry at all and assuring that she would certainly bring her husband back to them safe and fully restored in health soon, she set out on her pilgrimage to Ganagapur along with her husband.

The couple, after great difficulty, reached the outskirts of Ganagapur and although the wife was very exhausted, she was highly elated that they could reach the holy precincts. She left her husband in a place nearby, asking him to rest and saying that meanwhile she would go into the town first and find out the whereabouts of Guru Nath and would come back to take him along with her for the darshan. She went into the town and was told that Sri Guru Nath had gone to the Sangam. She came back to the place where she left her husband for rest. Alas! the husband, because of the exhaustion of the journey possibly accentuating his sickness, meanwhile collapsed and died. She was aghast and broke down completely with grief.

Savitri was not able to withstand the situation. She started crying aloud, 'I have brought my husband away from his parents telling them that with Sri Narasimha Saraswati's grace I would bring him back to them restored fully in health. What can I do now? What can I tell them, how can I ever face them? Everything for me is dark and dismal, and there is no way out for me except

death along with my husband.' She was furious at Guru Nath
and started shouting. 'You have belied all my hopes. All my faith
in you has been misplaced. You have cheated me. Before I end
my life, I will tell everybody and proclaim to all how you betrayed
me and my hopes. I fancied that you were *Mangala Murti*. Instead
you have proved to be the very opposite … you are heartless …'
After giving vent to her wrath against Guru Nath, she fell on the
body of her husband and burst into sobs again, 'Oh, my beloved,
why have you left me? Didn't you know how much I loved you?
You were dearest to me, how can I live a moment without you?'
Meanwhile, the people nearby, seeing the sad event, gathered
around her and were trying to console her. At this juncture, Sri
Guru Nath himself, in the guise of a *tapasvi,* with *rudraksha
malas* around his neck and his whole body smeared with *vibhuti*
and holding a *trisula* in his hand, appeared there. He also started
comforting and consoling her. He told her, 'Who can escape
Prarabdha Karma? Death is inevitable for whoever is born. Some
die early and some die later. But none can escape death. What a
delusion is life! How deluding are all family relationships! Wife
and husband, father and children, it is all *maya,* a scene for a
while. Two logs of wood floating separately in a stream come
close to one another and flow together for a while and again drift
apart and float again separately each going its own way. There is
no permanent relationship at all between any two persons. Each
one has his or her own destiny to suffer, each according to his or
her karma of his/her past lives. In life, the only certainty is death,
and of what avail is bemoaning the inevitable and inescapable.
We have to accept things as they come, and reconcile ourselves to
the inevitable. Yet at the same time, we should not forget the
higher purpose of life and the ultimate goal, and should strive to
attain it, irrespective of whatever calamities befall us in life.'

Guru Nath's presence, and especially his words, soothed her heart a little. A sense of reconciliation to her fate and preparedness to face the event with courage came upon her. She prayed to Guru Nath to tell her what she should do, and explain about *Stree-Dharma* after one loses her husband.

THUS ENDS THE THIRTIETH CHAPTER OF SRI *GURU CHARITRA* DESCRIBING THE PRETANGANA SOKA.

Glory to the all-merciful, the omnipresent and the ever-responsive Guru Nath!

Supreme Power of Chastity

This chapter deals with *Pativrata dharma*, the duties and disciplines for a married woman.

Siddhamuni continued with the narrative to Namdharak.
Savitri, after having calmed down a little, requested the *tapasvi* to tell her about the duties of a woman in family life and also her duties after she is widowed. She wanted him to give her guidance and enlighten her on *Stree-Dharma* and *Aachar* (the duties and code of conduct for women). Thereupon the *tapasvi* narrated the following.

Once there lived in the city of Kasi the great Agastya Rishi. His wife's name was Lopamudra. She was like Anasuya in her chastity and was the most ideal wife. Agastya was renowned for his austerities and for his spiritual knowledge, wisdom and prowess.

Once Narada Rishi paid a visit to the Mountain-King Vindhyachal. Narada Rishi praised Vindhyachal for his great qualities. He, however, added that the Meru Mountain (the king of the Himalayas) though inferior to the Vindhya in its grandeur, yet because of its height, is ranked as superior and is called the sovereign of mountains. Vindhyachal took it to heart, and then started growing taller and taller, almost touching the skies like the Meru Mountain. The result of this was that sunlight was not reaching the southern region, plunging it into darkness. People were not able to perform their *nitya vidhis* (daily rituals and oblations to the deities) and thereby Indra and the other gods were deprived of the daily offerings which people have to make. The gods, therefore, along with the *rishis* approached Bramha Deva and prayed to him to find a remedy for this. If *nitya vidhis* are not performed, it will disturb the harmony in the cosmos and evil will befall the people and the world. Bramha Deva advised them to go to Agastya Rishi and request him to do something in the matter, as Vindhyachal was a disciple of Agastya Rishi and was greatly devoted to him.

Indra and the *rishis* came to Agastya Ashram at Kasi. They explained to him the plight of the southern regions. Agastya agreed to help them in the matter.

Agastya went to Vindhyachal. Seeing his Guru (Master) Vindhyachal bent down to offer his obeisance to the Guru. Agastya said that he was going on a pilgrimage to some of the holy places in the southern region, and he (Vindhyachal) should remain in the same position till he returned. Vindhyachal said he would be happy to do whatever command his Guru would give him. Agastya crossed over to the south, thereby opening the blocked way for the sun. Agastya a saved the gods thus and also restored the wellbeing and prosperity of the southern region and its people.

Agastya Rishi's wife was an example for all women. All the gods and even Brihaspati acclaimed Lopamudra as peerless and as an ideal for women for all times. Now the *tapasvi* recounted to Savitri what Brihaspati said to the *rishis,* describing the duties of married women, taking the example of Lopamudra. He said for a woman the husband himself is God. Service to him should take all priority and precedence in woman's duties. The husband should be considered and worshipped as God himself. Husband's *Pada-Theertha* (the water used to wash the feet of the husband) is even more sacred for a woman than *Vishnu-Theertha*. She should never disobey him, and should faithfully and respectfully obey all his commands whatever they be. All the household duties will have to be faithfully discharged, and all shastric injunctions, like *Atithi Puja*, etc., are to be done by the wife, to bring a good name to the husband. She should respect and serve her husband's parents as her own parents. Even if the husband is afflicted with disease, or whatever difficulties befall him, she should share the sufferings and serve him with all love and dedication.

The *tapasvi* then said that when the woman loses her husband, there are shastric injunctions as to the disciplines of life she should strictly observe. She should realise that with her husband's loss, she should take to many austere disciplines.'

THUS ENDS THE THIRTY-FIRST CHAPTER OF SRI *GURU CHARITRA* DESCRIBING PATIVRATA NIRUPAN*.

Glory to the All-merciful, the Omnipresent and the ever-responsive Guru Nath!

---

* Reading should not be broken (stopped) at this chapter. The next chapter, i.e., Chapter 32, should be also completed along with this.

Triumph over Death with Guru's Grace

> This chapter describes how Savitri's husband regained his life by Guru Nath's grace.

Siddhamuni continued with the narrative.

The *tapasvi* described to Savitri all the duties that pertain to women in their family life. He also described the duties that pertain to them after one loses the husband. He said that a woman who has lost her husband will have to adjust herself to the new situation. In grief, in olden times women used to enter the funeral pyre along with the husband's body, which was called Sati or *Sahagamana*. They believed that life with one's husband was a relationship of continuous companionship, not only in this world but in the life beyond as well. It denoted both worldly as well as, or actually even much more, spiritual companionship between the wife and husband. According to the belief, a *Pativrata* who mounted the funeral pyre along with her husband's body certainly attained liberation.* But it was intended to be a totally voluntary and subjective act undertaken wholeheartedly. It was not to be a matter to be forced upon the

---

* The views expressed in this chapter is not relevant to modern times. One needs to understand the same in the context of the days when these thoughts were prevalent.

woman, but one based on her conviction and her own volition and choice.

There were exemptions or exceptions provided for, regarding *Sahagamana*. A woman carrying and a nursing mother were forbidden to take to *Sahagamana*. If a widow chose to live her life as per shastric injunctions and tradition, she was not needed to take to *Sahagamana*. If she lived a pure and austere life during her widowhood, she was supposed to earn as much merit as she would have got through *Sahagamana*.

The disciplines to be observed by a widow as per shastric injunctions or tradition were described by the *tapasvi*. She was not supposed to wear the head-dress (hair). She was expected to take meal only once a day; observe *Chandrayan Vrata*, i.e., increase and decrease her food intake as per the *Kalas* (phases) of the moon; restrict her food and give up the comforts of life to whatever extent possible; take to austere habits; occasionally go on pilgrimage to holy places; perform *tarpan* (food and water offerings to the soul of the departed husband) if she is without a son; observe the bathing rituals in the months of *Vaisakh, Magh* and *Kartika*; offer *ghritdan* (ghee), *jalkumbh-dan* (tumbler), *deep-dan* (lamp), food, clothes, fruits, etc., in the name of her husband in charity to Brahmins; discard bangles and wear white saree; take only a subordinate position in the household; abstain from demanding too much and from exercising her authority; and abide by the will of her son, who of course was expected to revere and love her as a dutiful son and respect her wishes. It was understood that the woman would surrender and transfer her responsibilities of the household to her son and daughter-in-law, and devote more time in the memory of her husband and contemplation of God.

In the above way, Sage Brihaspati narrated all the *Pativrata achara dharmas* to the *rishis* and gods who had assembled at Agastyasram. And now the *tapasvi* (Sri Narasimha Saraswati in disguise) recounted the same to the woman who had lost her husband, and who sought advice and guidance as to the duties and mode of life for the woman, in her different stages of life.

Thus the *tapasvi* tried to console and comfort her in her bereavement and advised her to pick up courage to face the irretrievable situation and pursue her duties as ordained for women, but ever remembering the transitoriness of all life, and the eternity of the spirit.

The woman was very much touched by the solicitude of the *tapasvi* for her ultimate welfare. She expressed to him that her mind was much pacified, and she profusely thanked him for dispelling her ignorance and freeing her from the meshes of illusion of the mundane life. She told him that he was her all— mother, father and God. She however said in a determined and resolute manner that she had chosen to do *Sahagamana* along with the body of her husband.

The *tapasvi* gave her *bhasma* and told her to besmear her husband's forehead with it. He gave her four *rudrakshas* to be tied to the husband's ears and the body, before it was consigned to flames. She was also asked to perform *Maharudra abhisheka* before the cremation and thereafter visit the Sangam and seek the blessings of Guru Nath there before the final ceremony.

The woman now got all the preparations done for the funeral and her *Sahagamana*. She invited the priests and asked them to start the funeral sacraments with the chant of the prescribed mantras. She took her bath, adorned herself with all her ornaments and the bright-red *kumkum* mark on her forehead. She took the dead near the river, carrying also the fire in her hand.

All the men and women of Ganagapur gathered there, hearing of the sad event. They were all moved to tears, because the woman was so young, hardly sixteen years of age, and so beautiful. They were trying to persuade her not to do the

Sahagamana saying that it was not proper, they said, for a young girl of her age. She was almost a child still.

But the woman adamantly stuck to her resolve. She got the firewood piled up. She called the *Suvasinis* there and gave away whatever she had. She requested them to bless her, and further to send word to her in-laws that her husband and herself were doing very well at Ganagapur, and that none should let them know the truth as it would break their hearts. When she was about to mount the funeral pyre, she remembered suddenly the instructions of the *tapasvi*. She tied the *rudrakshas* given by him, two to the earlobes, and two on the chest of her husband's body. She applied the *bhasma* on his forehead. Then she rushed to the Sangam to seek Guru Nath's blessings before taking to *Sahagamana,* as previously advised by the *tapasvi.*

The woman approached Sangam and saw Guru Nath seated under the Audamber tree. She fell prostrate at his feet. The Guru blessed that she would soon be the mother of good children— 'Suputra praptirastu'. The people who accompanied her told Guru Nath that she had lost her husband, and she had come to Him to seek blessings for her *Sahagamana* along with her husband's body.

Sri Narasimha Saraswati told them to bring the dead body to Him at the Sangam. The body was brought. Just at that time four Brahmins came there to offer their worship to Sri Narasimha Saraswati. Guru Nath asked the Brahmins to sprinkle *Charan Theertha* on the dead body. This was done, and lo! the dead body rose to life as if from sleep. The revived man noticed his wife whose face lit up with wonder and joy at seeing the unbelievable, and asked her how they happened to be there. The woman told all that had happened, how Guru Nath retrieved him from the realm of death and restored to her the *Mangalya* and thus protected the lives of both of them. Both of them fell at Guru Nath's feet and bathed them with their tears, which were welling out from the innermost depth of their hearts.

THUS ENDS THE THIRTY-SECOND CHAPTER OF
SRI *GURU CHARITRA* DESCRIBING HOW
FAITH TRIUMPHED OVER DEATH WITH
GURU NATH'S GRACE.

Glory to the all-merciful, the omnipresent and the ever-responsive Guru Nath!

Rudraksha Mahima

This chapter describes *Rudraksha Mahima* and illustrates upon the merit earned by those who wear *rudrakshas* on their bodies.

Siddhamuni continued his narrative explaining to Namdharak the power of the rudraksha.

When the *tapasvi* gave to the woman four *rudrakshas* and asked her to tie them on the body of her dead husband, the woman asked him what purpose it would serve. The *tapasvi* who was Guru Nath himself in reality, told her briefly the *Rudraksha Mahima* and also the *Rudrabhisheka Mahima*.

Wearing of *rudraksha* and applying *vibhuti* on the forehead confer great sanctity to the wearer. They are most purifying and ward off all evil. None can harm the wearer and even the Lord of death would keep away from him. They confer happiness in this life and ensure happiness in the life beyond. The *tapasvi* narrated the following story to illustrate the power of the *rudraksha*.

There lived in Kashmir once upon a time, a king named Bhadrasena. He had a son named Sudharma. His minister-in-chief also had a son, named Taraka. Sudharma and Taraka were of nearly the same age, and they grew up in closest friendship. Each loved the other very much, and they used to be always together. They both were highly devoted to Lord Sankara. Instead of wearing princely jewellery and ornaments, they used to wear *rudraksha malas* and also used to apply prominent *vibhuti* marks on their foreheads, as both *rudrakshas* and *vibhuti* are believed to be very dear to Lord Sankara. Their parents however were not happy about the ascetic tendency of their sons from such a tender age.

Once Parasara Rishi came to the court of Bhadrasena. The king received him with great honour and veneration. The king told him of his worry about his son, who was taking to ascetic ways of life even at such an early age. He further said that he was equally worried about his minister's son. Parasara Rishi told the king that he should not feel worried at all, but instead rejoice at the devotional temperament and conduct of the prince and his friend. He then said that it was because of the great merit they had earned in their previous lives that they were born in this life with such devotional temperament, especially with fascination and attachment to the holy *rudrakshas*. Parasara Rishi told the king about the previous lives of the prince and the minister's son.

In the bygone times, there lived a courtesan who was very beautiful. She was very intelligent, shrewd and artful, and was very good in singing and dancing. She used to attract many people.

The courtesan had a *natya-mandap*. She had two pets, one a monkey and the other a cock. She taught them also to dance. She used to deck both of them with *rudraksha malas*. One day a rich merchant came to be entertained by her. He had an ornament in the form of Sivalinga, made of precious stones, which he was wearing on his neck. He was wearing *rudraksha malas,* and was having *Bhasma Tripundra* marks on his forehead. Looking at all these signs of piety, the woman felt a liking and attraction for him. She particularly felt a strong fascination for his Sivalinga-ornament made of precious stones. She told him if he gifted that ornament to her, she would live with him for three days as his mate. He wanted from her an oath of assurance that she would keep the bargain faithfully. She agreed and after her taking oath by placing her hand on the Sivalinga, the merchant gifted her the precious ornament and she started to live with him. The first night went off happily and well for both of them. On the second night unfortunately, when they were asleep, the *natya-mandap* caught fire and the fire started spreading to where the Sivalinga-ornament was kept and it was also about to be caught up in the flames. The merchant tried to retrieve the ornament from the spreading fire, but he too was caught in the flames and was burnt to death. The courtesan-woman was aghast at this sudden tragedy. As she promised him that she would be his woman for three days, and as he died during this period, she resolved herself to take *Sahagamana* with him, like a faithful wife. Meanwhile all neighbours gathered around, and seeing her preparing herself for the *Sahagamana* along with her merchant customer, they tried to stop her, telling her that she was not a wedded wife to him and she should not take to such an extreme step. But they could not prevail upon her and she jumped into the fire. But lo! instantly Lord Sankara appeared there, caught hold of her hand and pulled her out of the fire. Lord Sankara said that he was very much pleased with her, that though she was a courtesan, yet she kept up so steadfastly and unswervingly to the vow of truth and was determined to sacrifice her life for the pledged word. He said that he only wanted to test her and created the fire artificially. As he was pleased with her for her devotion to truth, he promised to grant her any boon she would ask of him.

She said to Siva that she had no desire at all, except that she, along with all her relations, friends and servants, should be blessed with *Kailasha Pada*. Thus she attained Kailash with all her people and won liberation for herself and all of them too.

Parasara Rishi further told the king, that when the fire burnt the *natya-mandap*, the courtesan's pets, the *markat* (the monkey) and the *kukkut* (the cock) also died in the fire. But as they had the *rudraksha malas* around their necks and especially at the moment of death, it won for them great merit. The *markat* was born as the king's son and the *kukkut* was born as the son of the chief minister. 'Such was the power of *rudraksha,*' said Parasara Rishi to the king.

THUS ENDS THE THIRTY-THIRD CHAPTER OF
SRI *GURU CHARITRA* DESCRIBING
THE RUDRAKSHA MAHIMA.

Glory to the all-merciful, the omnipresent and the ever-responsive Guru Nath!

34

Rudrabhisheka Mahima

This chapter refers to the *Rudradhyana* and *Rudrabhisheka Mahima* and the story of the prince who died at a very young age but got back his life again.

Siddhamuni continued narrating to Namdharak on Rudrabhisheka Mahima *as told by Guru Nath to the woman in the guise of* tapasvi.

King Bhadrasena, after listening to the account of the past life of his son and that of his minister, prayed to Parasara Rishi to throw some light on how his son's future was going to be. The *rishi* was hesitant to say anything in reply to the king. As the king was persistent, the *rishi* said that the prince had only eight days more to live. The king fainted in grief on hearing this. When he recovered, he fell at the *rishi's* feet and prayed that he should show him the way so that his son's life could be saved. Moved by pity, the *rishi* said that if he could earn the grace of Lord Siva, the *Mrityunjaya,* there was the possibility of his son's life being saved.

Lord Siva is all powerful. It was Lord Siva who caused the Vedas to be manifest and gifted them to Bramhadeva to serve as a guidance to the latter in his function as the creator of the world of matter and the universe of beings. Along with the Vedas, he also gifted him the *Bramhopanishad,* in which there was a chapter titled 'Rudradhyaya' describing the *Rudrabhisheka Mahima.* Bramhadeva narrated the *Rudrabhisheka Mahima* to the *rishis* once, as described in the '*Rudradhyaya*' of the *Bramhopanishad.* His narration has been given as under:

The study of the Rudradhyaya and performance of *Rudrabhisheka* would expiate one of all his sins and would endow also liberation on him from the cycle of birth and death. He said that *Rudrabhisheka* was the panacea for all the ills of the mundane life. All the *rishis,* thereafter, as advised by Bramhadeva took to *Rudrabhisheka.* From the *rishis,* it spread among all people, and everywhere the echo of *Rudra Japa* and *Rudradhyaya* could be heard. Whenever and wherever Yama Dharma Raja's *dootas* visited, they were repelled by seething heat generated by the spiritual vibrations emanating from *Rudra Japa.* The *Yamadootas* narrated their plight to Yama Raja. The latter rushed to Bramhadeva and told him about the matter. Bramhadeva told Yama Raja that he should instruct his *dootas* that they should never approach anywhere near where *Rudradhyaya* and *Purushasukta* chanting would be going on and they could move freely only where such chanting is not there.

Parasara Rishi advised the king that he should invite one hundred Brahmins and arrange for performance of ten thousand *Rudrabhishekas* and bathe the prince with *Rudrabhisheka Theertha,* which alone could save the life of the prince. The king arranged for the performance of *Rudrabhishekas* as advised by the sage. On the eighth day, the prince fell down dead. But Parasara Rishi immediately sprinkled the *Rudrabhisheka Theertha* on the body of the prince, and bathed the body with the *Theertha.* Lo! the prince came back to life instantly. Just at this time Sage Narada came and told the king how blessed he (the king) and the prince were. Narada told them that *Yamadootas* were there to take away the prince to the *Yama loka.* But as soon as the body of the prince was bathed with the *Rudrabhisheka Theertha* the *Sivadootas* appeared there, snatched away the prince's *jiva* from the hands of *Yamadootas* and restored the life of the prince. *Yamadootas* ran back to Yama and reported the happening. Yama approached Lord Bramha and the latter told him that though the prince was to die at his twelfth year, the *Rudrabhisheka Theertha* bath bestowed on him a fresh, long lease of life, and the prince was thus blessed to live for a full span of hundred years. Enlightened thus about the *Rudrabhisheka Mahima*, Yama returned to his abode and instructed his *dootas* once again, that they should be very watchful and cautious and should not go near any one engaged in *Rudrabhisheka* or having *Rudrabhisheka Theertha* sprinkled on the body or even wearing *rudrakshas* on the body, because all such people are dear to Lord Siva and enjoy the protection of his divine grace.

THUS ENDS THE THIRTY-FOURTH CHAPTER OF
SRI *GURU CHARITRA* DESCRIBING
THE RUDRADHYAYANA MAHIMA.

Glory to the all-merciful, the omnipresent and the ever-responsive Guru Nath!

35

Somavara Vrata Mahima

This chapter narrates about the *Somavara Vrata Mahima* and the story of Princess Simantini. It also tells how the mantras forfeit their potency if they are made overt, and that for a woman the *vratas* are far more beneficial than the mantras.

There is a higher power than destiny. Mad-Bhaktah Napranasyati—*(my devotee never perishes) is the eternal assurance of the Lord. But the Lord also knows what is good and what is appropriate for his devotees and he has his own way of dispensation of his grace. Leaving it all to his will and mercy, let us surrender unto him.*

Siddhamuni continued the narrative of the Guru Charitra *to Namdharak as under.*

Savitri's heart was overflowing with gratitude and devotion towards Guru Nath who had restored her husband's life. The husband looked quite hale and healthy with no trace of his former disease at all. Savitri now prayed to Guru Nath to give her *Mantropadesa,* which would protect them (herself and her husband) against all the turmoils of life in this world, give them a safe passage to the life beyond and liberate them for ever. Guru Nath told her that for a woman, no mantra is needed. It is only *patiseva* that is needed for a woman and that this alone would safely ferry her across the ocean of *samsara* to the heavenly shores beyond. For a woman the mantra is not as efficacious as *patiseva.* Further, a mantra needs strict *nishta,* secrecy, etc. A mantra cannot be given to anybody and everybody. It requires some merit on the part of the recipient. Otherwise it loses its potency and does not confer the due benefit. That was what happened in the case of the *Sanjeevani mantra* of Sukracharya, the preceptor of the *asuras*. Sri Narasimha Saraswati explained it further as follows.

Once a war was raging between the *devas* and the *asuras*. Sukracharya alone knew the *Sanjeevani mantra,* the chanting of which would revive the dead back to life instantly. Because of the power and protection of the *Sanjeevani mantra,* the *asuras* could remain invincible and the *devas,* as they had no recourse to and no protection of a mantra, were being routed in the battle. The *devas* had to flee away, utterly defeated and battered.

The *devas* then went to the Kailash and narrated to Lord Siva their woe and perilous condition and prayed to him to rescue them from the devastating onslaught of the *asuras* against them. Siva sent Nandi to fetch Sukracharya. When the latter was brought, Siva gulped him into his mouth. Sukracharya stayed for some days in the stomach of Siva, but one day managed to come out when Siva was lost in his *Samadhi.* He reached back to the kingdom of the *asuras* safe and the *asuras* were again emboldened that their Preceptor's full protection was restored to them. They became again a great menace and terror to the *devas*. The *devas* then hatched out a plan.

The preceptor of the *devas,* Sage Brihaspati had a son named Kacha. Kacha was sent to Sukracharya to be his disciple and to study under him. Sukracharya accepted him as his student because of his veneration for Brihaspati. Sukracharya's daughter Devayani caught a fascination and liking for Kacha. Once the *asuras* had caught hold of Kacha secretly and killed him. At Devayani's pleadings, however,

Sukracharya, by the power of his *Sanjeevani mantra,* revived him and brought him back to life. When the *asuras* caught hold of Kacha secretly the second time, they did not want the body to be left after slaying him, because Sukracharya might again bring it back to life. Therefore this time, they burnt the slain body to ashes, mixed the ashes in wine which they surreptitiously made Sukracharya to drink. As Kacha did not return home in the night, Devayani expressed her anxiety to Sukracharya about the safety of Kacha. Sukracharya saw through his *divyadrishti* that the ashes of Kacha were in his stomach and this he told Devayani. He told her that this time he would not be able to bring him back to life. If he were to try to bring him back to life, as Kacha would have to come out of his (Sukracharya's) stomach, he (Sukracharya) himself would be dying in the process. Therefore he would not be able to save him this time. But Devayani pleaded if he would teach her the *Sanjeevani mantra* and in the process of reviving Kacha if he (Sukracharya) were to die, she would chant the mantra and revive him (Sukracharya) also back to life. At her persistent pleading, he taught her the mantra. As he was uttering the mantra, Kacha heard it from within the stomach of his Guru and memorised it. Kacha was saved. Sukracharya also was revived back to life.

Later Devayani pleaded to Kacha that he should marry her. But Kacha pleaded that it would be a sacrilege to do so; they were like sister and brother to each other. First, she was his Guru's daughter; further, having emerged out from the vitals of Sukracharya by the result of the mantra, he also had become a child of Sukracharya. Furthermore, she having revived him back to life, she was like a mother to him. Therefore he said the marriage was unthinkable between them. Saying thus, he left and went back to his father.

The *Sanjeevani mantra* however had lost its potency for
good, having been given to a woman who did not merit the
mantra, and further having lost its secrecy, because of being
overheard by another (i.e., by Kacha) besides the one it was
intended to (i.e., to Devayani) at that time.

As Sri Narasimha Saraswati dissuaded Savitri, from being
desirous of taking mantra, the woman pleaded she be taught
some *vrata,* which would be as beneficial as a mantra. Sri
Narasimha Saraswati told her about the *Somavara Siva Vrata.*
He narrated another anecdote to illustrate the beneficial effects
of this *vrata.*

Once upon a time, in the olden days, there lived a king
by name Chitravarma in Aryavarta. He was in the line of the
great Nala. He was a great devotee of Lord Siva. He had no
children for a long time. At last a daughter was born to him.
She was named Simantini. The king consulted his court
astrologers about the future of the princess. They all said she
would grow into a very virtuous girl and would have a long
life, but at the age of fourteen itself, she was likely to become
a widow. The king's and queen's hearts were filled with
gloom and sorrow at the prospect of their daughter's
widowhood.

The princess reached the age of seven. The king started
searching a suitable alliance for her. Meanwhile, Simantini
learnt the *Somavara Siva Vrata* from Maitrayani, which is
believed to confer *mangalya* and auspiciousness to women.
From that very young age she started performing this *vrata.*
She was thereafter married to a young prince by the name
Chitrangada, the son of King Indrasena. The marriage was
celebrated in all regal pomp.

One day prince Chitrangada went to swim in the River
Kalindi along with his friends. There were also his guards
attending upon him. The prince was swimming in the
stream with his friends. He was suddenly caught in a

whirlpool in mid-stream and sank down. The guards tried to search for him and save him, but to no avail. Simantini said to her father and mother that she would throw herself into the stream and die to join her husband in the other world at least. Her grief was inconsolable. She was all fury against Siva, as in spite of her devout and strict observance of the *Somavara Vrata,* he had not protected her at all. She was being dissuaded by all from doing *Sahagamana,* because shastras did not approve of *Sahagamana* for a woman without the dead body of her husband by the side.

To add to the misfortune, as the king and the people were steeped in sorrow at the prince's death, one enemy-king attacked the kingdom of Indrasena and defeated the latter. 'Misfortunes never come alone but come in a chain'—is the old saying. So it was the case with regard to Indrasena, who lost his son as well as his kingdom. When Chitrangada was caught in the whirlpool, he sank down into the depths of the river. The damsels of *Nagaloka* sighted him and rescued him and took him to their kingdom in the netherworld. It was the kingdom of Takshaka, the great serpent-king. The Naga *kanyas* sprinkled *amrit* over the body of Chitrangada who was lifeless. The *amrit* revived him instantly. He was taken to King Takshaka who received him very kindly. Takshaka was happy to learn that Chitrangada was in the line of descent from the famed king Nala, who happened to be a dear friend of his in the olden times. Takshaka was very hospitable to him. The prince was looked after very well. The prince found that Takshaka's city was a very rich and beautiful one.

After some time, Chitrangada asked Takshaka to permit him to go back to his father. Takshaka gave him a very warm and loving send-off, sent a Naga prince for escort and also gave him many precious and handsome gifts. The prince and the Naga-prince who escorted him, emerged out of the waters of the mid-stream. They swam to the bank. Just at that time Simantini came to the river for the bath before her *vrata* as it happened to be *Somavara* (Monday). Although God seemed to have let her down, still she wanted to continue the *vrata*.

The prince recognised her as Simantini, the princess who was wedded to him. Her face was clouded with grief. He enquired of her who she was and why she looked so much grief-stricken. Although he had close resemblance to her dead husband, she did not take him to be her husband as she thought that her husband was lost for ever. The maids waiting for the princess narrated to the prince all about her misfortune, and how she lost her husband whom she loved so dearly. The stranger (the prince) said that he knew Chitrangada very well and that the latter was quite safe and would return to her soon. After saying thus, the prince, along with the Naga prince, went to his father's kingdom. Already by that time the enemy king was thrown back and Indrasena had got his kingdom back. The king was most delighted at his son's safe return. He sent messengers immediately to Chitravarma to inform him of the happy turn of events and of his son's safe return and that he, along with his son was coming over there, to his kingdom.

The joy of Simantini knew no bounds. Her faith in Lord Siva and the merits of *Somavara Vrata* were thus vindicated and she had got back her lost husband.

Sri Narasimha Saraswati thus impressed on Savitri the *mahima* of *Somavara Siva Vrata*. He told her that she should observe the *vrata* all through her life, and this *vrata* meant worship of himself (Sri Narasimha Saraswati) only.

Savitri and her husband then offered elaborate worship to Guru Nath, performed *Samardhana* and with the blessings of Guru Nath returned to their home town, Mahur. The parents of the young man were overwhelmed with joy at the safe return of their son and daughter-in-law and to see their son restored completely to good health. Their hearts overflowed with gratitude towards Guru Nath for the divine mercy which he had showered on the family.

THUS ENDS THE THIRTY-FIFTH CHAPTER OF
SRI *GURU CHARITRA* DESCRIBING
SIMANTINI AAKHYAN.

Glory to the all-merciful, the omnipresent and the ever-responsive Guru Nath!

36

*Achara Dharma**

This chapter describes the plight of the Brahmin woman who went for *parannabhojana.* Guru Nath explains to the Brahmin woman and her husband some of the Vedic injunctions.

Namdharak was all raptures and joy listening to the glorious narrative of Guru leelas from the lips of Siddhamuni. He said he was at a loss to know how he could express his gratitude to Siddhamuni who had come to him like the rising sun dispelling his ignorance and filling him with the light of wisdom. He said that his thirst and yearning to hear more and more of the Guru leelas was insatiably increasing. Siddhamuni, pleased with the yearning of Namdharak, continued his narrative.

Ganagapur had become a great centre of pilgrimage because of Sri Narasimha Saraswati's stay there and his association with the place. Thousands of people from different parts of the country started pouring in daily, seeking Guru Nath's darshan and blessings and for redress of their afflictions—of the body, mind and spirit through his divine grace.

In Ganagapur, at that time, there lived a Brahmin, who was very devout. He never accepted gifts from any. He never used to go to Samaradhana, where cooked food (*paranna*) was fed. He used to maintain himself and his family on dry alms (cereals

---

*   The rituals rxplained in this chapter needs to be understood in the context of the time whenthey were written.

offered to him). His wife had a bad temper. She used to tell him every day that he should accept *paranna* which would relieve their troubles to a large extent.

Every day many people used to come to Ganagapur and perform Samaradhana. At Samaradhana, couples are invited for *bhojan*. At Samaradhana, sumptuous feast is given with several preparations and delicacies. The Brahmin's wife felt that her husband's obstinacy was depriving them of proper and even minimal food when it was aplenty around. But the husband was never in an agreeable mood to their going to Samaradhana feasts.

Once the woman went to Sri Narasimha Saraswati and requested him to tell her husband to change his mind and to accept invitations to Samaradhana *bhojan*. To this Guru Nath agreed and prevailed upon the Brahmin to comply with the wishes of his wife once at least. How could anyone disobey Guru Nath's command?

When the Brahmin and his wife went to the Samaradhana feast, a strange thing happened. The woman had an obnoxious vision of dogs and swine hovering around her plate of food, and she felt a revulsion and nausea to partake of the food, though it was lavishly served and was rich with many delicacies. She got up from her seat and asked her husband also to leave from there all at once, and to come out along with her. She along with her husband, came to Sri Narasimha Saraswati and told him about the repulsive and nauseating vision, which she had at the Samaradhana gathering. Sri Narasimha Saraswati said that it was very much wrong on her part to have forced her husband through him (Sri Narasimha Saraswati), to change his principle and observance. The woman prayed to Guru Nath and also her husband that she should be forgiven for what she had done. As the Brahmin was feeling very sorry for having broken his rule, Guru Nath told him that he was not to worry about it any longer. No sin would touch him on that account because he did not go there of his own volition, and that in exceptional cases Brahmins can accept *paranna* from others' houses.

The Brahmin prayed to Guru Nath to enlighten him in which houses one can take food and in which houses it is to be avoided. Guru Nath explained about this in detail, as under.

There are many disciplines regarding acceptance of food. One can take food in Guru's house without any hesitation, so also in the maternal uncle's house, in the father-in-law's house, in the houses of brothers and in the houses of pious people. If there was no Brahmin priest available at the time of *shradh* ceremony, one can attend and take food, but on the next day he should do Gayatri Japa.

Anyway, food is most holy. It should be taken in the houses of the pious and *sattvic* people, and after taking God's name.

Homes of evil-minded people are to be avoided. Food is not to be accepted from: *(a)* greedy people; *(b)* people who are not doing their duty to their family; *(c)* people who are proud and egoistic; *(d)* people who indulge always in self-praise and talking ill of others; *(e)* people who are ill-tempered; *(f)* people of immoral conduct; *(g)* people who are addicted to drinking wine and other intoxicating drinks; *(h)* people who delight in harming others; *(i)* people who regularly live on *paranna* only, etc. If we accept food from such people, their sins will affect us. Through the food we take, the *gunas* flow into us. The food should promote *sattva guna*, i.e., a pure, cool and enlightened temperament in us.

The Brahmin requested Guru Nath to instruct him on *Achara Dharma*, the code of conduct for Brahmins.

Guru Nath said that *Parasara Smriti* laid down in great detail under *Achara Samhita* the code of conduct for the Brahmins, who are the spiritual custodians of the community and the society. The *Achara Samhita* is something like the Bhagwad Gita, for the Brahmins. It is, so to say, like a fifth Veda. It lays down daily disciplines to be strictly observed by a Brahmin from dawn do dusk. The disciplines laid down are as under and whoever meticulously observes them will attain everything and will never suffer from any want, nor will ever be subject to grief.

Early Morning Prayers: The Brahmin should rise in the early serene hours of the morning, which is called *Bramha Muhurta* (between 3.30 to 5.00 a.m.), during which time, the *sattva* quality will be prevalent in the atmosphere. As soon as one rises from the bed, he should remember his Guru first and offer mentally his obeisance to him; he should then offer his obeisance to God and the deities (Trimurtis, the sun god, the *Navagrahas*, etc.), then to the sages, the *pitridevatas* and to the parents. He should not let the mind wander away. He will have to dwell his thoughts on Guru and God only for some time at least. He is advised to have first the darshan of the cow (*Go-mata*), before he does anything else.

Achamana: After offering obeisance to the cow, he should (gargle his mouth and then) do *Achamana,* by sipping in a little water. *Achamana* is to be practised many times during the day. If there is no water available for the *Achamana,* if he just touches his right ear, that is said to be sufficient. The right ear is said to be the seat of Agni (Fire God), Varuna (God of seas and the air), Surya, Chandra and the other deities. *Achamana* is to be done, at the time of taking food, and while retiring to bed also. *Achamana* is believed to endow longevity as well as good health. *Achamana* is to be done taking the Guru's/God's name and chanting the appropriate mantras.

Swadhyaya/Vedic Chant/Meditation: Till sunrise and before he goes out for his morning ablutions, he will have to devote either to chanting of prayers, recital of Vedic mantras or meditation.

Morning Ablutions: After dawn one should attend to the calls of nature. At that time he should keep silent. He should then clean his mouth and teeth. The twigs of trees which are to be used for cleaning the teeth are listed. After this one should take his bath. It cleanses and refreshes the body and drives away laziness. It endows strength, longevity, intellectual brilliance, etc. It cleanses away the effect of bad dreams and also drives away poverty and all ills.

Bramhacharis are to bathe in the mornings and all householders both in the morning and in the afternoon and the ascetics in the mornings, in the afternoons as well as in the evenings, i.e., all three times during the day. Whatever water one would be using for bath, he should deem it as the waters of the holy Ganges flowing down from the feet of Hari, and which would endow both physical as well as mental and spiritual purity.

When water is not available or when one is sick, one should recite the *Apohista mantra,* and do *marjana* three times. This is called *Mantra Snana.* Doing *Vishnu Nama Sankirtan* is called *Manasika Snana.* Taking darshan of the Guru, or sprinkling the water after washing the feet of the parents is called *Theertha Snana.*

On the days of *vratas, shradhs,* or after the birth-ceremonies or death-ceremonies in the family—on the tenth day of the pollution period, hot water bath is prohibited. On auspicious occasions like marriage or other functions, cold water bath is prohibited. In flowing water of a river one should face opposite the current, and in tanks etc., one should face towards east and then take the bath.

If one takes oil-bath on Sundays, it could lead to disease, on Mondays it could lead to draining away of the energy, on

Tuesdays it could lead to death, on Wednesdays it endows wealth *(Lakshmiprapti)*, on Thursdays and Fridays it could cause the impairment and danger to the health of the children *(Santhana-Nashtam)*, and on Saturdays it brings in all auspiciousness, health and wealth. Housewives are not to take hair-bath daily.

On the days when one has taken oil bath, he is not to apply *bhasma*. On all other days and at all other times, he should necessarily apply *bhasma* on his forehead.

Gopichandan is to be applied by those devoted to the form of Hari. It is called *Urdhva Pundra* (vertical markings) and it is equally meritorious like *Bhasma Dharana* which is to be applied in horizontal lines (*Tripundra*). Whoever applies both *bhasma* and *Gopichandan*, he is equally dear to both Hara and Hari.

Sandhya Vandana: Sandhya Vandana which is done in the very early morning hours, before the stars disappear in the sky is most ideal *(uttama)*. The *Sandhya Vandana* done before sunrise, even though the stars have set, is of intermediate merit *(madhyama)*. The *Sandhya* done after the sunrise is of the lowest merit *(adhama)*. The evening *Sandhya* done before the sun has set is most meritorious *(uttama)*. The *Sandhya* done after the sun has set but before the stars have appeared is of intermediate merit *(madhyama)*. The *Sandhya* done after the stars have appeared is of the lowest merit *(adhama)*. The afternoon *Sandhya* also has to be done at the right time.

Arghya: There is much significance behind the *Arghya Pradan* rite. There are said to be 33 crore demons (evil forces) called *Mandehas**, who try to block the way of the

---

* Evil forces in man, caused by his obsession with his mind *(Man)* i.e., egoistic desires, and sense-cravings of the body *Deha,* which together block the way for the enlightenment of the intellect. The chant of the Gayatri Mantra drives away the darkness of ignorance and causes illumination of the intellect.

sun. The *Arghya Pradan* done together with the chant of Gayatri Mantra, drives away (destroys) the demons, and helps to clear the way for the sun. The sin caused by the destruction of the demons is absolved by the chant of the *Asavadityo Bramha mantra* while doing the *Pradakshina.*

All the three times of the day (mornings, afternoons and evenings) the Gayatri Mantra has to be chanted 108 times at least (each time). Chanting it a thousand times absolves from many of the (ordinary) sins. Chanting it ten million times annihilates all the sins. Gayatri Mantra is the very essence of all the Vedic hymns. It is the most potent and protecting mantra. If any interruption comes, for whatever reason, when doing the chanting, the right ear has to be touched. In case one is obliged to talk with anybody while doing the *japa,* he will have to recite the *Tadvishtoh mantra.* The chanting has to be done silently and mentally.

Auposan and the Pancha Yajnas: After performing the *Sandhya Vandana, Auposan* has to be necessarily done. *Bramha-yajna, Vaisvadeva,* etc., will also have to be done by the Brahmin.

Tarpan: To appease and please the Vasus, Rudras, Adityas, *devarishis* and *pitrus, tarpan* has to be offered. On Deepavali, three palmfuls of water (oblations) have to be offered to Lord Yama, Chitragupta, etc., to get rid of the troubles caused by disease, sins, Sani, etc. It will avoid premature death and endow longevity.

On the Krishnashtami day in the month of *Magha,* tarpan has to be offered to Bhishma. Thereby all the sins committed during the entire year will get absolved.

Wearing of the sacred thread is obligatory for a Brahmin. One who discards or does not wear the sacred thread loses his Brahmin rights. The thread is the sacred bond, linking man to God. It is symbolic of Gayatri, the eternal protector.

These disciplines are inviolable for a Brahmin. Whoever follows these injunctions and observes the disciplines, will never suffer misery. He will enjoy all joys and happiness. Unfortunately, in this *Kali Yuga*, as Brahmins have digressed away and have given up these disciplines, they are suffering all sorts of troubles and untold misery.

Brahmins must keep up their spiritual heritage. They must keep up their dignity by the purity of their conduct. Then alone they are worthy to be called Brahmins and can help the Bramhanic culture to survive and dharma to be sustained in the world.

THUS ENDS THE THIRTY-SIXTH CHAPTER OF
SRI *GURU CHARITRA* DESCRIBING THE ACHARA
DHARMA FOR THE BRAHMINS.

Glory to the all-merciful, the omnipresent and the ever-responsive Guru Nath!

37

Grihasta Dharma

This chapter describes the religious duties incumbent on a Grihasta.

Namaskara Priyaha Suryaha
Alankara Priyaha Vishnuhu
Abhisheka Priyaha Sivaha

'One meal a day makes a *yogi,* two meals a day makes a *bhogi* and three meals a day makes a *rogi.*'

The purity of one's mind depends on the purity of food he takes, not only through the mouth, but also through the five senses, namely eyes, nose, ears, limbs and the tongue.

Sri Narasimha Saraswati was lighting up the minds of people by giving instruction on the disciplines necessary for keeping up the spiritual flame. After soothing their body and mind, he used to start giving spiritual instruction to put them on the Godward-path, to help them evolve spiritually, so that they would be relieved for ever from the afflictions of birth and death. In the previous chapter, Guru Nath narrated to the Brahmin /couple the Acharavidhis for the Brahmins. In this chapter, he described to them Deva Puja Vidhi *(about the daily worship) and its* mahima.

Siddhamuni continued his narrative to Namdharak.

For Deva Puja, the shrine room should be kept clean, *Rangoli* should be done and the place should be decorated with flowers. The atmosphere should be filled with the fragrance of incense-sticks, sandalwood or other perfume-materials. The place should be specially congenial and soothing to the mind. It should make an instant appeal to the mind and bring it into devout and worshipful mood. The atmosphere should be such that the senses get sublimated, mind gets collected and calmed and the spirit gets uplifted and elevated.

Seated on a clean, comfortable seat, one should take to the Puja. The worship has to be done three times a day—morning, afternoon and the evening. If full and elaborate worship is not possible for want of time or for any other reasons one should at least do the Shodasopachara Puja (worship constituting the sixteen types of services) in the morning, Panchopachara Puja (worship constituting of five types of services) in the forenoon, and offering of the camphor light *(Nirajana)* in the evening, and perform the worship this way. Having been born as a Brahmin if he does not do the worship daily, he will be subject to the netherworld after death.

There are six types of Puja:

(a) Udaka Narayana Puja, i.e., worshipping God in water.

(b) Agni Puja, i.e., worshipping God in fire.

(c) Aditya Puja, i.e., worshipping God in the sun.

(d) Manasika Puja, i.e., worshipping God mentally.

(e) Pratima Puja, i.e, worshipping God in the icons.

(f) *Yajna* Puja, i.e., worshipping God through performance of *yajna*.

The Manasika Puja is the highest form of worship. Idol worship is a relatively lower type or form of worship compared to Manasika Puja, but it has also its place in the spiritual journey. Worship of the cow and a Brahmin, visualising them as God, is also an accepted form of Puja. The worship of Guru however, pleases all the Trimurtis.

In the *Kali Yuga,* as men are not capable of cultivating and cherishing such exalted form of adoration towards the Guru and of identifying the Guru with God, God has assumed the forms of Saligrama stones and of Linga-form stones, which are found on the banks and the riverbeds of the Narmada and the Gandaki rivers. Worship of the Saligrama or the Linga, absolves man from all his sins.

With Guru's *upadesa,* and worshipping the idol as per his instructions, God will respond even through idols and will fulfil all the desires of the worshipper.

Regarding the worship of the idol, first, one should seat himself before the shrine, should do *sankalpa* and then *Pranayama. Pranayama* helps to quieten the mind and centralises the consciousness for concentration. Water has to be sprinkled over the materials for worship. The idol has to be then installed in the *Simhasana.* On the left side of the idol should be placed the conch, and on the right side should be placed the bell. The flowers and other materials of worship of the previous day are to be removed. The lamp has to be lighted. Then worship has to be first offered to Lord Ganapati.

Then the Guru has to be remembered. The worship to the shrine has to be done. The tutelary deity has to be visualised in the shrine of one's own heart, and the same visualised form has to be then invoked and enshrined in or to be identified with the idol placed for worship. This is *Prana-Pratishta,* imparting living-reality to (or instilling life into) the idol. One should visualise that God himself has come and is standing in front of him. *Bhavana,* with true faith, is the very essence of the idol worship. Then to the visualised form of God, identified with the idol, *Padya, Arghya, Aachamana, Madhuparka, Snana*—all these *Upacharas* are to be done. Then chanting the prescribed mantras, *abhisheka* has to be performed with milk *panchagavya*, etc. The idol has to be then dried with a clean cloth and placed back on the shrine. Then *Vastra, Gandha* and *Yajnopavita* are to be offered and thereafter Puja has to be done with flowers, with materials and articles of fragrance, and with *Akshatas,* etc. While white flowers are ideal for worship, coloured flowers are not so sacred for worship. Lotuses, jasmines, and some other such flowers are good; Ganapati is not to be worshipped with *tulsi,* and Devi is not to be worshipped with Garika, Maredu *(bilwa)* is dear for Siva and *tulsi* for Vishnu. After the offerings of flowers, *dhoopa* has to be offered. During the Puja, appropriate mantras and prayers are to be recited with full devotion.

After the Puja, *Naivedya* will have to be offered to the Lord. Visualising that God had accepted the food offered, the devotee's hands are to be cleaned with water. Then *tambula* (betel-leaves) have to be offered. The Puja will have to be conducted with *aarti,* offering *mantra pushpa* at the idol's feet, followed by *Pradakshina* and *Sashtanga Namaskara.* The *Namaskara Vidhi* is also explained in detail, how to offer *Namaskaras* to the idol, to the Guru, to the elders, to parents, etc. The Puja *Theertha* has to be sprinkled on one's forehead, to be smeared on the eyes and should be sipped by the mouth. The Puja *Theertha* is most purifying; it purifies the body, mind and the spirit.

After the *Deva Puja* and before taking food, we have to offer oblations, the *Pancha Yajnas,* viz., *Deva Yajna, Rishi Yajna, Pitru Yajna, Bhuta Yajna* and *Atithi Yajna.* These *Yajnas* absolve man of the *Pancha-suna* sins which everyone invariably commits while doing the daily chores. The *Pancha Yajnas* are done through *Vysvadevatri.* From the food cooked, a little portion will have to be first offered to gods, *pitrus/*ancestors, *bhutas, rishis* and *atithis,* and only then will one take his food, considering it as *Yajna-sesha* (the remnant portions of *Yajna*).

If a guest happens to arrive, he should be welcomed and fed. *Atithi* is to be deemed as God himself in human form. After the guest is fed only the *Grihasta* has to take his food. When an *atithi* or a *bramhachari* comes for *bhiksha*, he should be offered *bhiksha* instantly even if *Vaisvadeva* and *Naivedya* have not been performed yet. If the *atithi* is pleased, all gods, all *pitridevatas* will be pleased. One morsel of food given to them brings mountain-size merit and one tumbler of water offered to them brings an ocean-size merit. One who does not offer food to *atithi* and eats by himself, will be born as a dog or donkey in his next life.

Strict silence is enjoined when taking food. Actually before taking food, there are other oblations to be done and observed. A circle with four cones *(mandala)* should be drawn with flour and the plate of food should be kept on that *mandala*. A little food has to be kept aside on the right side on the floor as *Bali*, in the name of Chitragupta, and thereafter only should one eat the food. One should visualise that God, seated inside him, is eating the food and that the food is also the Bramhin himself *(Bramharpanam, Bramha Havir, Bramhagnav, Bramhanahutam, Bramhaivathena gantavyam, Bramha Karma Samadhina).*

Pranaahuti and *Ausposana* mantras are to be recited at the beginning and after the completion of taking the food. At night when taking food, lamp should be lighted and one should not eat the food in the dark.

Moderation in food is also enjoined. Moderation is very much necessary in food. How many mouthfuls one should take, as per the day of the fortnight, i.e., *Chandrayan Vrata*, is described. The types of utensils and plates to be used for taking food, the metals out of which they are to be made, their shapes—are also described in some detail. There are also rules prescribed about drinking water, washing hands, washing eyes, face, etc. The auspicious sounds which one should hear, the sounds which are inauspicious, whose faces are auspicious to see and whose faces are not—are also described.

Sri Narasimha Saraswati teaches also about the types of food to be taken and those which are prohibited for a Brahmin. Food without a daily oblation, food made with too much salt, garlic, etc., are prohibited. On particular days some types of food and certain types of vegetables and fruits are to be avoided, like *padval* on Padyami day, *belphal* on Friday, *Shaniphal* on Tuesday, etc. A Brahmin should never take *nishiddha* food or food touched by a cat, rat, crow, dog, etc. He should not eat food that is stale, i.e., left-over food from the previous day. These impair the *sattvic* traits and promote *rajasic* and *tamasic* tendencies in him. A Brahmin should nurture and guard his *sattvic gunas* which are necessary and essential for his functioning as the community and the society as a whole.

In the evening the Brahmin should perform *sayam-sandhay*, i.e., chanting Gayatri mantra with three oblations of water and uttering *gotra*, *pravara* and with *auposan*. Thereafter only should he take his night meals. Before retiring to bed, one should read some sacred books, and then after offering his whole day's work as worship done to the Lord, he should go to sleep.

Sayana-vidhan (sleeping) is also described, i.e., regulations, relating to the cot used for sleeping by a Brahmin, etc. The cot should be clean. It should not have been made of *jambul* wood or tusks of a dead elephant. Days for weaving cots are also specified—they are either Sunday, Tuesday or Thursday. When weaving, certain deities are to be remembered. One should sleep with head towards east or south.

The places prohibited for sleep for a Brahmin are old temples, cremation grounds, at the foot of a tree, near ant-hill, near tanks, on foodgrains and in a dilapidated house. A Brahmin should not go to bed with wet clothes. He should not go to sleep without a garment. He is not to sleep under the bare sky.

A Brahmin should not indulge with his wife when she is in her monthly period or when she is wearing blue-coloured saree. There are injunctions on the wife as to how to conduct herself during her monthly periods and the things and disciplines she should observe. All these are necessary for bodily health as well as for moral and spiritual health, not only of the couple but also for the wellbeing and welfare of the progeny. All these have been codified by Parasara Rishi in *Parasara Smriti*.

With this chapter ends the Karma Kanda section* of Sri *Guru Charitra*.

THUS ENDS THE THIRTY-SEVENTH CHAPTER OF
SRI *GURU CHARITRA* DESCRIBING
VARNASHRAMA ACHAR VIDHI.

Glory to the all-merciful, the omnipresent and the ever-responsive Guru Nath!

---

*   The Karma Kanda section commences from chapter 25.

38

Miracle of the Poor Brahmin's Samaradhana*

This chapter describes how Guru Nath made the food prepared for a couple of persons *akshaya* and made it suffice for a large Samaradhana, for thousands of people to be fed sumptuously.

Siddha Yogi continued his narrative.

The influx of devotees to Ganagapur for Guru Nath's darshan was increasing day by day. They used to offer *bhiksha* to Guru Nath and they also used to do Samaradhana, i.e., feeding a large number of people of the town on that occasion. Not a single day passed without a Samaradhana in the town of Ganagapur.

One day a poor Brahmin by name Bhaskarayya came to Ganagapur for Sri Narasimha Saraswati's darshan and also with the intention of offering him *bhiksha*. But, as he could not afford much, the provisions he brought along with him for the purpose of the *bhiksha* were scant and would hardly suffice for two or three persons. He had Guru Nath's darshan and requested him that though he was poor, he would be privileged if Guru Nath accepted *bhiksha* from him too on one fine day. To this, Guru Nath gave no reply and kept silent.

---

* From this chapter begins the Bhakti Kanda section of Sri *Guru Charitra.*

Thus Bhaskarayya to remained at Ganagapur hoping that Guru Nath would accept his *bhiksha* some day. He used to stay in the *Math* itself and for his food, he used to go to the Samaradhana every day. The other Brahmins started criticising and ridiculing him that it was not proper for a Brahmin to be taking his food daily at the Samaradhanas only. But the Brahmin had no other means, and he carried on like this for three months, waiting for Sri Narasimha Saraswati to talk to him and accept his *bhiksha*.

Then one day, in the morning Guru Nath did send for Bhaskarayya and told him that he should prepare for the *bhiksha* that day. The Brahmin felt very happy. With the meagre provisions which he had brought along with him, he started cooking food for the *bhiksha*, which should suffice for Guru Nath and himself. Sri Narasimha Saraswati told all the Brahmins who came for his morning darshan not to leave the place nor go back to their homes without partaking of the food at the *bhiksha* and Samaradhana which Bhaskarayya was going to do at the *Math* on that day. All the Brahmins thought that Guru Nath must have provided from the *Math* all the provisions needed by the Brahmin for the Samaradhana. Sri Narasimha Saraswati then told the Brahmin to bring the food he had cooked and to place it before him. The Brahmin, with great trepidation and embarrassment, brought the scanty food he had cooked and placed it before Sri Guru Nath. Guru Nath covered the vessel containing the food with his shawl. The Brahmin offered his worship to Guru Nath. After the worship was over, Guru Nath asked the Brahmin to start serving the food to all the assembled Brahmins, but keeping the vessel containing the food, covered with the shawl. The Brahmin started serving and the food became *akshaya*, i.e., inexhaustible and undiminishing. Besides the Brahmins, people of all castes, their families and their children were also served food. Thereafter, Guru Nath asked the Brahmin to take his food. The Brahmin was told to remove the shawl that was covering the food all along. The shawl was removed and lo! whatever food Bhaskarayya had cooked and what was in the vessel originally, still remained! Bhaskarayya thanked Guru Nath, who asked him to feed dogs, crows, etc., for *Bhuta-trupti* and also offer it to the aquatic creatures (fishes, etc.) in the river waters. The little residual food still continued to remain undiminished.

The small measureful of rice which the Brahmin had cooked could feed thousands of men and several other creatures too! Faith and Grace can indeed work wonders!

THUS ENDS THE THIRTY-EIGHTH CHAPTER OF
SRI *GURU CHARITRA* DESCRIBING THE POOR
BRAHMIN'S SAMARADHANA.

Glory to the all-merciful, the omnipresent and the ever-responsive Guru Nath!

39

Aswatha Vrata Mahima

This chapter describes the birth of children to a barren woman past her sixties, as a result of Guru Nath's blessings.

Siddhamuni continues narrating to Namdharak the leelas *of Guru Nath.*

In Ganagapur there lived a Brahmin named Somanath Sarma and his wife Gangabai. They had no child and therefore, they were very unhappy. When the woman reached the age of 60, she felt a sense of desolation and frustration in life.

Gangabai used to visit the *Math* daily and have the darshan of Guru Nath. She used to perform *aarti* before him along with offering prayers. She kept up this practice for years.

One day Sri Narasimha Saraswati asked Gangabai why she always looked so sad. She told him she was sad because she had no child, and as she had no child, all the other women looked at her with contempt. Being childless, she had lost her status as a *grihini*. A house without a child is like a dungeon or a barren desert. There would be no joy in that house. Besides, all the scriptures also proclaim that the doors of heaven are for ever barred to childless-couples and therefore life beyond also would be as gloomy and joyless to them as life in this world, and may perhaps be even far more worse. She had seen how happy, contented and joyous, the women who had children were. She had undertaken many fasts, vigils and *vratas* and had also made many pilgrimages, hoping that she would be able to earn the merit to be blessed with a child. But all her prayers and vigils turned futile. And now that she had crossed her sixties, there was no hope at all of her having a child. That was why she was always seized with despair and gloom. Sri Narasimha Saraswati, looking at her with deep compassion, and told her not to lose hope at all. He told her to visit the Sangam daily and offer her worship with single-minded devotion to the Aswatha tree there. He assured her that the Aswatha tree would certainly fulfil her desires.

The woman prayed to Sri Narasimha Saraswati to enlighten her on the *Aswatha Mahima*. Guru Nath said that he would narrate to her what Bramhadeva told Narada Rishi about *Aswatha Mahima*.

At the foot of the Aswatha tree live all the deities including Bramhadeva. It is indeed the *Kalpavriksha*. When the *rishis* requested Narada to teach them the *Achara Vidhi* regarding the worship of the Aswatha tree, Naradamuni enlightened them on the following instructions.

The worship of the Aswatha tree should be started on an auspicious day. The days on which there is no moon (i.e., Chandra bala), the days on which *Sukra* is not on the ascent, especially during the months of *Ashad, Paush (Pushya)* and *Chaitra*, are not auspicious days for beginning the Aswatha worship. The worship is to begin in the morning. The worshipper should take a bath first, then place two *kalasas* filled with water near the tree. Worship is to be offered to the two *kalasas* while reciting *Purushasukta*. This is to be done seven times and then they should take a bath again.

After this, Lord Vishnu (as Datta), holding the divine weapons in his six hands, has to be remembered and homage has to be paid to him. Then a cloth or thread is to be wrapped round the tree, and *pradakshina* is to be done around the tree, while reciting the *Purushasukta* again. This *pradakshina* is equivalent to *pradakshina* around the supreme Purusha, Lord Vishnu, the Virat Purusha Himself. It would sanctify the worshipper completely, expiating all his/her sins and conferring immense spiritual benefits, besides material prosperity.

Thereafter, every day Gangabai used to go to Sangam, take a bath in the holy waters of the confluence there, and then offer her worship to the Aswatha tree. On the third night in her dream, a Brahmin appeared and told her to go to the *Math* and to do seven *pradakshinas* around Guru Nath himself and to eat whatever *prasad* Guru Nath would give her. Next day she did accordingly. Guru Nath gave her two fruits as *prasad* and told her that a son and a daughter would be born to her before long. Two beautiful children, a boy and a girl, were born to her as per Guru Nath's blessings. And the Brahmin couple were immensely happy.

THUS ENDS THE THIRTY-NINTH CHAPTER OF
SRI *GURU CHARITRA*.

Glory to the all-merciful, the omnipresent and the ever-responsive Guru Nath!

40

Dead Wood Grows into Tree by Guru's Grace

This chapter describes the miracle of fresh leaves sprouting out of a piece of dead wood and the cure of leprosy of a Brahmin by name Narahari, by the grace of Guru Nath. Guru Nath gives the illustration of the forest couple and narrates how their steadfast faith was rewarded.

Siddhamuni continued his narrative to Namdharak. Guru Nath was the reliever of all ills. He was Bhagawan Dhanvantari.

There lived a Brahmin named Narahari Sarma who was suffering from leprosy. He came to Sri Narasimha Saraswati to pray to him to be relieved of the dreadful disease. He related to him how the disease had made him a virtual outcaste and what misery it had brought on him. He said he was disgusted with life and had decided to end his life. But hoping that Guru Nath might save him, he had come to visit him.

Guru Nath was like a mother to all. The Brahmin's plight moved him with pity. Sri Narasimha Saraswati told the Brahmin that he had committed many sins in his former lives and his ailment in this life was the result of those past sins. However, he said, he would be relieved of the disease and should follow his (Guru Nath) instructions.

At this juncture, a man came over there carrying Audambar branches, which was almost dead and dry. The branches had been cut about five years ago. Guru Nath took that wood from the man and gave it to the Brahmin. He told the Brahmin to go to the Bhima-Amaraja Sangam and plant it on the bank there. He should then take a bath and offer worship to it. He should have a second dip in the water, fill his tumbler with water, and water the planted Audambar wood. He should water it thrice every day. The wood would sprout and put forth fresh leaves in the course of time. No sooner than the wood put forth leaves, he would be rid of his disease and would become completely well.

The Brahmin started on as per the above instructions with implicit devotion and faith in Guru Nath's words. Some of the people told Guru Nath about the great faith with which the Brahmin had been watering the dead wood. It was over a month since the Brahmin had planted the wood and had started watering every day. They said that the people were making fun of the Brahmin calling him mad and absolutely foolish to be watering a dead wood believing it would grow and put forth leaves. The Brahmin had become a butt of ridicule in the town.

Listening to them, Guru Nath told them that there was nothing that faith could not achieve. He narrated the story of the forest-man (Sabari), which had been narrated by Suta Muni to the *rishis* to illustrate the power of faith.

Once upon a time there was a king named Simhaketu who was the ruler of Panchal Nagar. He had a son named Dhananjaya. Once the prince went to the forest for hunting. He had one of the forest-men (Sabari), as his guard during the hunt. The prince was very tired and stopped for rest at a place. Meanwhile, the forest-man, wandering around sighted an attractive stone. He picked it up and brought it and showed it to the prince. The prince told him that it was a Sivalinga and explained to him about *Sivalinga Mahima*.

He advised the Sabari that since he (the Sabari) had found it, he should take it home and start worshipping it. He also told him how to do the worship. *'Bilwa* leaves are dear to Siva, you should therefore worship it with *bilwa* leaves and flowers. Incense is to be burnt, oil lamp lighted and *chitabhasma* (ashes) to be offered to the Sivalinga, as *chitabhasma* is most dear to the Lord.' The Sabari took the prince's instructions as *guropadesa* and he and his wife started following it with intense faith.

One day they could not find *chitabhasma* for their worship. The Sabari told his wife that as they could not let the Sivalinga go without *chitabhasma* he would burn his body and she should make the offering of that *chitabhasma* to the Lord and complete the worship. His wife however, offered to burn herself instead. Sabari said that she was too young and had hardly seen life, and as such she should not end her life when he was there. But his wife was not convinced and said that life was anyway like a bubble and age should be of no real consideration. If the *chitabhasma* of her body could serve as an offering to the Lord, what greater opportunity could ever be for this human birth? Seeing her determination, and as the time for the worship was passing away, Sabari had to consent and let her burn herself. She went into the hut, and he set fire to it from outside. He took the *chitabhasma* in his hands and was preparing to do the offering. As per his habit, obsessed with the worship and forgetting for the moment that his wife was no more, he called out to his wife by name, asking her to join him in making the *chitabhasma* offering. Siva was very much moved with the devotion, the spirit of sacrifice and their matchless faith in him. He gave back the woman her life. So in answer to the call of her husband, who had called her forgetfully, she rushed out to join him in the offering. The only thing she remembered was that when the hut was set on fire, she felt overwhelmed by sleep and was not aware of anything. She heard the call of her husband, which so to say, 'woke her up from her sleep', and she rushed to him. Lord Siva appeared before them and blessed them.

Guru Nath very much appreciated the Brahmin's faith in his (Guru Nath's) words and the implicit manner in which he was following them.

Thereafter, Sri Narasimha Saraswati set out towards Sangam for his daily routine and rituals. On the way the Brahmin saw him and offered his obeisance to him. Guru Nath sprinkled water from his *Kamandalu* on the Audambar wood which the Brahmin was watering daily. No sooner had Guru Nath sprinkled water, than new leaves sprouted out from the wood; and the dead wood changed into a live, healthy growing tree. The Brahmin's body too became clean and rid of the disease. The Brahmin fell at the feet of Guru Nath, pouring out his gratitude and singing praises of him. 'Oh Lord! my beloved Guru Nath! How much you love your devotees. Seated under the Aswatha tree, you are only waiting to welcome your bhaktas, and to shower your blessings on them. You so readily grant them all the boons and give them all happiness. Your effulgence and lustre outshine the light of crores of moons. Thou, the son of Atri and Anasuya and who named you as Datta, how beautiful you are! How charming you look with the garlands hanging down on your body! Just as *Ankush* alone can control and tame the wild elephants, so also devotion to your feet and your grace alone can control the wayward minds of men being chased wildly by the *Shadripus,* the six inner enemies.

'I bow down to you, my beloved Guru Nath! Oh the Master of the Five Elements! Oh Sree Vallabhesh Nayak! Oh the lotus-eyed! Thy lotus feet are my sole refuge. Pray, never forsake me ...'

The Brahmin offered elaborate worship to Guru Nath. He performed Samaradhana. Sri Guru Nath was very much pleased with the Brahmin's intense devotion. He named him Yogesh. He taught him the *Vidya Saraswati* mantra. He asked the Brahmin to go to his house and to bring his wife and children to live at Ganagapur. The Brahmin did accordingly and thereafter constantly stayed with Guru Nath, serving him most devotedly.

THUS ENDS THE FORTIETH CHAPTER OF
SRI *GURU CHARITRA*.

Glory of the all-merciful, the omnipresent and the ever-responsive Guru Nath!

41

Sayamdeo's Unflinching Devotion

This chapter describes Sayamdeo's coming to Guru Nath and the test of faith he was put to by Guru Nath. Guru Nath relates the story of Twasta who sets out with determination to fulfil the impossible demands of his Guru and the latter's family members.

This chapter is an allegorical description of self-realisation. Sayamdeo is the *sadhaka,* the aspirant. The dark night with heavy downpour symbolises 'the dark night of the soul'. Fire represents knowledge and wisdom. As Sayamdeo returned to (near) the Sangam, he heard the chant of the Vedas i.e., *Anahata Nada*—the *Omkara Dhwani,* which is always reverberating in one's own heart as well as in the entire universe. There he had a glimpse of the Sadguru, in full splendour of the moonlight. Clouds of ignorance cleared off; the fire of knowledge was lit, and Sayamdeo had the clear vision of the Sadguru. That was *Sakshatkara,* the state of realisation.

Namdharak said to Siddhamuni that listening to Guru Charitra was like drinking nectar. He said his mind was getting rid of all doubts and dross and was being filled with new light. He said he felt so blessed indeed! He told Siddha Yogi that he felt very much interested to know the details about his ancestor Sayamdeo who was a devotee and close disciple of Guru Nath and who used to earlier live at Vasar-Brahmeshwar but later at Ganagapur itself. Sayamdeo used to be very dear to Guru Nath, and he was happy

that he was born in the line of such blessed devotees of the Lord.
Then Siddhamuni narrated as under.

Sayamdeo came to know that Guru Nath was now residing
at Ganagapur. It was Guru Nath that saved him from the claws
of death, from being killed by the Muslim chief 16 years ago. He
was eager to have Guru Nath's darshan again and spend the rest
of his life in the service at his feet. He trekked to Ganagapur. He
fell prostrate at Guru Nath's feet and prayed that he should not
forsake him. He poured out his prayers to Guru Nath. He said,
'Your lotus feet is the confluence of the holy waters of all the
sacred rivers and all the holy places. All the nectar of the heavens
is in your *Kamandalu* only. Your *Charan Theertha* drives away
death, and just a little sprinkling of it is enough to resurrect the
dead. It is too presumptuous on my part to try to put into
articulation your inexpressible and infinite glory!...' Tears of joy,
welling out from the depths of his heart were trickling down
from his eyes drenching the feet of Guru Nath.

Guru Nath was pleased, and clasping Sayamdeo closely told
him that his grace would be for ever on him and his family. He
asked him to go to the Sangam and bathe there, which would
wash away all his past sins. He asked him to come back to the
Math after the bath for food.

After Sayamdeo had his food, Guru Nath enquired of him
with great solicitude all the details of his family and their
welfare. Sayamdeo told him that he would now come away
permanently to live at Ganagapur for serving the master. Sri
Guru Nath said that it was not easy for anyone to do service to
him properly and satisfactorily. It would be too arduous for
anyone. But Sayamdeo stayed on there, trying to serve the
master. Guru Nath wanted to test him.

One day Guru Nath took Sayamdeo along with him to the
Sangam. Guru Nath sat down under the Aswatha tree and went
on conversing with him till late after dusk. Then suddenly

stormy winds started blowing, accompanied by thunder and lightning. There was a very heavy downpour of rain. Sayamdeo was shivering, unable to bear the cold. Nevertheless, he was trying to put up a bold face. Sri Guru Nath told him that he himself was also feeling the cold too much and therefore, he (Sayamdeo) should go to Ganagapur and bring some fire from there. He told him that he should not look sideways at all, either while going or while returning. Sayamdeo put his own shawl over Guru Nath's shoulders to cover him and to keep his body warm, and then left in the direction of Ganagapur.

It was pitch dark then and nothing was visible, except when there were flashes of lightning. With great struggle Sayamdeo was able to reach Ganagapur. He put some fire (burning coals) in a pot and started on his return journey, towards the Sangam. Unable to find the way and forgetting Guru Nath's instructions, he looked sideways. Oh! there were two huge five-headed serpents, one each on either side, following him. He got very much frightened and almost lost his way. Struggling much and praying to Guru Nath, he at last managed to reach the Sangam.

Lo! what does he find there? There are thousands of lights shining brightly all round. There is the *Omkara nada* resounding and the chant of Vedic mantras reverberating everywhere. Guru Nath is seated under the Aswatha tree, shining with the splendour of thousands of moons and looking like Lord Siva himself. It was a divine vision! Sayamdeo, dazed by the vision, fell prostrate at Guru Nath's feet.

Guru Nath then ended the vision and lifted Sayamdeo, smiled at him and comforted him. He told him that he was very much pleased with his devotion, and added that it was he (Guru Nath) himself who sent the two serpents along with him for his protection. He further said, that he should never forget that Guru Bhakti is the supreme protection in one's life and its power is incomparable.

Sayamdeo requested Guru Nath to tell him about *Guru Bhakti Mahima*. Guru Nath said he would narrate what Lord Siva told Parvati about *Guru Bhakti Mahima*.

In the line of Bramha, there was one boy born who was named Twasta. When the boy attained *Upanayana* age, the *Upanayana* ceremony was performed by the father and the boy was sent to the Gurukul. The boy was serving the Guru very dutifully.

One day there was a big storm, and the Guru's cottage collapsed and its roof was blown off. The Guru called Twasta and told him, 'You must build me a good, strong house; it should look beautiful and should have all comforts.' The Guru's wife then came and told Twasta, 'You should get me a good dress. It should not be woven of thread. It should look very beautiful and fit me well.' Then the Guru's son came and told Twasta, 'You should get me a pair of shoes, just of the correct size for me. The shoes should be such that mud will never stick to them and they will never get soiled, and further I should be able to walk with them even on water and they should be able to take me instantly to wherever I just think of going.' Then the Guru's daughter came and said, 'You should get me ornaments for my ears, and an Ivory Toy-House made from the single tusk of an elephant. You should also get me utensils for cooking. They should be such that they will not turn black with soot when food is cooked in them.'

Twasta was at a loss to know as to how he would be able to procure all these and fulfil the demands, but he felt confident and certain, that his Guru's grace alone will help him to fulfil all the demands of the Guru and his family.

Twasta, praying to his Guru only, started walking towards the nearby forest. He sat down there praying to his

Guru, that he should help him to fulfil all the demands and to get through the ordeal.

As he was praying thus all of a sudden an *Avadhut* appeared before him. The boy was overjoyed at seeing him. The *Avadhut* enquired of him as to what was worrying him. The boy told him the impossible tasks set to him by his Guru and his (Guru's) family members and that he was at a loss to know how he would be able to discharge them all satisfactorily.

The *Avadhut* then said, 'Dear child, do not despair about this. You will surely succeed. There is nothing impossible for those who win Lord Visweswara's grace. It is through Visweswara's grace only that Bramha could earn the capacity to create the worlds; it is through Visweswara's grace again that Vishnu could gain the capacity to sustain the creation and to grant the prayers of his devotees. Therefore, for success in fulfilling the demands of your Guru, you go to Kasi, serve Lord Visweswara there and earn his grace. He will certainly bless you. He will make you even Viswakarma and will enable you to earn an eternal name and fame.'

The *Avadhut* continued, 'Therefore I advice you to visit Kasi. You should undertake there the *pancha-krosa yatra*, in and around Kasi, visiting all the holy shrines and the *theerthas* therein. The *pancha-krosa yatra* will earn for one as much merit as one gets through the performance of an Aswamedha *Yajna*. Even the thousand-tongued Adisesha cannot describe adequately the merit that accrues by pilgrimage to Kasi.'

Twasta said, 'Oh Mahatma! Where is Kasi? How far is it? I am a lad, how can I reach there?' Then the *Avadhut* said, 'I will also come along with you to Kasi. Thereby I too will get the merit of Lord Visweswara's darshan.' Saying thus, the

Avadhut took the boy to the holy Kasi in a trice, through the power of his Siddhis.

Twasta was overjoyed. He said, 'Oh Mahatma! You are indeed Lord Visweswara. You have come to save me! Please let me know in detail what places are to be visited, what rites are to be done, and explain to me the whole *Kasi yatra Vidhana* fully.'

THUS ENDS THE FORTY-FIRST CHAPTER OF
SRI *GURU CHARITRA* DESCRIBING
KASI KHAND YATRA.

Glory to the all-merciful, the omnipresent and the ever-responsive Guru Nath!

42

Lord Viswanath's Grace on Twasta

This chapter describes Twasta's *Kasi yatra* and how he
earned Lord Visweswara's grace and was able to fulfil all the
impossible demands of his Guru and his family members.
This chapter teaches us that there is nothing which cannot
be achieved through faith.

Siddhamuni continues the narrative as under.
The *Avadhut* instructs the young celibate about the *Kasi
yatra Vidhi* – (a) *Griha yatra*, (b) *Dakshina Manasa yatra*, (c)
Uttara Manasa yatra, and finally, *(d) the pancha-krosa yatra.*

Early in the morning, after taking the bath in the Ganges,
one should first offer worship to Dhundi Raja and then offer his
worship to Lord Visweswara. *Ganga Snana* confers the same
merit which *Dhyana* did in the *Krita Yuga, Tapas* or penance in
the *Treta Yuga, yajnas* in *Dwapara Yuga.* In the *Kali Yuga, Ganga
Snana* is the most meritorious rite and endows one with the
Moksha Saamrajya, i.e., sovereignty/freedom of the spirit. As
soon as one rises from bed, if he just thinks of the Ganges River
three times, he will be purified of all sins. There is no other easier
saving path in the *Kali Yuga* than a bath in the holy Ganges.

Kasi is called Avimukta Kshetra, Ananda Kaanana,
Mahasmasana, Rudrageha, etc. Every bit, every inch of it is most
holy for five *krosas* around Kasi. Within the sacred precincts of

this five-*krosa* area, there are many sacred lingas, *theerthas,* etc. Therefore whoever does this *pancha-krosa yatra,* will have had darshan and will have done *Pradakshinas* of so many holy lingas and sacred centres, and the merit which this endows is limitless indeed.

Lord Visweswara has conferred special merit on Manikarnika. It is as meritorious and sacred as the Viswanath Temple itself. One has to take bath in the Chakra Pushkarini, then perform oblations to *devas* and *pitrus* and offer charity (ies) to Brahmins. Thereby, all his ancestors are redeemed and they attain *Akshaya Punya Lokas* (eternal life in heavens/divine realms).

Every day one has to do the *Antargriha yatra,* and then the *Dakshina* and Uttara Manasa yatras. One has to bathe in Jnanavapi and worship Sringara Gowri. On Tuesdays and Sundays especially, Bhairava has to be worshipped, which will endow great merit. On Ashtami, Navami and Purnima days, Mother Annapurna has to be worshipped. It will endow all good and auspiciousness. Vishnumurti, Dhundi Raju, Bindu Madhava are also to be worshipped. During the *Sukla Paksha* and *Krishna Paksha,* every day, in the prescribed way, all will have to bathe in the particular *Theertha* and worship the particular lingas, doing the *abhisheka.* One should stay as many days as possible in Kasi, and in his own name enshrine one Sivalinga there. By doing this, and offering worship and *abhisheka* to Lord Visweswara, one would get *Sakshatkara*—the direct vision of the Lord. After giving these instructions to the young lad, the *Avadhut* disappeared.

Twasta realised that it was none else but the Guru of Gurus, the Adi Guru, Lord Visweswara himself who had come in the form of the *Avadhut* to help him.

Twasta devoutly followed all the instructions of the *Avadhut* and took darshan of all the shrines and performed all the *vidhis.* Lord Visweswara was very much pleased with the devotion of the boy. He appeared before him and asked him to seek a boon. The *Bramhachari* prayed, that he may be blessed to fulfil all the tasks set by his Guru and the Guru's family members and that thereby, be able to please them all. The Lord blessed him and granted him all the boons and asked him to return to his Guru's place. Twasta was able to fulfil all the tasks set for him, with Lord Visweswara's grace and blessings. The Guru, his wife and children were pleased with the boy beyond all measures. The Guru imparted to Twasta all scriptural knowledge and spiritual wisdom. And Twasta became perfect in knowledge and an enlightened being. He became Viswakarma, Master of all the arts and skills, and came to be known as Twasta Bramha. Here ended the *Guru Bhakti Mahima* as related by Lord Siva to Parvati.

Sayamdeo thanked Guru Nath for enlightening him on *Guru Bhakti Mahima* and started extolling him again. 'Oh Guru Nath! You are Lord Dattatreya, the Trinity—Bramha, Vishnu and Maheshwara unified in One. You were the originator of the Vedas. Whenever dharma starts declining, you incarnate in the world to destroy the wicked and to protect the good, to resuscitate dharma and to reestablish it again on earth. You were the ordainer of the *Varnasrama Dharma* for the unkeep of harmony, order and happiness in the human society and the world. You are the giver of all auspiciousness and you are an ocean of mercy. You are always seated under the Audambar tree, ever ready to receive your devotees and to offer them your divine and loving protection at all times. You are *Bhaktavatsala* Lord! You are the tree, I am the creeper nestling around you. You are the *Kalpavriksha* come on earth. Your mere darshan is enough to destroy the accumulated store of sins of all our former lives. You are the fulfiller of the four *Purusharthas* of life. Please permit me to stay at your lotus feet, and bless me that I shall never be separated from you.'

Sri Narasimha Saraswati told Sayamdeo that he could bring his family and stay at Ganagapur.

Sayamdeo had four sons, the eldest was Nagnath who became the most ardent devotee of Guru Nath. He became very dear to Guru Nath and was loved by him very much.

One day Guru Nath asked Sayamdeo to perform *Ananta Padmanabha Vrata* as it happened to be the *Ananta Padmanabha Chaturdasi* day. Sayamdeo said the Guru Nath himself was his Lord Ananta and he would only worship Guru Nath. Guru Nath said that *Ananta Padmanabha Vrata* had very great significance and that by performing it, Kaundinya had earned great merit and attained an eternal abode in the starry heavens. Sayamdeo requested Guru Nath to tell him how Kaundinya happened to perform the *vrata*.

THUS ENDS THE FORTY-SECOND CHAPTER OF
SRI *GURU CHARITRA* DESCRIBING THE KASI YATRA.

Glory to the all-merciful, the omnipresent and the ever-responsive Guru Nath!

43

Ananta Padmanabha Vrata Mahima

This chapter describes the *Ananta Padmanabha Vrata Mahima* and the story of Kaundinya Rishi, who, through the grace of Lord Ananta, earned an eternal abode in the realm of the stars in the heavens (skies). Guru Nath asks Sayamdeo, that he should also perform *Ananta Padmanabha Vrata*, especially because he too belonged to the *Kaundinyasa Gotra*.

*N*amdharak was highly excited with joy and enthusiasm listening to the close association of his ancestor Sayamdeo with Guru Nath. He was all eager to know more and more details of their association. He pressed Siddhamuni to continue the narration. Sri Narasimha Saraswati's narration to Sayamdeo regarding Ananta Padmanabha Vrata *was recounted in this chapter by Siddhamuni.*

Yudhishtara was one of those who performed this *vrata* as advised by Lord Krishna. This is how it happened. The evil Duryodhana induced Yudhishtara to play the game of dice, and in that through deceit and foul play he defeated Yudhishtara. The bet in the game was that whoever lost the game was to go into exile for 12 years, and in the thirteenth year they should live incognito. In case they were found in the thirteenth year, the cycle of exile would start all over again. Because of the defeat in the game, the Pandava princes had to forsake their throne and had to go into exile along with their Queen Draupadi. They were put to many hardships. The evil Duryodhana was not letting them live in peace even in the forest. Yudhishtara's adherence to dharma and his pledge to honour the commitments of the bet made him bear it all. Although he and his brothers could crush Duryodhana and his people in physical combat, they were restraining themselves so as not to bring a blemish on their vow of dharma and adherence to truth.

While the Pandavas were in great despair as to how they could get over the difficulties without violating in the least even a single rule of dharma and vow of truth on their part, they saw to their great delight that Lord Krishna had come to visit them. The Pandavas ran forward and fell at the Lord's feet. They worshipped him with great devotion. Yudhishtara then told the Lord that the thought of Krishna and constant remembrance of Him alone was their sustenance and sole strength in being able to withstand all the ordeals that they were passing through. He, however, prayed that the Lord should advise them as to how they would be able to pass through the exile safely and would be able to recover their kingdom which they had been deceitfully deprived of by their cousins.

Lord Krishna told them that they should do *Ananta Padmanabha Vrata* which would earn for them great merit and would be a great protection to them always, and would certainly help them to pass through all the ordeals unscathed, triumph over the Kauravas eventually and win back their kingdom. Ananta Padmanabha, the lotus-navelled Lord of Eternity, was indeed Lord Krishna himself. This *vrata* was to be done on *Chaturdasi* day of *Sukla Paksha* during the Bhadrapada month. Lord Krishna further said that this *vrata* was done in olden times by Kaundinya at the instance of his wife Sushila and Lord Ananta Himself, and he thereafter explained how Kaundinya started performing the *vrata*.

Sushila was the daughter of a Brahmin by the name Sumantha. Sushila's mother was Deeksha, the daughter of Bhrigu Rishi. Deeksha passed away when Sushila was still a child. Sushila, though a child, used to manage the household very well, also while attending upon her father. Sumantha married again; the second wife's name was Karkashi. She was a very hot-tempered person, and was always quarrelling with her husband. She was not disposed kindly towards Sushila, either. Sumantha was anxious and desirous of getting his daughter married off soon. One day Kaundinya happened to come to their house. Sumantha offered his daughter in marriage to Kaundinya to which the latter consented. Sushila's marriage was thus performed with Kaundinya. Kaundinya stayed for some days in Sumantha's house after the marriage. Finally, on an auspicious day, Kaundinya along with his bride set out on their journey back home. All that Sumantha could give his daughter was a little quantity of millet-flour packed in a piece of cloth, at the time of her departure, and even that too, much against the will of his wife. By midday they reached a river; they took a break here so that Kaundinya could perform his midday oblations. Sushila was very much charmed by the sylvan surrounding and was enchanted by the beauty of the forest and the river. While she was looking around, drinking in the beauty of mother nature, she was at a little distance from a group of women engaged in some religious ceremony. She went to them and enquired about the ceremony which they were performing with such great devotion. The women told her that they were doing *Ananta padmanabha Chaturdasi Vrata,* which earns great merit for the performer. They said that the fruits of the *vrata* were also Ananta, and that the *vrata* fulfils all human desires and ferries the person safely across all the tribulations of life. They told her that she too could join the *vrata* along with them. Sushila also then performed the *vrata*, most meticulously and devoutly, observing all the instructions laid down for the *vrata* as told her by the women. She used the millet-flour, given to her by her father, for the *vrata* and offered it to the Brahmin-priests who conducted the puja. After the puja was over, wearing the red (14-knotted) sacramental thread and taking leave of the women, she came back to join her husband. They then resumed their journey.

They reached a town called Amaravati. At the very outskirts of the town itself, the town's people greeted and welcomed them. In one voice they said, 'You are the most learned and holy person. You are a great *tapasvi* as we can see the yogic splendour and radiance in your face. You must stay in our town only. We would not let you leave from here.' They led Kaundinya and his wife to a spacious house in the town and made them stay there.

Kaundinya was honoured and respected very much by the town-people. He became very prosperous. His house was ever aplenty with wealth, paddy, cattle, etc.

One day Kaundinya happened to see the red sacramental thread on the wrist of his wife and asked her what it was. He thought it was a charm she was wearing to entice and enslave him. She told him that it was the sacramental thread of the *Ananta Vrata* which she performed regularly. 'It was all due to Lord Ananta's Grace only that we are so prosperous,' she said. Kaundinya became furious. 'It is all nonsense what you say. All this wealth and prosperity is a result of my greatness alone.' Saying thus, he tore the thread from her wrist and flung it into the fire without listening at all to the pleadings of his wife. No sooner did he do this, than misfortune befell Kaundinya. All the people turned away from him. He lost his wealth. His house caught fire. He became penniless and shelterless. He realised that all this catastrophic turn of events in his life was due to nothing else but the blasphemy and sin he had committed against Lord Ananta. He was in great remorse. He started crying out to Ananta for forgiving him. He vowed he would not touch food unless Ananta forgave him and blessed him with darshan. He set out frantically searching for Ananta everywhere.

Crying 'Oh Ananta! Oh Ananta!' he went on roaming from place to place. 'I will end my life if you will not give me your darshan,' he was wailing. As he was wandering thus, he came across a tree richly laden with fruits. But there was not a bird to be seen on the tree even though the tree was overladen with luscious-looking fruits. Kaundinya plaintively asked the tree whether she had seen Ananta and whether she could tell him where to find him. The tree answered in the negative. After proceeding further in his search, he came across a cow and a calf; the cow was not able to graze due to its blistered tongue. Kaundinya asked the cow whether she had seen Ananta and whether she could tell where he could find him. The cow nodded a negative reply. Kaundinya went searching further and he came across a bullock. He put to the bullock also the same question which he had asked the tree and the cow earlier. The bullock also nodded a negative reply. Kaundinya then came across two adjoining lakes full of lotus flowers. He put to the lakes too his question whether they had seen Ananta, and the reply was again in the negative. Thereafter he came across an ass and an elephant. There was no affirmative response from them either. Kaundinya was in great desperation; he was terribly exhausted and fell down. His life breath seemed to be ebbing out. He was still frantically crying in a choking voice, his heart bursting out with great anguish for Lord Ananta's darshan. At that critical moment, one old man appeared, Lord Ananta himself in an assumed form. The old man asked him what his anguish was all about. Kaundinya cried out his request to him also whether he could take him and get for him Lord Ananta's darshan. The old man asked Kaundinya to accompany him, giving him a helping hand to walk along. There appeared a gorgeous and splendorous city; as they entered it, they saw a golden throne studded with diamonds and Lord Ananta seated on it. Oh! the vision dazzled him; his heart leapt up in joy inexpressible. He fell prostrate at Lord Ananta's feet. He sang praises in adoration of the Lord. He said, 'Oh Ananta! Oh! Lord resting on the serpent couch, my life has found its fulfilment today; forgive all my sins and lapses. You have graced me with your glorious vision; Oh the creator of this Bramhanda! Oh Ananta! Oh the infinite ocean of mercy! Please never forsake me!'

Ananta was pleased with Kaundinya's outpouring adulation.

Kaundinya asked the Lord that he was intrigued about the tree laden with fruits but without a bird around, about the cow that was unable to graze and also about the other things he had sighted on the way.

The Lord said to Kaundinya thus, 'The tree laden with fruits but without a single bird around, was a very learned Brahmin in his previous life, who always wanted to keep the knowledge to himself and never taught anyone. A lamp should light up other lamps. A person of knowledge will have to impart the knowledge to others, then only the knowledge finds its fulfilment. As this Brahmin was miserly with his knowledge in his former life, he was born in this life as a tree. You see that the tree is burdened with fruits but not a bird coming near it.

'As to the cow, in its former life it was a human being. That man gave a piece of land in gift to a Brahmin but that piece of land was barren and uncultivable. That was why in this life, the cow was unable to graze and satiate its hunger, nor that of its calf.

'As to the bull, in its previous birth, it was a rich Brahmin. Though rich, he never gave even a pie in charity to the poor and the needy.

'As to the lakes, they were in their previous lives sisters. When it came about that they had to do some *daan* (charity) in a religious ceremony they did it but each sister gave her charity to the other sister only, instead of some other poor and merited person.

'As to the ass and the elephant, they were your own anger and your passion.

'The old Brahmin who brought you to my presence, was none else but I, myself. I was moved to pity by your desperation. I bless you! You will have all wealth and prosperity. Your name and fame will for ever remain. You should do this *vrata* for 14 years, on every Bhadrapada Suddha *Chaturdasi* day. After this life for you, I will provide an eternal abode in the *Nakshatra Mandala,* i.e., in the starry skies.'

Kaundinya then returned and joined his wife. They enjoyed all prosperity and were for ever happy.

Lord Krishna further said to Yudhishtara, 'Agastya Rishi performed this *vrata* and earned an eternal name and fame. Kings like Sagara, Dileepa, Bharata, Harischandra, Janaka, etc., all of them used to perform this *vrata*. Yudhishtara performed this *vrata* and, as a result, was able to win victory in the Kurukshetra war and regain his kingdom. You also do this and all your woes will end for ever'.

Guru Nath thus explained to Sayamdeo the *Ananta Padmanabha Vrata Mahima,* and also about the detailed mode of the *vrata*, how it is to be performed, etc. He told him, that he being in the lineage of Kaundinya (as he belonged to the *Kaundinyasa Gotra*) must necessarily perform this *vrata*.

Sayamdeo performed the *vrata* as instructed by Guru Nath. Sayamdeo thereafter, remained with Guru Nath serving him with the greatest devotion and dedication.

Namdharak was thrilled with joy and elation listening to the account given by Siddhamuni regarding his blessed ancestor Sayamdeo, and also that he belonged to the lineage of the great Kaundinya Rishi.

THUS ENDS THE FORTY-THIRD CHAPTER OF SRI *GURU CHARITRA* DESCRIBING THE ANANTA PADMANABHA VRATA MAHIMA.

Glory to the all-merciful, the omnipresent and the ever-responsive Guru Nath!

44

Tantuku's Pilgrimage to Srisailam

This chapter describes Sri Narasimha Saraswati taking the
weaver Tantuku to Srisail parvata in a trice on the holy
Sivaratri day by his mystical power, and his narration of
Sivaratri Mahima and the story of King Vimarsan. Tantuku
sees none else but his Guru's form even in the Sivalinga at
the Srisailam shrine. A true disciple should visualise his Guru
alone in all the Gods. For him all the Gods get subsumed in
the form of his Guru.

*Siddhamuni told Namdharak that he would narrate to him
an anecdote of a weaver who was a great devotee of Guru
Nath. His name was Tantuku.*

Tantuku used to come to Guru Nath daily for his darshan.
He used to sweep and clean the precincts of the *Math* every day.
A little before Sivaratri, people were setting out on a pilgrimage
to Srisailam for Lord Mallikarjuna's (Jyotirlinga) darshan.
Tantuku's parents also decided to go and they wanted their son
also to accompany them. Tantuku knew that Guru Nath was
Lord Mallikarjuna and, therefore, there was no need at all for
him or anybody to go all the way to Srisailam for the Lord's
darshan. The parents could not prevail upon him to join the
pilgrim-party and the son stayed behind, while all his relations
and parents went.

On the holy Sivaratri day, as usual, the weaver took his bath
in the Sangam and came to the *Math* for the darshan of Guru

Nath. Guru Nath asked him why he did not go to Srisailam along with his people. The weaver said that his Srisailam was Ganagapur only and Guru Nath was his Mallikarjuna. Guru Nath was pleased with the weaver's devotion and faith. He asked him to sit near him and to keep his eyes closed. No sooner than Tantuku did this, he found himself at the foot of the Srisailam mountain and with Guru Nath only by his side. Guru Nath asked him to go and take his bath in the holy Patala-Ganga River and thereafter to perform the ritualistic *vidhis* and visit the temple for Jyotirlinga-darshan. As he walked down to the river, he found his parents and relations there. They were surprised to see him; the parents rebuked him saying that he could have as well come along with them instead of deciding to come all along later. The weaver told them that he did not come by himself there, but it was Guru Nath's will and grace that brought him there. They did not take his reply seriously. After the bath when he went into the temple, he found Guru Nath only in the place of the Jyotirlinga. Guru Nath was seated there in the place of Linga, and was accepting all the offerings being made by devotees and was receiving the unending *abhishekas*. The weaver's ecstacy knew no bounds for having had the darshan of his Guru Nath on the holy Sivaratri day in the sacred Jyotirlinga-shrine of Srisailam, which is the Lord's eternal abode.

The weaver then fell at the feet of Guru Nath and pleaded with him to enlighten him on *Srisaila-sthana mahima*. Guru Nath told him that the *Srisai-parvata mahima* have been described in the Skanda Purana and which he would recount to him.

In Kirat desa, there lived a king named Vimarsan. He was a very valiant person. He made many conquests and was always victorious. But he was a very sensuous person. He lacked moral rectitude. But even so, he had one saving virtue, that was his devotion to Lord Siva. Every month, on the Sivaratri day, he used to do the 'Jagarana', i.e., keeping awake the whole night worshipping Siva. On other days, he used to mostly enjoy himself with women, music and dance. His wife Kumudvati was a very pious lady. She was always worried about her husband's licentious nature. She always tried to persuade him that he should change his mode of life. She used to tell him that while he professed his devotion to Siva, his behaviour and conduct were most unbecoming of a devotee. She told him that she was at a loss to understand how with such a sensuous and indulgent nature, he ever came to cherish devotion to Siva at all. Thereupon the king started narrating the account of his previous life.

In his previous birth he was a dog wandering in the streets of the city of Pampa. On one Sivaratri day, curious to know what was happening inside the temple where thousands of people were going in, he also went in. He was also hoping that he would be able to get something to eat there and allay his hunger. As soon as he entered inside the precincts, the people there took hold of a stick to drive him out. The dog started running, but inside the temple compound itself. While being chased, it ran round the main temple of the shrine three times. While running it could get the glimpse of the holy shrine inside where Sivaratri Puja was being performed. But it got a good beating. Not being able to get anything to eat, it had to go without food that night. Because of the severe beating it received, and added to it, due to hunger, the dog died. But the merit which it got through the darshan of the puja, the *pradakshinas* and the fast it underwent, although unknowingly and with the least intention, resulted in it being born as a king in the next life. But he was not able to shed the habits (*Samskaras*) that characterised his previous life as a dog. If he as a dog had done the *pradakshina* and fast with a little understanding at least, he would have been able to shed the 'dog-*vasanas*' completely and would not have had this wayward and sensuous mind in this life.

The queen asked the king if he could also tell what her previous birth was and let her know about it. The king told her that she was a pigeon in her previous birth. One day she saw a large piece of meat lying on the ground. She picked it up in her beak. While she was flying in the sky with it, a kite saw it and started chasing her. The pigeon started flying with all its strength, and in the process of being chased and in its flight for escape from the kite, it happened to fly around the Srisaila parvata three times. In the end, however, the kite caught hold of it and killed it and then ate it up. But because of the three *pradakshinas* which she happened to do, though unintentionally, the pigeon earned great merit and was born as a queen in this life. The queen was very keen to know if the king could tell her how her future birth would be. The king told her about that also. He said that both of them, after a few more births as king and queen, would be attaining salvation and would be free from the cycle of birth and death for ever.

Guru Nath told the weaver about the Sivaratri *mahima* thus, at the holy Srisailam itself. Guru Nath asked the weaver to touch his *padukas* and then close his eyes. No sooner than the weaver did this, he was back in the *Math* at Ganagapur, seated in the presence of Guru Nath.

THUS ENDS THE FORTY-FOURTH CHAPTER OF
SRI *GURU CHARITRA* DESCRIBING SRISAILA MAHIMA.

Glory to the all-merciful, the omnipresent and the ever-responsive Guru Nath!

45

Guru Nath Cures Brahmin's Leprosy

This chapter refers to the anecdote of a Brahmin, called Nandi, who was suffering from leprosy and who went to Tuljapur and other holy places and did great austerities. Goddess Parameswari directed him in his dream to visit Ganagapur and seek the blessings of Sri Narasimha Saraswati for the cure of his disease. He thereafter becomes a close disciple of Guru Nath.

Namdharak was rapturous listening to Guru Charita. *He said to Siddhamuni, 'Your narration is regenerating me; all the cobwebs of doubts infesting my mind are being cleared and swept off. New light is filling my mind. I had never in my life experienced such joy and peace. Please tell me more and more of the Guru leelas.' Siddhamuni started the following narrative.*

There was a Brahmin suffering from severe leucoderma and leprosy. He made pilgrimage to Amba Tuljapur. He performed worship and *upasana* there with steadfast devotion for over three years and most of the days observing fasts. But his condition showed no improvement and he did not find any relief from his dreadful disease. He was feeling very desperate and wanted to end his life. Then one night Amba Devi appeared in his dream and asked him to go to the temple of Chandala Parameswari and offer worship to her. He went there and for seven months he was offering his prayers and worship and observing fasts. Goddess Parameswari also appeared in his dream like Amba Devi earlier, and advised him to go to Ganagapur and have the darshan of Sri Narasimha Saraswati, which would relieve him from his dreadful disease. The Brahmin got annoyed and angry and said, 'If you, the Goddess-Mother of the universe, cannot cure me, who else will be able to do it? I am being fooled by you. You have no consideration and compassion ... I will not move from here.'

The Brahmin brushed aside the advice he received in his dream and continued to stay there only doing his *aradhana*. The Goddess appeared in dream again and this time said sternly, that unless he obeyed her command his disease would get aggravated and he would become only worse and would have to repent greatly.

The Brahmin, in deference to the command of the Goddess, set out for Ganagapur. After reaching there he went to the *Math*. But Guru Nath was not in the *Math* at that time; he was at the Sangam. He waited at the *Math* and when Guru Nath returned to the *Math* he bowed down before him and prayed that he should be relieved of his dreadful disease. Guru Nath said, 'What can I, a mere human, do when Goddess Parameswari could not herself cure you?' Guru Nath just retorted back what exactly the Brahmin expressed in scepticism and anger to Goddess Parameswari when she first appeared in his dream and advised him to go to Ganagapur and seek redress from Sri Narasimha Saraswati.

The Brahmin realised his folly and prayed to Guru Nath that he should be forgiven for his sceptical remarks made in ignorance. He poured out to him his woeful tale, how he was forsaken by his wife and even by his parents because of this loathsome disease of his. He said that unless Guru Nath showed mercy on him and freed him from the disease, he would end his life.

Sri Guru Nath was moved by the desperation of the Brahmin. He asked a devotee of his to take the Brahmin to the Sangam.

He told the Brahmin that he should bathe in Sangam and then worship the Aswatha tree by taking three *pradakshinas* around it. After that, he was to wear the new clothes which would be given to him. The Brahmin took the bath in Sangam, worshipped the Aswatha tree and after discarding his old clothes, put on the new ones given to him by Guru Nath. Lo! the disease disappeared mostly, except for a few white patches here and there. Guru Nath later explained to him that the few patches remaining were due to the sceptical feelings entertained by him originally.

The Brahmin was overcome by a surge of devotion to Guru Nath and sang many hymns in praise of him. He told him that having passed through the ordeals of 84 lakhs of births, and finally being born as a man and much more than that, as a Brahmin, he was still steeped in ignorance! alas! always plunged neck-deep in the waters of *sansara* he had no peace. How torturous is birth! What turmoils one has to go through, all because of one's ignorance and lack of correct perspective of life and the ultimate realities! Only refuge at Guru Nath's feet saves one from such pitiful existence. The Brahmin stayed on there composing many hymns on Guru Nath. Guru Nath used to call him 'Kaveeswara'. Slowly, with continued exposure to Guru Nath's grace and love he was totally rid of his disease; the few patches that remained earlier had also slowly disappeared completely. He became famous as Nandeeswara Kavi.

THUS ENDS THE FORTY-FIFTH CHAPTER OF
SRI *GURU CHARITRA* DESCRIBING
THE DWIJA KUSHT-HARANAM.

Glory to the all-merciful, the omnipresent and the ever-responsive Guru Nath!

46

Poet-Devotee of Lord Sri Kalleswara

This chapter refers to the anecdote of a poet who was a
devotee of Lord Kalleswara and who did not believe in Sri
Narasimha Saraswati's divinity and therefore, was talking
disrespectfully to him. But he soon realises the great
mistake of his assessment and becomes a staunch devotee
and close disciple of Guru Nath.

Siddhamuni continued with the narrative of the Guru leelas.
Once, one of the devotees of Sri Narasimha Saraswati
requested him to visit and grace his house in Hipparage village.
Guru Nath visited the house. The devotee worshipped Guru
Nath with elaborate rituals.

In the same village, there lived a pious and devout Brahmin
named Narakesari, who was also a poet. He used to go daily to
the Kalleswara Temple in the village and, after completing his
worship, used to compose a few poems in praise of Lord
Kalleswara. This was his routine every day. Some of his friends
told him that Sri Narasimha Saraswati had come into the village
to a devotee's house. They told him that he should also come
and take his darshan. They further asked him to compose some
poems in adoration of Sri Narasimha Saraswati and to recite them
before him. To this Narakesari reacted with disdain and said
contemptuously, that his poetry was not meant for a human
being, however great he be. He did not go for Guru Nath's

darshan, and as was his wont, went to the Kalleswara Temple and started his worship. But as he started it, he fell asleep and had a dream.

In the dream, he saw Sri Narasimha Saraswati seated there in the same place as of the linga, and heard him telling, 'You have been all along worshipping me, a mere human being. Why are you worshipping a mere human being and moreover, one for whom you have no respect at all?' The dream ended thus, and Narakesari came to his senses. Realising what a great mistake he had committed by not paying heed to his friends' persuasion and advice, he hurried to the devotee's house for Guru Nath's darshan. As he was offering his obeisance, Guru Nath said, 'Why are you offering obeisance to me, a mere human being?' Narakesari burst into sobs, praying Guru Nath to forgive him for his ignorance and error. He sang poems in adoration of Guru Nath and worshipped him. Guru Nath was pleased and blessed him.

Narakesari thereafter came to live at Ganagapur, devoting his life in the service of Guru Nath. He composed many songs, hymns and rich poetry in adoration of Guru Nath.

THUS ENDS THE FORTY-SIXTH CHAPTER OF
SRI *GURU CHARITRA.*

Glory to the all-merciful, the omnipresent and the ever-responsive Guru Nath!

47

Guru Nath's Omnipresence

This chapter describes how Guru Nath visits the homes of seven of his devotees in the different villages during Deepavali and stays with each one of them, while also being present at Ganagapur at the same time.

Siddhamuni was very much impressed and pleased with Namdharak's earnestness and insatiable longing to listen to more and more of the glorious accounts and leelas of Guru Nath. He told him that he was indeed a very blessed soul. He told him, 'You have become a "Shriman". You have become morally and spiritually very rich. Very few would have such a blessed opportunity as you have had in listening to the Guru Charitra in such great detail. Let me tell you one more anecdote which tells us of Guru Nath's omnipresence and omnipotence.'

One year, some time before Deepavali, some of the devotees had come for Guru Nath's darshan from other places and each one of them requested Guru Nath that he should come to his village and grace and stay in his house during Deepavali and bless him, his household and his village. Everyone thus wanted that Guru Nath should specially visit his particular village and his house and bless him. To everyone of them Guru Nath was replying in the affirmative, and assuring them that he would certainly visit each one's particular village and would stay with him during the Deepavali festival. This was intriguing to everyone and they were all wondering how Guru Nath would be able to fulfil his promises of visiting at the same time all the different places. He promised at least seven devotees from different places (villages) to this effect.

On *Trayodasi* day itself, Guru Nath was present at the door of each one of the devotee's house, whom he had promised. Thus he made his appearance simultaneously in different villages. He was received by the household of each one of the devotees of those places; all the three days, i.e., from *Trayodasi* to *Amavasya*. At the same time, he was at Ganagapur too; actually he had not left from that place at all. He was fully present at the Deepavali festival in the *Math*.

On *Kartike* Purnima day when all devotees came to Ganagapur for *Deeparadhana,* the devotees from the different villages were pouring out their gratitude to Guru Nath for having graced their respective villages during Deepavali. The people of Ganagapur were getting wonderstruck as Guru Nath was amidst them at Ganagapur only, during the Deepavali.

Everyone realised and understood the omnipresence and omnipotence of Guru Nath. Everyone burst into singing the glories of the Lord. Guru Nath indeed is the Supreme Purusha of the *Purushasukta* – 'Sahasraseersha Purusha, Sahasraksha Sahasrapad', with his hands, eyes and feet everywhere.

THUS ENDS THE FORTY-SEVENTH CHAPTER OF
SRI *GURU CHARITRA.*

Glory to the all-merciful, the omnipresent and the ever-responsive Guru Nath!

48

Farmer's Rich Harvest

This chapter describes how Guru Nath helped his farmer-devotee to get a rich harvest of crop, while all the crops of that area during that season were devastated by the cyclone.

Siddhamuni narrated to Namdharak another wonderful miracle of Guru Nath.

Every day, Guru Nath used to go to the Sangam for bathing and performing his *Anusthan*. Each time he went to and came back from the Sangam, a farmer, whose field was on the wayside, used to come forward and offer prostrations at his feet. The farmer was cultivating this field as a tenant, the owner being one of the landlords in the village. Twice every day the farmer used to have darshan and *pada-namaskar* of Guru Nath. One morning, while on his way to the Sangam, Guru Nath asked the farmer why he was so particular about his darshan that he would not miss it even on a single day. The farmer replied that his darshan was the protection for him and his family; it conferred him with immense benefits; his fields always yielded an excellent crop and had never experienced any crop failure though his neighbour-farmers suffered from frequent crop-failures. Because of this, he had not defaulted even a single time in his payment of rent to his landlord. His family had never been suffering from want over the years, ever since he started doing his daily prostrations to him. The farmer added, 'And your darshan is ever a feast of joy for my eyes, it is the sustenance for my heart and soul. I can never afford to do without your darshan.' He prayed to Guru Nath that he should step into his field and bless it with the casting of his look and the touch of his feet. Guru Nath was pleased with the simple-hearted and guileless faith of the farmer and blessed him walking to the field, stepping in it. The farmer's joy knew no bounds at this.

Guru Nath took a glance at the whole field. The *jowar* crop planted was coming up well; in a month's time, the crop was to be ready for harvest.

Guru Nath said to the farmer, 'Will you listen to me and do what I say?' The farmer immediately replied, 'Master! I will do anything, whatever you want me to do.' Guru Nath said to him, 'Cut down the crop, up to the stalks, today itself,' and went away on his way to the Sangam. The farmer rushed to his landlord, to fix the latter's share for the year's crop. The landlord said, as the prospect for that year's crop was very good and as it was much better than in the previous year, he should pay him twice the quantity of grains over that of the previous year. The farmer instantly agreed to it and rushed back to the field. He hired a few labourers and started cutting down the crop. His wife and neighbours rushed there, trying to stop him. Has he gone mad to cut away the crop when only a few more weeks of waiting would yield a rich harvest? They wondered. They even went and complained to the landlord asking him to intervene. The farmer sent back word to the landlord, that he (the latter) had no business to interfere. He said, 'I have enough stock of grain in my house from my last year's harvest. Whatever quantity of grain I agreed to give him from this year's harvest, I will give it away now itself, from my old stock. Nobody has any right to stop me. Sri Guru Nath told me to cut off the crop today itself and I must carry out his command, even at the cost of my life.' To this his wife protested, 'What does the ascetic know of farming? Both yourself and your Guru Nath are mad!' She started crying; so also the children. Brushing them all aside, he went ahead and chopped off the crop before midday itself.

When Guru Nath was returning from the Sangam, he saw what the farmer had done. He said to him, 'What have you done? I only told you jokingly and you went ahead and cut off the crop, without any forethought.' To this, the farmer replied, 'Master, I do not care what will happen. Your word is all that matters to me. What I ever need is only your grace.' Guru Nath said, 'So be it!' and then went away to the *Math*.

Hardly had a week passed after the farmer cut off the crop, than his wife was creating hell in the house all the time for what he had done. Then all of a sudden, there was a heavy cyclone. All the crops were submerged under water and were destroyed. The food that had come near the mouth was snatched away by the cruel hands of Nature. All the long months of labour of the farmers had become a total waste. But lo! what has happened to the devotee farmer's land? The roots of the cut crop, now watered well by the cyclonic rains, put forth stalks and soon yielded a very rich harvest. The year's yield was many more times than what he ever got in any of the years ever before.

The wife and the children were overjoyed and realised Guru Nath's solicitude for them and the grace he showered upon them. The wife greatly repented for her quarrel with her husband and especially for having tauntingly remarked, 'What does the ascetic know of farming?'

The farmer and his wife went to Guru Nath, paid their obeisance to him and offered him worship. Guru Nath was pleased with them and blessed them saying that they would always be prosperous and Goddess Mahalakshmi would be residing in their house for ever. Further, he also told them that both the husband and wife would attain liberation in this life itself and would be freed from the cycle of birth and death for ever.

When the farmer went to deliver the agreed share of the grains to the landlord, the latter, now realising the goodness and the devout nature of the farmer, refused to accept the excess and took only the quantity that he used to normally take every year.

The farmer distributed a lot of the harvest grains to other farmers and to the people of the village who had lost the crops that year.

THUS ENDS THE FORTY-EIGHTH CHAPTER OF
SRI *GURU CHARITRA*.

Glory to the all-merciful, the omnipresent and the ever-responsive Guru Nath!

49

Holiness of Ganagapur

This chapter describes *Theertha Mahima* of Ganagapur and the Bhima-Amaraja Sangam and of *Papavinasini Theertha,* etc., and how Guru Nath's sister Ratnai was cured of her skin disease. Guru Nath is also said to have narrated about Guru Gita to his disciples in this chapter. Guru Gita is full of spiritual import. The primeval and Supreme Guru, Lord Siva himself has given the Guru Gita to humanity. The Lord says, 'Except through Guru, there is no other way to God.' The same is implied in the saying of Lord Jesus, 'I am the way; I and Father are one.'

Namdharak asked Siddhamuni why did Guru Nath love Ganagapur so dearly that he came there and made it his abode almost permanently, and what was the merit possessed by Ganagapur to become the Dattatreya Punya Theertha. *Siddhamuni said that Sri Narasimha Saraswati himself had once explained this and narrated it as under.*

On the occasion of one *Aswiyuja Bahula Chaturdasi,* preceding Deepavali, devotees from various places, as usual, came to Ganagapur for Guru Nath's darshan and for offering their worship to him. Guru Nath said to them, 'Let us all make a pilgrimage and have the darshan of Kasi, Gaya and Prayaga.' The devotees were all excited and said to him, 'Please permit us to get prepared for the journey; we will bring along with us our families too and so also the provisions required for the journey.' Guru

Nath laughed and said, 'Where do you think are Kasi, Gaya and
Prayaga? They are all in the precincts of Ganagapur itself, believe
me. I will show them all to you today itself.'

Guru Nath took the devotees to the Sangam and said, 'This
Bhima-Amaraja Sangam itself is Prayaga. This is as holy as
Prayaga. Besides, as the Amaraja River flows here as Uttara
Vahini (in the northern direction), this place is as holy as Kasi
itself. There are eight most sacred *theerthas* in and around here.
It will not be possible for even the thousand-tongued Adisesha
to describe the glory and power of these eight *theerthas*.' The
devotees asked Guru Nath to tell them about the origin of the
Amaraja River. Guru Nath told them that in the Jalandhara
Purana, the origin of the Amaraja River was described. This was
narrated briefly as under.

Jallandhar was an *asura*. He was mighty in strength and
conquered all the gods. A mysterious and strange power was
protecting Jallandhar and made him invincible. If his head
was chopped off, a new head would sprout up in its place
instantly. If a drop of blood was shed from his body, out of
that a new demon would be born. Thus the armies of
Jallandhar went on multiplying, for outnumbering the
armies of the gods. The gods were routed in the battle waged
by Jallandhar and they had to flee from their heavenly
abode. Indra fled to Lord Siva and narrated to him their
plight, and prayed that he should save them. Lord Siva
created *Sanjeevani Udak Ghat* (the vessel of *Sanjeevani*
water) and gave it to Indra and told him if the *Sanjeevani*
water was sprinkled on the dead bodies of the *devas*, they
would also rise alive. While Indra was carrying the vessel of
the *Sanjeevani* water, a little water from the vessel spilled
over and fell on the earth, and it became the Sanjeevani
River, and this river later came to be called the Amaraja
River. A bath in the river at the time of solar and lunar
eclipses and on new moon and *Ekadasi* days, will be most

sanctifying and will confer great merit. There are many other great *theerthas*, namely the *Manohar Theertha*, the Aswatha tree which is indeed *Kalpavriksha* itself, Sankar Bhuvan, Sangameswara and Nandikeswar, etc. He further narrated one anecdote.

There was once a *Bharadwaja Gotra* Brahmin called Goswami, in the village called Nagesa, which is not far away from here. He was very pious and devout. He had rid himself of all worldly attachments and spent all his time in worship and meditation of Lord Siva. He had two elder brothers named Eswara and Panduranga respectively. Once both the brothers planned to make a pilgrimage to Kasi. They asked their younger brother Goswami also to accompany them in the pilgrimage. But the latter replied, 'Visweswara is here only; this place of ours itself is the holy Kasi. All the *theerthas* abide here only. I see them all here only, why go to distant Kasi?' The brothers said that if it was really so why was it that they were not able to see it all themselves. Goswami then prayed to Siva that he should make all the holy *theerthas* of Kasi get manifest there so that his brothers also could see and get convinced. Instantly, the manifestations began to make their appearance around there. The *murti* of Visweswara made its appearance out of one of the *kundas* there; they saw the Bhagirathi waters welling out from a spring. The brothers could witness all the *theerthas* which they heard to be existing in Kasi. They were thrilled and spellbound.

Sri Narasimha Saraswati described to them the *Sangam Mahima* which is no less than that of the holy Kasi. He took them to the *Papavinasini Theertha*, which is a few miles away from there and told them the merit one would earn by bathing in there. He said, 'The waters of *Papavinasini* will cleanse the *jiva* of all the sins accumulated over all the past births. Ganagapur is itself the veritable Kasi.'

Siddhamuni told Namdharak about Papavinasini Mahima, *through another anecdote.*

Sri Narasimha Saraswati had a younger sister called Ratnai. She was overtaken by leprosy due to a grave sin she committed in her former life. A cat had just given birth to five kittens in a pot. The woman without seeing, had poured water in the pot and put it on fire for getting hot water. The new-born kittens had died. As a result of this, the woman in her new birth was afflicted with leprosy. She came to Sri Narasimha Saraswati praying to him to relieve her of this dreadful disease. Sri Narasimha Saraswati told her of the sin she had committed in her previous life, of causing the death of the five kittens, although it was done unknowingly. He asked her to go to the *Papavinasini* and stay there and to take bath daily in the holy waters there. She was soon relieved of her disease.

Sri Narasimha Saraswati took the devotees along with him to *Koti-Theertha* and explained its *mahima* to them. He took them to *Rudrapad-Theertha* also and said that it possesses all the power and merit of the *Gaya-Theertha*. The devotees performed there all the rites enjoined upon when one visits Gaya. Guru Nath took them to the other holy places also, namely Kalleswara shrine, *Manmadh Theertha*, etc. He told the devotees to be doing *abhisheka* to Kalleswara throughout the month of *Sravana,* and *Deeparadhana* in the month of *Kartika.*

Guru Nath thus explained the *Ganagapur Mahima* and *Ashta Theertha Mahima* in and around Ganagapur.

THUS ENDS THE FORTY-NINTH CHAPTER OF
SRI *GURU CHARITRA.*

Glory to the all-merciful, the omnipresent and the ever responsive Guru Nath!

Note

In some versions of *Guru Charitra,* it is said that Guru Nath relates the Guru-Gita to the disciples in this chapter.

The Guru-Gita is from the Skanda Purana. It was said to have been narrated to Mother Parvati by Lord Siva, when Parvati entreated him to enlighten her about the path by treading which the *jiva* can attain enlightenment and liberation. The Lord then narrated to her the Guru-Gita, which says, 'It is by devoted service at the feet of the Guru alone, that one gets cleansed of all sins and, ultimately, attains the Supreme.'

The Guru-Gita emphasises that without the helping hand of the Guru, one can never hope to reach the goal. The Guru indeed is the way to reach the goal; he is indeed the link between man and God between the *jiva* and Bramhan. Unless the Guru transmits his own soul-impulses to the disciple the later will not gain spiritual wisdom.

The Guru-Gita advocates that the keys to the doors of the mansion of wisdom remain only with the Guru. It also describes the characteristics of the Guru. Unless one is fully enlightened and had intuited the Truth himself, he is not entitled to be a Guru. The Guru-Gita also tells how one should approach the Guru. One should approach the Guru with great humility, with full and unwavering faith (*sraddha*) and with a burning yearning to attain liberation.

The Lord concludes the Guru-Gita observing that the importance of my words will be truly appreciated by those noble aspirants who are devoted to the Guru and God in equal measure, and do not differentiate at all between the two. The truly wise man always dips in the holy waters of Guru-Gita, for it cuts at the root of *sansara* and snaps asunder the ties of bondage. It opens the gates to freedom – to the consciousness and awareness of the reality and the universality of spirit.

The Upanishads have given 'The Four Sacred Maha Vakyas' (The Grand Proclamations), for the disciple's *sadhana*. These are—

(a)   *Prajnanam Bramha* (pure consciousness or awareness is Bramhan): this is called Guru's *Upadesa Vakya.*

(b)   *Tatwamasi* (that thou art. The goal you are seeking is indeed thine own self): this is called Guru's *Adesa Vakya.*

(c)   *Ayamatma Bramha* (this self of mine is indeed itself the Bramhan, the absolute self): this is *Abhyasa Vakya.*

(d)   *Aham Bramhasmi* (I am myself the Bramhan. The pure consciousness within me—the core of my being is indeed itself the Bramhan): this is the *Anubhava Vakya.*

The Guru from his *Anubhava* (from his personal experiences) gives the *Upadesa* and *Adesa Vakyas,* which the disciple listens to with full faith and devotion. This is *Sravana.*

The disciple then contemplates upon the truths enunciated by the Guru. He does *Manana* over the statements made by the Guru and then takes to *Nidhidhyasana* upon the truth, with full and implicit faith and devotion. When the disciple's whole mind gets gradually focused on the self, the mind melts off and the truth of the self flashes itself in his (the disciple's) awareness. He also then gains the *Anubhava Jnana,* like his Guru. He exclaims in divine awareness 'Aham Bramhasmi—Sivoham'.

As per the *Bhramara-Keetaka Nyaya,* whereby the (ugly-looking) beetle gets metamorphosed and transfigured into the beautiful Bhramara itself, so also the *jiva,* stricken with ignorance and all the afflictions of the worldly life, attains enlightenment and blossoms forth and begins to shine in his atmic (Divine) splendour, just like his Guru, through *Nidhidhyasana* on the Guru and the *Guropadesa.*

For this great and grand attainment in one's life, what is the primary and indispensable requisite is implicit faith in Guru's words and devotion to him. Then Guru's grace flows by itself and lifts the *sadhaka* to the higher and exalted states of consciousness and to the ultimate truth and reality.

50

Guru Nath's Blessings on the Nawab

This chapter illustrates the merit one earns by visiting holy people. The Nawab who was a washer-man in his previous life but born into a royal family in this life because of the blessings he had from Sri Sripada Srivallabha, gains the darshan of Sri Narasimha Saraswati and gets cured of his physical ailment and also attains spiritual liberation.

Siddhamuni, earlier told Namdharak the story of the rajak*, the washer-man devotee of Sri Sripada Srivallabha.*

The *rajak* used to serve Sripada Srivallabha with great love and devotion. Sripada Srivallabha was very much pleased with his services and as a reward for the services he rendered, blessed him so that he would enjoy all regal pleasures and would be freed from his life of drudgery. Actually the *rajak* was secretly longing in his heart of hearts for regal pleasures. Sripada Srivallabha, divining the *rajak's* thoughts uttered his blessings; but then the *rajak* said that he was too old already, and any joys were worth enjoying only when one was young. Therefore, he prayed that the fulfilment of the blessings of the Guru be deferred to his next birth. The Guru said, 'Let it be so!'

---

* Although the *rajak*, too had his sense-cravings like most of us, yet his devotion to the Guru was the greatest redeeming feature in his case. If our sense-cravings do not drown down and obliterate away our faith in God, we too can hope to be saved. The episode of the *rajak*-turned-into-Nawab holds out this hope to us all — the weak-minded and sense-crazy mortals.

The *rajak* was born in his next birth in the Muslim Nawab's family of Vaidurinagar (Bidar). When he became the ruler, he was very kind to all the subjects, treating the Hindus and the Muslims alike and all the subjects as his own children. He used to respect Brahmins very much. The *maulvis* used to feel envious and jealous of this. They tried to turn him against the Hindus, but the king never heeded them. He was very spiritual-minded and believed that all the religions—even Hinduism and Islam— are but different pathways to the same God. He firmly believed all the Hindu gods are but different facets of the same Allah and that the various idols and forms which Hindus worship are but an aid for purifying and to bring the mind to one-pointedness, which ultimately leads to experiencing and realisation of the Formless—the *nirankara,* the concept of Allah in Islam. He was trying to establish harmony and cordiality in the relationship between the two religious communities. By and large, he was loved equally by both the communities among his subjects.

The Nawab developed an ulcer on his body. He tried many *hakims* and *Vaidyas* but none could cure him. The pain and irritation was acute and was becoming unbearable for him. He was advised that if he visited the *Papavinasini Theertha* and took bath in its holy waters, he might get cured. Further he was told that a Mahapurusha darshan like that of Sri Narasimha Saraswati who resided at Ganagapur, would certainly cure him of his ailment.

Sri Narasimha Saraswati foresaw that the Nawab was planning a visit to Ganagapur for redress of his ailment. He envisaged also that hereafter, besides the already heavy influx of Hindus and Muslims, people from other communities also would be pouring into Ganagapur with the result that the serene atmosphere of the place would be disturbed. He thought that it was time now for him to renounce his incarnated form and assume his invisible self. However, this would mean that the influx of people desiring to meet Guru Nath and seek his blessings for the mere fulfilment of their worldly desires or out of sheer curiosity would be arrested, though his sincere devotees and earnest spiritual aspirants would still continue to come to Ganagapur.

The Nawab came with his retinue up to *Papavinasini Theertha*. There he saw a *yogi* coming to him. The Nawab, after making his salutations to the *yogi*, prayed him to help his ailment to be cured. The *yogi* told him the same what was advised to him earlier by the Brahmin priests – that with the mere darshan of a *Mahanubhava* anything could be cured, and even death would flee away from him. Indeed such a *Mahanubhava* was Sri Narasimha Saraswati of Ganagapur. The *yogi* told him that he should proceed to Ganagapur and take the darshan of Guru Nath. To implant faith and conviction in the Nawab about *Sant Darshan Prabhav* (the great benefit one earns by visiting a holy person) the *yogi* narrated the following anecdote.

There used to be one Brahmin living in Avanti Nagar. The Brahmin took to licentious life. He started eating meat also, besides being addicted to women and wine. He took to a concubine called Pingala but who was quite faithful to him. One day a Muni named Rishabha happened to knock at Pingala's house, asking for *bhiksha*. Pingala received him with great respect. The Brahmin also joined her in honouring him. They both worshipped him with flowers, smeared his body and bathed his feet with perfumed water. They sipped his *Charan-Theertha* and entertained him with delicious food. They made him rest there. They massaged his feet and he had a sound sleep and rest. They kept awake the whole night attending upon him. Next morning, the ascetic-guest very pleased, left after blessing them. After a time, both the Brahmin and Pingala died.

Because of the Muni's blessings, the Brahmin was born in a royal family in his next birth. His father's name was

Vajrabahu and the mother's name was Sumati. The king had many other wives, but Sumati was the queen-consort (Patrani). The king and queen were very happy at the birth of the prince. But the other wives of the king were very jealous of Sumati and they were all the more worried that thereafter, because of his love for the child, all the king's attention would be centred on Sumati alone exclusively, and that they would be totally neglected and would be relegated to an inferior status. They plotted to kill the queen and her child and they one day poisoned the food served to the queen and the child. The bodies of the queen and the child developed most unsightly lesions. There started oozing out pus from the lesions, emitting foul odour. The *Vaidyas* tried their best to cure the lesions but it was of no avail. The disease was proclaimed incurable.

The king became very averse to the queen and the child; his other wives also weaned him away in their favour. He came to a decision to get rid of the queen and the child. One day he called his charioteer and asked him that he should take the queen and the child into the recesses of the forest and leave them there as a prey to the wild animals. The charioteer took the queen and the child and left them in the forest. The queen and the child could not find anything to eat; they were very hungry. She was plaintively crying, praying to God that he should end their lives as they could not bear the misery any longer. Hearing the wailing, some cowherd-boys came to her and asked her and the child to accompany them. They soon came to know that she was a queen. Although both of them had been overtaken by a dreadful disease, they took them to the palace of their Vaisya-king, whose name was Padmakar and who was very kind-hearted. The king entrusted the mother and the child to the care of the maid-servants, asking them to look after the two very well. Although Sumati and her child were being looked after very well there, their disease was however becoming worse and worse. One day the son died, and the mother was inconsolable. At this juncture, Rishabha Muni happened to come to that place. Hearing the wailing, he enquired as to what had happened. When he heard about the death of the prince, he could intuitively know who the child was. He recognised that the boy in his previous life was the same Brahmin who served him, though for a day but yet served with great devotion together with Pingala when he had visited the house of the latter. Accompanied by the king, the Muni approached the woman and tried to comfort her. He said life is like a bubble which is transient anyway and would burst off anytime. He said as death cannot be defied by anybody, we will have to reconcile ourselves to it and face it. But the woman was inconsolable and she was preparing to kill herself. The Muni was moved with pity. He smeared the dead body of the child with sacred ash (*vibhuti*) uttering some mantras, and also put a little of it in the child's mouth. He gave the *vibhuti* to Sumati also and asked her to smear it all over her body. Lo! the child rose up as if from sleep, his body shining golden bright and having no traces at all of the disease. Same was the case with the mother. The queen fell at the feet of the Muni and poured out tears of gratitude.

The boy later came to be called 'Bhadrayuver', i.e., one who has secured (assured) longevity. When he grew up, he became king and lived for a long time. Such is the power of the darshan of a *Mahanubhava*.

After narrating, as above, the *yogi* told the Nawab that if he also sought the darshan of a saint and had his blessings, he would also certainly get rid of his disease. The *yogi* asked the Nawab to go to Ganagapur. The Nawab came to Ganagapur, and started enquiring where he could meet Sri Guru Nath. He was told that Sri Narasimha Saraswati had gone to the Sangam. The Nawab went to the Sangam. He saw Sri Narasimha saraswati there and paid his obeisance to him. Guru Nath said, 'Oh, *rajaka*! Don't you remember you were a washer-man and you used to worship me? Why have you taken so long to come to me?' As Guru Nath was talking thus his whole previous life flashed in the Nawab's memory. He fell at the feet of Guru Nath, with tears of devotion and gratitude welling out from his heart. All the devotion he used to have for Sripada Srivallabha in his previous life surged forth again.

The Nawab prayed that Guru Nath should relieve him of his ailment. Guru Nath told him, 'Show me where is your ulcer?' As the Nawab was trying to remove his coat and show him his ulcer, lo! there wasn't any trace of the ulcer at all. The Nawab's joy knew no bounds. Further, in the presence of Guru Nath, he felt as much intense joy as does a long lost son on finding his mother again.

The Nawab prayed to Guru Nath that he should visit his kingdom and bless it. Guru Nath said that it was then getting late for his forenoon *anushthan* and he had to rush to *Papavinasini Theertha* immediately. He told him he could come and meet him there later. Saying thus, Guru Nath, along with his retinue of disciples, disappeared and in a trice reached Papavinasini, which is 44 *krosa* away from Ganagapur. Some of his devotees, prominent among whom was Nagnath, the son of Sayamdeo, came for his darshan there. They worshipped Guru Nath and performed Samaradhana. Guru Nath at that time graced their houses and blessed all their family members. It was nearing evening time and Guru Nath told them that the Nawab would be arriving now with all his royal retinue for his darshan.

The Nawab and his retinue, riding on their horses, reached Papavinasini by the evening and had Guru Nath's darshan. He fell at Guru Nath's feet and again prayed that he should visit his kingdom.

Guru Nath visited Vaidurinagar. He was accorded the grandest welcome. All streets and houses were decorated with festoons and flowers. The roads were sprinkled with fragrant water mixed with musk and sandal. The queens received him doing *aarti*. The Brahmins sang Vedic hymns.

Sri Narasimha Saraswati was made to sit on a specially decorated throne, bedecked with precious stones, garlands, etc. The Nawab himself was waiting upon him. Guru Nath asked the king whether all his *Vasanas* were fully satiated yet or not. The Nawab said he had enough of them and what his heart yearned for now was only doing service at the feet of the Master. Guru Nath advised him that he should now leave the throne to his son and retire to Giri Parvata (Srisailam) and take to a life of contemplation. He assured him he would give him darshan there and grant him liberation. Saying thus to the Nawab, Guru Nath returned to Ganagapur.

The Nawab did as advised by Guru Nath. He took to intense meditation. He had the vision of Guru Nath and earned liberation — the freedom of the spirit, the true sovereignty.

THUS ENDS THE FIFTIETH CHAPTER OF
SRI *GURU CHARITRA.*

Glory to the all-merciful, the omnipresent and the ever-responsive Guru Nath!

51

The Mahaprasthan

In this chapter, the Mahaprasthan of Guru Nath is described. Guru Nath has decided to withdraw his physical form. He sets out from Ganagapur leaving his *Nirguna padukas* there after enshrining his presence and power in them. He leaves for the holy Srisaila Parvata with four of his disciples. From there, he sets out on a flower-float on the waters of Patala Ganga to his eternal abode. He sends back a cluster of flowers as a token of his message and blessings to his disciples, which comes floating against the current.

The final message of Guru Nath to humanity is embodied in a nutshell in this chapter. He assures that through mere remembrance of him one can earn his grace. He also tells about the great merit which the *Guru Charitra Parayana* confers.

Mad-Bhaktah Yatra Gayanti,
Tatra Thisthami Narada

Oh Narada! My true abode is where people sing my name with devotion...

As we have seen in the previous chapter, Siddhamuni told Namdharak about the visit of Guru Nath to Vaidurinagar at the pleading of the Nawab. Siddha Yogi continues the narrative.

Guru Nath was accorded a most regal welcome by the Nawab and was received with overwhelming devotion by all the sections

of people of the city. Following the visit, Guru Nath's name and
fame spread far and wide, and many Muslim people also started
pouring into Ganagapur for Guru Nath's darshan and for redress
of their difficulties. With the constant influx, the serene
atmosphere of Ganagapur was getting disturbed. Guru Nath had
already been hinting to his devotees for some time past, that he
would be leaving for the *Kadali-Van* (banana-grove) at Srisaila
Parvata before long.

One day he called all his devotees and the people of
Ganagapur to the *Math*. He announced that he was bidding
goodbye to Ganagapur and was setting out on his pilgrimage to
Srisailam. All started sobbing. What would be Ganagapur without
Guru Nath? Guru Nath was its sole life and light. Seeing how
grief-stricken all were, Guru Nath announced that although they
would not be able to see his physical form at Ganagapur, yet he
would be abiding there for ever, in his invisible form (in his grace
body). He would continue to answer all prayers, and would
continue to shower his grace on all the supplicants. He further
said that wherever he be, he would continue to visit the Sangam
in the mornings every day for his bath, and by midday he would
be visiting the *Math* unfailingly, though he would not be visible
to the human eyes. He assured them that he would be in his
Nirguna padukas in the *Math* and that they would be the reservoir
and repository of all spiritual power and that worship offered to
them would be reaching him only. He further said that worship
offered to the Aswatha tree was worship unto the *Kalpavriksha*.
The Aswatha tree would fulfil all the desires of the supplicants.
Comforting and assuring the people thus, he set out from
Ganagapur. He asked his disciples, except four of them, to go
out on pilgrimage, and assured them that he would be ever with
them.

All the people of Ganagapur were following him. Guru
Nath told them that they should return to their homes. He again
assured them, that his presence would continue to be felt at the

Math, by all devotees, by the mere remembrance or recall of his name.

The people had to retrace their steps with a heavy heart homewards. They were feeling that their life-breath had ebbed out of them. The void caused in their life by Guru Nath's leaving from Ganagapur could never be filled up and would remain so for ever. Their hearts sank down in despair and gloom.

At the *Math* they all stopped, their feet refusing to move from there. Why not we all end our lives here? that was their thought at the moment.

Lo! there was a flash of light in the *Math.* Guru Nath revealed himself before their eyes, smiling and holding out his *Abhaya Hastha* (the raised palm indicating assurance and benediction). The people were enlivened. Their gloom had melted away; and with faith enriched in the omnipresence of Guru Nath, they slowly returned to their homes.

Guru Nath along with his four chosen disciples, reached the *Kadali-Van* on the banks of Patala Ganga at the foot of the Srisaila Parvata. Thereafter, Guru Nath asked the disciples to prepare a float with banana trunks and leaves. The float was prepared. It was bedecked with flowers. Guru Nath asked them to place the float in the river. He stepped into the float and seated himself on it. The disciples offered obeisance and worship to him, while their hearts were bursting out with grief at the impending separation from their beloved Lord. Guru Nath cheered them up and told them: 'My dear children, I am fully aware of the anguish of your hearts at the thought that I am leaving you. But, I assure you again, I shall be with you forever and especially at Ganagapur. I will be showering my full grace there on all supplicants, who are sincere, earnest and faithful. Only to make myself inaccessible to agnostics, atheists and the faithless, I am taking to this *Prasthan.* But even so, every day I will be present at the Amaraja Sangam for my morning bath, and will be visiting the Ganagapur *Math* for receiving the *bhiksha*. Be sure about this, and do not give place to any doubt. I will never be leaving Ganagapur. I will be accepting all worship that will be offered at the *Math*. Convey the following advice of mine, which I am giving to you now, to all ...

'All pilgrims to Ganagapur should first take their dip in the holy waters of the Bhima-Amaraja Sangam. If they bathe in all the *Ashta theerthas*, the merit will be even far more and will be several-fold. The Aswatha tree, which is near the Sangam, is as holy as the *Kalpavriksha* itself. They should make *Pradakshina* around the Aswatha tree. They should offer worship to the *Nirguna padukas* at the *Math*. All three times of the day, they should do *aarti* to the *padukas*. Whoever offers worship to the Chintamani Ganapati deity there, will earn fulfilment of all his desires. Believe me, I will be residing in the house of every devotee, ever serving them and showering all grace on them. I will be like the Kamadhenu in the front yard of their house, like the *Kalpavriksha* in the backyard of the house and like Lakshmi, Saraswati and Parvati residing inside the house. With mere remembrance of me, I will respond to everyone.

'Remember also how fond of music I am. Therefore, during *Devataarchana* time, (during the worship-time) you should invariably also do bhajan. There is nothing like bhajan to bind me down in your homes and hearts. In whichever house my name is chanted, there is no scope for poverty or diseases to come anywhere near there. Poverty and disease, all quickly take to flight from there. The inmates of the house will be blessed with longevity; that house will be ever prosperous and aplenty. The house will be ever happy and joyous with healthy and playful children and will never be in want of anything.

'Further, let me also tell you about the supreme merit one will earn by listening to or reading my *Charitra* (*Guru Charitra*). It will be the panacea for all ills. In the *Kali Yuga*, it will be like the *Kalpalatika,* the ever wish-fulfilling celestial creeper. It will be like *Chintamani,* the celestial diamond, bestower of all prosperity. Now I bid you adieu, you stay back. I will be sending flowers as my *prasad* to you, no sooner than I reach my destination. The *prasad* will confer on you immense good.' Saying thus, he disappeared out of their sight.

It was *Bahudanya* year, *Uttarayana, Bahula Padyani,* Friday. The *Nakshatra* was *Pushyami* and was especially an auspicious time with *Brihaspati* entering the *Kanya Rasi.* Such was the time of the Mahaprasthan of Guru Nath.

The disciples stayed on there only, unable to decide what to do and, so to say, immobilised. Their minds were blank. At this juncture, a boat came towards them. The boatmen told them they had a message for them from a *yatri sanyasi* who gave his name as Sri Narasimha Saraswati. They said that they saw on the waters a *Yati,* golden-splendoured body, holding a *danda* and a *kamandal,* and wearing golden *padukas.* He was speeding fast on a flower chariot. He told them, (the boatmen) that they should give this message to his disciples. 'Tell them it is the ardent wish of their Guru, Sri Narasimha Saraswati, that they should soon get back to Ganagapur and that he will be sending them *Prasad-Pushpa* as a token of his blessings.' No sooner did the boatmen say thus, than four big flowers of celestial beauty came there floating against the current. The boatmen picked up the flowers and gave the disciples one flower each. The four disciples were Sayamdeo, Kavishwar Nandi, Narahari-Kavi and Siddha himself.

Siddhamuni said to Namdharak, 'As you have been born in the line of Sayamdeo, you have won the merit of listening to this glorious Guru Charitra. *In narrating this to you, I feel greatly blessed by Guru Nath and feel supremely happy.'*

THUS ENDS THE FIFTY-FIRST CHAPTER OF
SRI *GURU CHARITRA.*

Glory to the all-merciful, the omnipresent and the ever-responsive Guru Nath!

EPILOGUE

Listening to Siddhamuni's narrative, Namdharak was lost in ecstacy and was plunged into *Nirvikalpa Samadhi,* the super-conscious state. His body and breath became still and immobile but his face was shining with a new radiance and splendour, reflecting the inner state of bliss and beatitude, the bliss of *yogic* union with the Lord of his heart, namely Guru Nath.

Siddhamuni was happy seeing the spiritually exalted state of Namdharak; listening to (*sravana* of) *Guru Charitra* and his absorption in it had elevated him (Namdharak) into the realms of divine consciousness, releasing the spirit into freedom from the bondage of ignorance and from the thraldom of the body–senses–mind complex (the physical, vital and mental sheaths). Siddhamuni quietly touched him and brought him back to his normal consciousness, i.e., on to the physical plane of consciousness. Namdharak fell at Siddhamuni's feet, pouring out his gratitude to him for narrating the *Guru Charitra,* which had obliterated and removed his ignorance and endowed him with a clear vision of the only truth and reality, i.e., Guru Nath, who is the divine self seated in the hearts of all and in the entire creation.

Namdharak was a blessed soul. We too should be able to attain that state of realisation, provided we too, like Namdharak, shed our ego and surrender ourselves at the feet of the Guru and flood our hearts with devotion to him. The *Guru Charitra,* the spiritual treasure box as bequeathed to us by

Saraswati Gangadhar, will come to our succour in the spiritual ascent, as it did in the case of Namdharak. Let us take resort to it and constantly seek guidance for it.

A Quick Resume

Before we close the reading of the book presently, with salutations to Guru Nath, perhaps a brief review of the contents of the book, much more so, a deeper look into it, so as to grasp the inner significance of the various anecdotes narrated in the chapters, will not be without its reward and benefit to us. The inner import of the various anecdotes narrated may not become patent and clear to us, with just a single reading of the book. Hence let us have at least one more glimpse into it.

It is said that *sravana, manana* and *nidhidhyasana,* i.e., listening to or reading, dwelling upon what has been listened to or read, and contemplating upon the truth/s, is the whole process of spiritual *sadhana.* Thus *adhyayana* (reading and re-reading), and doing *vichara* (making mental enquiry and intellectual effort to grasp and understand the inner truths), is necessary to derive the full benefit of any scripture, and this is what is expected to be done by us in the case of *Guru Charitra* too. Here we will analyse the broader features of the entire text.

Guru Charitra is a sacred confluence (triveni sangam) of karma, bhakti and jnana.

We should bear in mind that *Guru Charitra,* so to say, is a confluence of the three main paths of *sadhana* viz., karma (the path of dedicated work and selfless action), bhakti (the path of worship and devotion) and jnana (the path of enquiry and knowledge). All these find a homogeneous integration in *Guru Charitra.*

From the first till the twenty-fourth chapter, i.e., from Namdharak's setting out upon his spiritual quest till Trivikrama

Bharati had *Viswarupa* Darshan, it is considered as 'Jnana Kanda'. The culmination (fruition) of the path of Jnana is when one is able to experience the self, i.e., the oneness in all. Trivikrama Bharati gets a vision of Guru Nath in all, in everyone and everywhere. That indeed is an instance of the attainment of the state of Jnana.

From the twenty-fifth chapter which describes the egoistic and fame-greedy pandits' boastful challenge till the thirty-seventh chapter wherein is delineated in detail what is dharma (the righteous actions and righteous way of living) and what is adharma (unrighteous actions and unrighteous way of living), it is called Karma Kanda. Karma is indeed synonymous with dharma.

From the thirty-eighth chapter wherein thousands of people are sumptuously fed in Samaradhana from a meagre quantity of food cooked from a small measureful of rice by a poor devotee, till the Mahaprasthan chapter, it is Bhakti Kanda.

Karma, Bhakti and Jnana are all equally important in spiritual evolution. *Guru Charitra* integrates and harmonises them all.

Karma is necessary till one is able to get over his obsession with body. One will have to weaken down the sway of his ego, make his heart more expansive with concern for others. One should get over the feeling 'I am just this body'. Karma will also purify us of the *mala* (the impurities of the mind).

In Bhakti, one's ego gets sublimated, he feels he is but a servant of God. His emotions, thoughts and love—all get focused on god (alone). He feels that he is nobody and that God is all. Bhakti also helps us to quell the 'Vikshepa', the agitations and turbulences in our mind.

In Jnana, one would have transcended all senses of separateness. He will experience the essential—oneness and unity of all existence. He sees God in all and all in God, and his love encompasses all beings. He clearly experiences the divine principle linking together all the creation. He does not feel himself as a separate being and as apart from others. He feels he is part and parcel of the divine whole. (Jnana will also dispel 'Avarana' and remove the veil of ignorance, which deprive us of our atmic vision and awareness). Thus Karma, Bhakti and Jnana are all necessary to bring in total purification and regeneration of our mind and in our attaining of self-realisation.

Guru Charitra is the panacea for all the human-ills.

Guru Charitra is the panacea for all human ills, of the body, mind and spirit. It provides succour to all, viz., *arthas* (those who are in distress), *arthathis* (those who are seeking worldly and material benefits), *Mumukshus* (spiritual aspirants) and *Jnanis* (those who are established in and are well advanced on the spiritual path). Many of the anecdotes of *Guru Charitra* vouchsafe this truth. Its power in this respect is experienced even to this day. There is nothing which cannot be achieved through surrender at the feet of the Guru, and with his grace one's preordained destiny even can be overcome and circumvented. Law of faith outweighs and overrules the law of karma. At least it endows on us mental strength to bear through the vicissitudes of life with courage and equanimity. We will have to however leave things to his will and seek from him what will only be ultimately good for us.

Guru Charitra is a manual of moral and spiritual codes.

Guru Charitra emphasises first on ethical purity and excellence. One should adhere to dharma (to his ordained duties). When we all adhere to our dharma, then alone the harmony in the cosmos will sustain; otherwise we will transform the cosmos into chaos.

The codes of conduct for men and women have been enunciated in detail in *Guru Charitra*. It enjoins on Brahmins as the spiritual custodians of the community, extra responsibilities and rigorous disciplines. They are expected to conduct themselves as examples and guide for all others. They should always be radiating purity and moral, ethical and spiritual excellence.

Man is an imperfect and erring being. *Guru Charitra* accepts this human weakness. But error is not to be perpetuated nor can it be let off unatoned for. It has to be corrected and atoned for. For this, in *Guru Charitra,* the sins which we are prone to commit, the retributive consequences thereof unless we make atonement for them, are all listed. Sincere repentence, prayers, mantra-chanting, Rudra Japa, surrender at the feet of the Guru, etc., are said to expiate all sins. Sincere prayer smashes down mountain-loads of sin.

We come across incidents of *Bramha Rakshasas* in some of the chapters. *Bramha Rakshasa* are indeed none else but those who are ethically fallen and are paying for their sins through suffering. Without ethical excellence no progress will ever be possible in the spiritual path. *Guru Charitra* provides the correctives for man to gain moral rectitude and at the same time to secure also a foothold and scaffolding for his spiritual ascent. Behind all the anecdotes, in all the chapters throughout the text, there is a strong spiritual undercurrent flowing. The goal of human life is to attain union with Godhead, the *Antaryamin,* the in-dweller and controller of our hearts. In Namdharak we have the clearest example of how the mere listening of the *Guru Charitra* can lead one to the blessed state of realisation.

***

Lessons of Wisdom from Nature

It will be of interest here to know that Lord Dattatreya says that we will have to however learn initially the lessons of wisdom from Nature herself, who is the best teacher. He cites his own example to illustrate this truth and tells us from whom he had learnt and what each one of them teaches us.

(a) Earth (symbol of forbearance—Titiksha)

The earth teaches us the virtue of forbearance (endurance) by its own supreme example. It bears with unmatched and unexcelled patience all the injuries we inflict upon it and, furthermore, it does only good to us always by providing crops, fruits, etc. It looks after our very sustenance, in spite of our doing so much harm and injury to it.

(b) Water (the symbol of purity)

Water teaches us the quality of purity. Further, it cleanses and purifies whosoever and whatsoever comes into contact with it. Like water, we also should be ever pure, getting rid of lust, greed, anger, ego, jealousy, selfishness and such unspiritual traits and demonic qualities and should endeavour to exert a similar purifying influence on others too.

(c) Air (the symbol of non-attachment)

Air moves freely anywhere and everywhere, but it does not get attached to any place or object. We too, thus should imbibe the virtue of non-attachment.

(d) Sky (the symbol of untarnished personality)

The air, the clouds, the stars, the moon and the sun, all have their habitation in the sky. Yet the sky remains apart from them all. From this we learn that though the self, our true and real personality and being, looks to be in conjunction and mixed up with our body-mind complex, is in fact always apart and remains alone, untarnished and ever pure *(kevala)*. We should not, therefore, get mixed up and bound by the *upadhis* (adjuncts) and the superimpositions on our true self (on our true being).

(e) Fire (the symbol of spiritual wisdom)

Fire teaches us that we should always remain bright and be ever aglow with knowledge and awareness of the self, of our innate divine nature and potential.

(f) Moon (the symbol of intrinsic immutability, though appearing as constantly changing)

The moon is ever full but appears to be waxing and waning due to the shadow of the earth falling upon it and eclipsing its full form. Likewise, our Atman also, which in truth is ever the same and changeless, appears to the indiscriminate to be changing and undergoing all sorts of modifications, which actually only the *upadhis* (physical adjuncts), the superimpositions on the Atman are undergoing, but not the self itself.

(g) Sun (the symbol of the one self in all—Ekatmata)

The one sun when reflected in many pots of water appears as many. So also, the one Bramhan appears manifold by its reflection in so many bodies and forms. Atman (which is Bramhan) is always indeed one only.

(h) Pair of Pigeons (the perils of attachment)

There were once a pigeon-couple and their little ones. One day, the young ones got caught in the net of a fowler. Due to attachment to the young ones, the mother pigeon also flew after them and got caught in the net. Due to the attachment to the female-pigeon, the male-pigeon also flew near there and met with the same fate. Thus, all of them fell a prey to the fowler. Attachment leads to one's own ruin.

(i) Python (the symbol of contentment)

Just as the python does not move about for its food but lies in one place only, content with whatever it gets, so also the wise should learn to be content with whatever Providence provides for them.

(j) Ocean (the symbol of equanimity)

Hundreds of rivers will be flowing into it but the ocean remains unmoved. Thus whatever may come and happen in our lives, we should always maintain our equipoise.

(k) Bees (the evil of avarice)

Taking great pains, the bees collect and store the honey. But alas, the honey-gatherer comes and takes it all away. Similarly, man struggles all his life for amassing and hoarding wealth. And then death, which may knock him down any time, deprives him of all, (if he has not been deprived of it by others already meanwhile).

The snares of the senses, viz., sound, touch, sight, taste and smell are illustrated in the following examples: *(l)* to *(p)*.

(l) Musk Deer

The musk deer is a slave to its sense of sound (ear). The hunter entices it away by playing music, and it gets caught in his trap.

(m) Elephant

The elephant is a slave to the sense of touch. The male elephant, driven by lust, falls into a pit attracted by a dummy female-elephant put there as a trap by the elephant-catchers.

(n) Moth

The moth is a slave to the sense of sight (eye). Attracted by the brilliance of fire, it flies into it and gets burnt to death.

(o) Fish

The fish is a slave to the sense of taste (tongue). Coveting food, it bites the bait and is caught and meets its end.

(p) Black Bee

The black bee is a slave to the sense of smell (nose). Attracted by the fragrance of flower, it hops from flower to flower and gets stuck in the petals and dies.

The earlier examples *(l* to *p)* teach that if we yield ourselves to the lures of the senses we are doomed, but if we can restrain our senses we will be saved. We have seen that enslavement to one sense alone has caused such havoc in the above instances. Man has all the five senses, and if he pampers them, alas, what doom will he be meeting?

(q) The Dancing Girl—Pingala (the virtue of desirelessness)

One night, Pingala was tired looking for customers and felt disappointed and worried. But she thought, 'Why not remain content with what I have?' With this thought, instantly, a sense of peace came over her.

It is desire that brings and breeds worry. Contentment, desirelessness and abandonment of hope, always endow peace and true happiness.

(r) The Raven (the evil of clinging to possessions)

Once a raven picked up a piece of flesh. It was pursued and hurt by other birds. But when in desperation she dropped the piece of flesh, all the chasing birds left her and then she felt completely relieved and was happy.

It is our possessions which we hug to and that is the cause of all our miseries.

(s) The Child (the virtue of Prapatti—i.e., total reliance on God)

The suckling child is free from worries and is cheerful, as his mother takes total care of him. Let us also leave ourselves, through self-surrender, to the care of God.

(t) The Girl from the Poor Household (the virtue of cultivating loneliness)

Once suddenly a party visited the house of a poor man for the purpose of negotiating alliance with his daughter for their boy. It happened that the girl was alone at that time in the house, her parents having gone to another place on some work. The girl herself had to therefore prepare the food for the guests. She started pounding the rice (grains). As she had only glass bangles on her wrists, they were making much noise while she was doing the pounding. Afraid that the noise will only expose their poverty to the guests, she started removing the bangles one by one, but retaining just two on each wrist. But these too continued making some noise. Then she removed one more bangle from each wrist leaving only one bangle on each wrist. Lo, there was no further noise!

The spiritual-aspirant, especially the ascetic, will have to learn to live alone in solitude, so as to avoid strife and discord with any.

(u) The Serpent (the virtue of unconcern for self-possessions)

The serpent does not build its own abode. It lives in holes already built by other creatures. So also spiritual-aspirants, especially ascetics, will have to spend their days in caves and temples already existing, but should not try and waste their lives in building houses and homes.

(v) The Arrow-maker (the virtue of one-pointedness)

Once an arrow-maker was so absorbed in his work of sharpening and straightening an arrow that he did not notice even the king and his big retinue passing by. Later, when the minister of the king came and asked him in which direction the king and his party went, alas, he had to plead his ignorance!

For achieving perfection in anything, one should have single-minded dedication in what one does.

(w) The Spider (our desire-infested mind alone is the cause of our bondage)

The spider pours our of its mouth long threads and labours to weave our webs but unfortunately, gets stuck up in its own web. Likewise, man also builds with his desires his own bondage and forfeits his freedom.

(x) The Bhringi (as the mind thinks so one becomes)

The *Bhringi Bhramara* (beetle) catches hold of a worm and throws it into a mud nest. The worm is all the time worried that the beetle is going to come and sting it, and thus its attention is all the time anxiously focused on the bettle sitting outside the opening of the nest. With its mind thus constantly focused on the form of the *bhramara,* it gets soon metamorphosed into a *bhramara,* shedding out its (ugly) worm-body.

As one thinks, so he becomes. If we constantly think of God, we, too, will become divine for sure.

Glossary

aarti	:	a ceremony performed in worshipping a god; a dish holding a lamp, burning ghee, incense, etc., is moved in a series of circles before the idol
abhisheka	:	rituals involved in bathing an idol with water, milk, honey, ghee, and so on
adhyayana	:	learning
akshata	:	auspicious rice tinged with turmeric and vermilion powder
akshaya	:	inexhaustible, imperishable
amrit	:	divine nectar that gives immorality
ananta	:	limitless, eternal, endless
anushthan	:	daily rituals
asrama	:	one of the four stages of human life Bramhacharya, Grihasthasrama, Vanaprathasrama and Sanyasa
avadhut	:	one of the attributes of an attributeless and formless infinity, manifesting in a finite human form. An avadhut is beyond the boundaries, grants only benedictions and grace on whoever comes in contact with him. Lord

Dattatreya (the guru of all the gurus) and his incarnations are regarded as avadhuts. Lord Dattatreya is the only avatar who has not come to destroy evil. He conquers evil. Normal human beings cannot respond to the attributeless and formless infinity, i.e., God, hence God, out of immense compassion, manifests as a human being so that devotees can enjoy the presence of God

bahudanya year : fertile and fruitful year for agriculture. According to Hindu astronomy 60 lunar years constitute one cycle and Bahudanya is the twelfth lunar year. It is considered to be the year of prosperity and abundance as per Indian astrology.

bhakti : path of devotion

bhikshu : a holy man living by begging alms

bhogi : person deeply attached to and enjoying worldly pleasures

bhojan : food

bilwa : bel tree (*aegle marmelos*)

bramha hatya : killing of a Brahmin

bramha jnana : self-realisation

bramha rakshasa : brahmin taken to Rakshasa Guna in behaviour

bramhachari	:	celibate, a pilgrim on the path of realising 'Bramha'
brihaspati	:	Jupiter
chandan	:	sandal wood
chandrayan	:	fasting according to the phases of the moon
daan	:	charity
darshan	:	seeing the holy person or idol of God
deep aaradhna	:	worshiping with the holy light
deepavali	:	festival of lights
dhoop	:	incense stick
dhyana	:	meditation
dvapara yuga	:	the third *Yuga;* copper age
ekadasi fast	:	fast kept for ritualistic vow falling on the eleventh lunar day
five elements (pancha mahabhuta)	:	earth, water, fire, air and sky
gandha	:	sandal paste
Gayatri japa	:	the sacred Vedic verse chanted at dawn, noon and dusk to illuminate the intellect
gotra	:	genetic heritage flowing from great rishis
grihini	:	housewife
guna	:	intrinsic nature
guru daksina	:	reverential offering made to a Guru

gurukul	:	the Guru's abode where he initiates his teachings to his disciples
gyana shakti	:	capacity to acquire knowledge about any area which one desires
iccha shakti	:	power of fulfilling wishes and desires
jijnasu	:	spiritual seeker
jiva	:	individualised soul; the 'I' consciousness
kalakas	:	verses
kali yuga	:	the fourth *Yuga;* iron age; the present dark age of materialism
kamandalu	:	water bowl used by ascetics
kanya	:	Virgo. It is the sixth sun sign
kartik maas bathing	:	'kartik' refers to the period between mid-October to mid-November. To perform the bathing ritual, the individual, at sunrise, immerses half his body in the holy river water facing the sun.
Krishna paksa	:	fifteen days from full moon to the new moon
krita yuga	:	the first *Yuga;* golden age
kriya shakti	:	power to overcome obstacles while performing any work; can be achieved by chanting AUM
leela	:	divine play
linga	:	oval-shaped stone symbolising the cosmic nature of Lord Siva

magha poornima	:	full moon night in the month of *Magha* (February–March)
mahanubhava	:	sage or holy person
mahapurusha	:	great soul; he who is free from all dual experiences of attachment and hate
mahima	:	miracles
manana	:	recitation or memorisation
murti	:	idol
naivedya	:	food offered to God
nakshatra	:	there are total 27 nakshatras. Pushya is the eighth nakshatra.
navagraha	:	according to Indian astrology they include the sun, moon, Mars, Mercury, Jupiter, Venus, Rahu and Ketu
nirguna	:	without attributes (as the ultimate being)
Omkar or ॐ	:	the primal divine sound which sustains the cosmos; symbol of Bramhan; also known as *Pranava*
padukas	:	sandals
parranna bhoja	:	intake of food prepared by somebody else.
pitri devata	:	departed ancestors
pradakshina	:	circumambulation
pranava nada	:	chant of AUM or ॐ
pranayama	:	yogic exercise for controlling breath
puja	:	ritual worship

rajas	:	represents vigor, aggression, passion, etc.
rakshasa	:	demon
rangoli	:	decorative designs drawn on the floor with white and coloured powders
Rasi	:	sun sign, there are 12 sun signs in total
rishi	:	sage who possesses purified consciousness and clarified intellect
sadhana	:	spiritual discipline; realising one's destiny
saguna	:	having attributes
sandhya	:	morning, midday and evening religious rites during which Gayatri Mantra is recited
sankalpa	:	will, determination
sansara	:	worldly life
sanyasa	:	hermitage
sattva guna	:	represents virtues such as gentleness, calmness, compassion and selflessness.
sattva	:	purity; goodness
shastra	:	ancient scripture; religious treatise
siddhi	:	parapsychic and spiritual powers; occult powers
simhasana	:	throne
Sivaratri	:	a festival worshiping Lord Siva observed on the fourteenth day of the waning moon in the month of *Magha* (February–March); the night symbolises the ushering of the dawn of realisation

sravana	:	fifth month of the Hindu calendar (August – September)
sukla paksa	:	fifteen days from new moon to full moon
tamas	:	represents sloth, lethargy, etc.
tapasvi	:	ascetic practitioner
trayodasi tithi	:	thirteenth lunar day
treta yuga	:	the second *Yuga;* silver age
tulasi	:	basil
upacharas	:	services
upadesa	:	teachings; spiritual initiation
upnayana sanskara	:	a ritual in which sacred thread is worn and Gayatri Mantra is initiated
uttarayana bahula padyani	:	a very auspicious day both according to *tithi* (day according to the lunar calendar) and *yoga* (occasion).
vaidya	:	physician
vairagya	:	renunciation; detachment
vasnas	:	cravings for sensual and material pleasures
vastra	:	clothes
vidhidhyasa	:	contemplation
vidhis	:	religious ceremonies or rituals.
vrata	:	a religious vow; acceptance of a particular code of conduct
yajna pavita	:	sacred thread worn at the time of the thread ceremony

yajna	:	sacrificial rites performed before the sacred fire reciting *Vedamantra* to counteract all evil forces
Yama	:	presiding deity of death
yoga	:	a disciplined path that leads to union with God
yogini	:	women who practices '*Yoga*' for realisation of god; female ascetic who has mastered the senses and mind
yuga	:	age; era; the four *Yugas* according to Hindu mythology are *Krita*, *Treta*, *Dvapara* and *Kali*

About the Authors/Translators

Having originated in the study circle conducted by Sri Sathya Sai Seva Samithi (Chembur), the idea of translating *Guru Charitra* into English received active encouragement from Sri P.B. Paranjape, founder of Shree Swami Samarth Vishwa Kalyan Kendra. The translation process had been attempted by Sri L.N. Joshi and finally initiated and completed by Sri K.V. Rao.

Sri Laxman Narayan Joshi (1901-81)

He was born on 31 January 1901 at Pune. Son of Sri Narayan Vinayak Joshi and Smt. Laxmibai, Sri Joshi had his school education at Sholapur, and his college at Pune. He did his graduation (B.A.) and also completed the teachers' training courses (B.T. and S.T.C.).

Sri Joshi served as a teacher at Thane, Uran (Kolaba Dist.), Agashi (near Virar) and Bombay (Chabbildas Boys' School, Dadar). After retirement from regular service, he was conducting a Tutorial Institute at Lonawala. In the year 1980, he came away to Bombay to be with his son, Dr M.L. Joshi.

Sri Joshi was a well-read person and was totally devoted to Sri Akkalkot Swami Samarth Maharaj.

It was during his stay at Lonawala, that Sri Joshi conceived the idea of bringing out *Guru Charitra* in English and started working on it.

He left his body on 30 October 1981, to ever abide at the lotus feet of Sri Swami Samarth Maharaj.

Sri K.V.R. Rao (1920-86)

Sri K.V.R. Rao, son of Kuchimanchi Venkata Subbarao and Achutamma, was born in Andhra Pradesh on 26 March 1920 and originally belonged to Amalapuram in the east Godavari District.

Having done his post-graduation (M.Sc.) in pharmaceutical sciences from the Andhra University Colleges, in 1943, he spent most of his service career with The Boots Company (India) Limited, Sion, Bombay. He retired in March 1978, but was still closely associated with the company as its Technical Consultant.

He was also the President of the Poona Andhra Association and A.S. Telugu Library in the year 1947 and was Vice-Chairman and also General Secretary of Andhra Education Society of Bombay for many years. Since 1965, he was closely associated with Bhagawan Sri Sathya Sai Seva Samithi of Bombay and was also its Vice-Chairman.

On behalf of Sri Sathya Sai Balvikas Publications, he brought out books like *The Path Divine, The Saints of India, Immortal Heritage*, etc., and was also involved in compiling with (late) Sri N.S. Karandikar's *Biography of Sri Swami Samarth Akkalkot Maharaj*.

SHREE SWAMI SAMARTH VISHWA KALYAN KENDRA
|| Sri Swami Samarth Jai Jai Swami Samarth ||

Sri Swami Samarth, The most recent incarnation (Avatar) of the Datta Sampradaya, stayed in Akkalkot for about 20 years, teaching the common man spiritual precepts, taking them to *poornatva*, i.e., God.

By his grace Sri P.B. alias *Sri Nana Paranjpe* has been educating people about the teachings of Sri Swami Samarth, for over 40 years. To do this more effectively, he set up the **Shree Swami Samarth Vishwa Kalyan Kendra** (A registered Public Trust) at Apata Phata, (about 50 kms from Mumbai) in 1983. This Trust set up a spiritual campus with a beautiful idol of Sri Swami Samarth in a temple on the banks of the Patal-Ganga River, enables devotees to pursue their sadhana. In this temple, while Puja and *abhishek* is done daily, the festival of 'Guru Purnima', 'Datta Jayanti', 'Sri Swami Samarth Prakat Din' (i.e., Sri Swami Samarth's Appearance on earth), Jayanti's (birthdays) of Sri Krishna Saraswati Maharaj and Sri Namdeo Maharaj are celebrated with great enthusiasm. Hundreds of devotees participate in these celebrations, perform their Abhishek and partake in Mahaprasada.

With a view to enabling devotees to reside in this spiritual campus, Nana proposes to set up 'Anand Bhuvan'. Along with spiritual practice, skills would be imparted to the poor. Health centre, Yoga training, discussions by *Yogis* and saints are also planned.

'Anand Bhuvan' is planned as a three storied structure. It will have an area of 8,000 sq. ft., comprising of dining hall, meditation hall, auditorium, etc. The top floor will have rooms for devotees to stay. Two of the three floors have been constructed at a cost of over Rs 45 lakhs. To complete the construction another Rs 25 lakh will be required.

Sri Swami Samarth taught that self-realisation comes through self-development. The setting up of the spiritual campus and 'Anand Bhuvan' is to fulfill this aim. The 'Sri Swami Samarth Vishwa Kalyan Kendra' will not rest until this message and training reaches all.

Shree Swami Samarth Vishwa Kalyan Kendra

Main Centre:

Apta Phata, Post Bara Pada, Karnala, Tal. Panvel, Dist-Raigad-410206. Tel.: 952143-226480

Regd. Office:

9/A Kamgar Nagar, Kurla (E), Mumbai 400 024
Tel.: 25223473

SHREE SWAMI SAMARTH VISHWA KALYAN KENDRA
MUMBAI
Application for Membership

To,
Hon. Secretary
Shri Swami Samarth Vishwa Kalyan Kendra

Sir,
I _____, the undersigned is a devotee of Sri Akkalkot Swami Samarth Maharaj and follower of his teachings. I am a resident of
_____.
I have read the rules of your trust and they are acceptable and will be binding on me. I request you to accept me as Patron/Life member. I am ready to pay/ enclosing herewith a Cheque/DD of Rs. _____ towards the membership fees. I can/cannot devote_____ hours/days in a week/month for the activities of the trust.
I am interested in the following activities of the Trust :

Religious   Educational   Medical   Fund Raising

Full Name & Address   _____
                            _____
                            _____
Telephone / Fax   _____
E-mail   _____
Date Of Birth ———   Education ———————————
Other Members of Family   _____
Business Address   _____
                            _____
Telephone / Fax   _____
Date_____   Signature of Applicant _____
Name of Proposer   P.B. Paranjpe
Signature Of proposer
Application of membership is accepted/rejected
in M.C. Meeting dt.   _____
                            _____

President / Hon. Secretary
Shri Swami Samarth Vishwa Kalyan Kendra
Send your cheque/DD in favour of 'Shri Swami Samarth Vishwa Kalyan Kendra'

SHREE SWAMI SAMARTH VISHWA KALYAN KENDRA
An Appeal

Parampujya Sri Nanasaheb Paranjpe is engaged in the work of enrolling devotees as lifetime members of Shree Swami Samarath Vishwa Kalyan Kendra on the directive which he has got from Sri Swami Samarth Maharaj himself.

Till date over 900 devotees have enrolled as lifetime members of Shree Swami Samarth Vishwa Kalyan Kendra and we would like to appeal other devotees to follow their footsteps. The amount raised by membership will enable the kendra to take care of all future needs.

A spiritual campus has already been established for the practice of yoga, organisation of medical camps, yoga camps and other activities intended towards the welfare of the society. All those contributing over Rs 10,000 to Rs 19,999 will be honoured with their names on a plaque. Those giving over Rs 20,000 will have in addition, Abhishek been performed on any one day of their choice, with prasad being mailed to them, with a prayer to Sri Swami Samarth and Parampujya Nana Paranjpe to bless all.

All Donations to the Shree Swami Samarth Vishwa Kalyan Kendra Fund are tax-exempted under IT section 80G.

For membership please contact us:
+91-9890799547; +91-2114-273913
Email: milinddeshmukh1@rediffmail.com;
nana_paranjpe@rediffmail.com
Website: www.swamikrupakendra.com